THE BOYS IN BLUE WHITE DRESS

William F. Lee

authorHOUSE®

AuthorHouse™
1663 Liberty Drive, Suite 200
Bloomington, IN 47403
www.authorhouse.com
Phone: 1-800-839-8640

First published by AuthorHouse 10/1/2007

ISBN: 978-1-4343-2727-7 (sc)

Library of Congress Control Number: 2007907034

Printed in the United States of America
Bloomington, Indiana

This book is printed on acid-free paper.

ALSO BY
William F. Lee

The Bottom of the List
The Light Side of Damnation

PREFACE

This book is based on authentic experiences. The Marine names are fictitious, except for the mention of the Drill Team members. The dialogue in the book is based on some actual conversations, however literary license has been taken to enhance readability.

The story takes place in Washington, D. C. at the oldest Post of the Corps, Marine Barracks, 8th and "I" Street, SE. It provides special insights to the JFK funeral. It also captures the seriousness of the men to their ceremonial duties along with the roguish and rowdy life style of the company grade officers stationed at this beautiful old post.

These men stand tall and ramrod straight with high and tight crew cuts, wide shouldered and square, fit, and narrow at the hips during ceremonies. True poster Marines.

However, beneath this patriotic picture beats the mischievous hearts of rowdy Lieutenants and good-natured, roguish Captains. First Lieutenant Barney Leslie Quinn becomes part of this waggish group of rascals as if born to it.

This light side of spit, polish, shine clean-cut ceremonial life will give you unpublished insights to recognizable and serious events, and also provide amusement and laughs at these, Boys in Blue White Dress.

My appreciation to those special comrades that may think they recognize themselves in the telling of these tales. Remember, it is just a story. A novel. Fiction for sure, I think. Regardless, the telling is always better long after the events, and by another.

However, the historical moments are real and the experiences as well.

A personal letter to the author

Dear Bill,

Just a note about "An Evening Parade in Blue and White Dress." After reading your last book, and seeing the title of this one, it brought back memories of my time at 8th and I. This poem is written to take the reader through a Friday evening parade. I hope the poem honors all of the "Boys in Blue White Dress" who've taken the field over the years.

I came to The Barracks in 1964 as just one of your Snuffies; three years later, I left as a Marine Sergeant. I'm sure as I read this book, I'll see a lot of you in the exploits of Barney Quinn.

You inspired a young Marine to be the best that he could be and I will always be grateful.

With deepest Admiration,

Thomas Lee
2nd Platoon & Body Bearers
Marine Barracks
1964-1967

An Evening Parade
In Blue White Dress

The evening slips slowly off into night,
As the lights of the ramparts bring the bugler aglow.
The audience is seated as the bell sounds the time,
Officers draw swords and give the command;
Marines snap to attention ready to enter the field,
At the end of this field is "The President's Own",
They proudly step off playing a march
Written a century ago by one of their own.
Chesty is here, a feisty old dog,
Named for a legend, he's part of the Corps.
It's the Commandant's Own, they're ready to play,
They start with the drums and all move as one
Keeping time with the beat.
Bayonets now fixed there's silence again.
The parade is now formed only one thing awaits,
The lights grow dim as the Colors enter the field;
The audience stands to honor our flag
As the Color Guard moves to their honored place.
The Drill Team is ready; perfection is near,
Not a command will be given nor a word spoken.
All that can be heard is the slap of the wood,
The Rifle Inspector now enters the Drill,
Rifles are thrown and pass in the air,
Each movement is perfect, they're the best in the world.
Now it's time to Pass in Review
The Band plays the Hymn we know by heart.
Those in the stands rise to their feet,
Not just for those who pass in review,
But all Marines who have served.
Taps is now heard bringing an end to the day;
Others will follow and answer this call.
Marines who will march in Blue and White Dress,
While serving at the oldest Post of the Corps.

Dedicated to:
Captain William F. Lee
Company Commander
Ceremonial Guard Company
Marine Barracks

Written by
Thomas P. Lee
Sgt., Marine Barracks, 1964-1967

The Boys in
Blue White Dress
By
William F. Lee

In memory of
Brigadier General Ernest Reid, USMC (Ret'd)
1925 – 2006

And of

Captain Francis Shafer, Jr   Lieutenant Shelton Eakin
1938 – 1968   1935 - 1966
Panel 47E - - Line 15   Panel 09E - -Line 79

CHAPTER 1

Washington, D.C.
Friday afternoon
22 Nov 1963

THIS IS A GREAT FRIDAY. The Inspector General's annual inspection of Ceremonial Guard Company, my company, and the Marine Barracks here in Washington, D. C., is over. I took my Drill Team Platoon through the PT training portion this morning and just greased it. The IG chose us to take the test. Probably didn't think a bunch of ceremonial prima donnas were in shape, could cut it, you know, look pretty and can drill, but can they fight syndrome! Well, if so, they were way off base. These Drill Team troops are good at anything they do and unfortunately for me at times this includes some wild liberties. The tipped over cannons in Leutze Park are a tribute to the latter.

This afternoon, we're having organized grab-ass time. It's a clear and cool November day, with light rain forecasted later. Don't know where the name organized grab-ass came from, but it's one of those Marine Corps things. Years ago, some Snuffy, which is a term of endearment for the troops, tagged it with that name. It stuck and thusly some Marine became a "Snuffy Extraordinaire." Anyway, it's organized athletics today, and the Drill Team is playing the Color Guard/Body Bearer Section in six-man flag football...jungle rules. I'm playing with the DT so this gives the Snuffies a free and legal shot at an officer. I've been hit hard three times already, but only twice by CGBB players. I think one of my own

1

troops took a free shot for the hell of it. That's okay; I've gotten in several good licks myself. It's all clean fun...well, fun.

It's half-time and we're taking a short break. *Oh man, the day's almost over and no Camp David detail this weekend. I'm going to see Gabrielle tonight, as well as tomorrow and Sunday. We're goin' to have a ball. Just the two of us.* I'm brought back by someone excitedly shouting my name from across the field. I look and see that our transportation has returned to pick us up here at the athletic field, across the Anacosta River from the Navy Yard and our barracks. *Wonder why? It's early.* There's a sedan with the bus, and a trooper is barreling across the field towards me. He's the source of the hollering. He comes to a sliding halt in front of me, salutes and says, "Lieutenant Quinn, sir, I've been told to tell you that you and all the troops are to return to Guard Company immediately. There's an emergency, sir."

"Okay, Lance Corporal Burke. Calm down, catch your breath." I know him from the guard unit at The Barracks proper. He's one of the front gate sentries, and sharp. "Now then, what's the emergency?"

"Sir, the President is dead!"

"What? Our President?"

"Sir, yes, sir. President Kennedy, sir. Just a little while ago, in Dallas, Texas, sir. He was shot."

"Shot! Oh Jesus!" I blow out a deep breath, and then continue, "What the hell hap...Okay, okay. I'll get the troops rounded up and we'll be back in a jiffy. Go ahead, and tell Captain Kemp I'm on my way."

"Yes, sir."

As Burke leaves, I turn to Gunnery Sergeant Elms, the DT Platoon Sergeant, who has come up to see what's going on, and say, "Gunny. Get everyone loaded on the bus. ASAP. President Kennedy has been shot. He's dead. My bet is we will have to get the Death Watch troops ready to go quicker than a duck on a June bug."

"Aye aye, sir."

"And, Gunny, this means both units. The Body Bearer guys, along with our Drill team troops, will be the first ones going out. Get 'em back, and ready to go."

"Yes, sir." He turns, hollers at the troops to form on him immediately and they do so rapidly due to instilled discipline and the no-nonsense, gruff, gunny tone. He informs them of the situation, although

2

the few close to me when I got the word already know something is up and the Magpies are spreading the word. As soon as all are officially told, and dismissed, we race for the bus.

* * *

Back at our barracks, Building 58, in the Washington Navy Yard, I meet with Captain Robert Kemp, our Company Executive Officer. He says, "Lieutenant Quinn...Barney, President Kennedy was assassinated this afternoon in Dallas."

"By who? Who the hell--"

"Barney, let me finish. He was shot at 1230 hours, Dallas time, during a motorcade. Apparently, he died several minutes later. The announcement was made on TV, at 1340 our time. That's all I know right now, except you and the DT, specifically the Death Watch, need to be ready to go ASAP. The S-3 has called and said the Military District of Washington (MDW) informed them that the Death Watch unit will head out as soon as they get some details. Also the body bearers. Any problems?"

"No, sir. None. I got the ball. Have informed Gunny Blank to have the body bearers and color guard ready to roll, and to stay tight with you since I'll be gone. Any news on who, and why?"

"No. I've told you all I know. Watch the news as you get ready, and I'll keep you informed as well. Get goin'." Kemp says hurriedly.

"Yes, sir. No problems. I've conducted three solid training periods on the Death Watch. We're ready...will cover any details on the way. No sweat."

"Good."

I return to my platoon office and brief Gunny Elms and Sergeant Hapgood. They know as much as me, if not more. They've been glued to the TV. My Death Watch unit is getting ready. This unit and I, along with the other services, will be the uniformed honor guard around the casket while the President lies in repose and in state. He could lie in repose anywhere, but my guess is that it will be in the White House. He will lie in state in the Rotunda of the U. S. Capitol. Anyway, we're blowin' and goin', and prepared.

* * *

I've discovered through the TV and relayed reports from The Barracks S-3 Alpha, my friend Captain Milsap, that President Kennedy was shot by Lee Harvey Oswald, a former Marine. I think, crap, that's just great! That's all we need. The President died at 1239 hours at a hospital in Dallas, Parkland, I think it said on TV. It's late afternoon now. I'm getting edgy, waiting for the word. I want to get movin', get on with it. My Dress Blue uniform is ready; the brass hilt on my sword and the brass on its scabbard are shined; medals and brass buttons shined and on; shoes spit-shined and I have a bag with shaving gear, change of skivvies and socks, and shine gear set to go.

Captain Kemp comes into my office and says, "Barney, it's a go. The President is being flown back here. The word is they will take him to Gawlers Funeral Home in Bethesda. The Death Watch is to go there, immediately."

"Why there? That seems strange. Is he going to lie in repose there?"

"No, he'll eventually be taken to the White House. I don't know anything other than what I've been told, and that is you are to go to Gawlers, now. They're probably the people preparing him for burial. A van is on the way here to pick up you and your Death Watch detail and take you to the funeral home. Are you all set?"

"Yes, sir. Ready." Captain Kemp flushes, looks nervous and probably is, but he's cool as dry ice in getting things done. I add, "I bet it's a mad house out there now. It's almost dark. Evening time; on a Friday; in this city; and now this."

Captain Kemp says, "The van will have a police escort. It's on the way here as well. It will meet up with the van outside our building. Don't leave without them, Barney."

"Okay, got it, sir. We'll be dressed and outta here in just a few minutes."

"Take care, Barney. Keep in touch with me if you can, when you can. If you can't, you can't. Do what makes sense."

"Will do. We'll be fine. No sweat, Cap'n."

Captain Kemp winks, turns and leaves the office. A lot is happening, and there is a lot to do. The coming days will be emotional, passionate, and hectic to say the least...a tragedy for our country. I feel the pressure of the moment. My adrenaline is flowing freely, but the bottom line, as cold as it may sound, is that this is another ceremony, and we've stood 'em all, day in and day out. We'll stand this one as well, as cool as an ice floe, but underneath, I sense we all are like an underground hot spring. Gunny Elms, my Platoon Sergeant, comes back in to get ready. He's already informed the troops. I turn to my locker; check my unnie and accoutrements one more time. It's a go, and I start getting dressed.

* * *

The police car is here. We board the van. In the van, we stand, and hang on to the overhead straps, like evening commuters on a city subway. This keeps our uniforms wrinkle free. We never sit down on the way to a ceremony. Our van looks like a bread truck only painted Marine green. It can hold about a dozen or so men. We use it all the time for small ceremonies, such as a firing party and body bearers going to Arlington for a funeral detail. The police car leads us out the M Street gate of the Navy Yard, hangs a left down M Street heading toward downtown, and probably Wisconsin Avenue. Dusk is dropping like a curtain on the last act of a closing play, and traffic is already crazier than an insane asylum dining hall. As we close on the bridges and monuments area, it's more congested.

I hang on the strap, swaying with the van as it weaves in and out of traffic, horn honking, following the police car that hits its siren every few minutes. *How did this happen? Why? What kind of nut is Oswald? Was the DT, me, practicing the Death Watch an omen?* I know that has nothing to do with anything, other than it was timely. Nevertheless, it seems appalling just having it flash through my mind.

The police siren blares again; I lean over to peer out the windshield. Traffic is a mess. We're downtown. Must be a jillion cars out here. Everyone is blowing their horn. It's a massive gridlock, like a checkerboard with all the squares filled. People goin' home; others coming into work; some probably goin' to bars to watch TV and try to make some sense of all this, if there is any; and others maybe not even knowing where they're headed. Merely dazed people going somewhere with the radio tuned to the news as if anything else is on. The city looks as if it is in a state of panic. Maybe in a way it is. The police car has its red light flashing now, and is hitting the siren more often. We follow closely, honking.

I straighten up, switch hands on the strap and hang on as this ole' bread truck sways and rolls. Its suspension system feels worn out and it's top-heavy to boot. It seems to roll more than a small boat in the North Beach pipeline surf. I may need some Dramamine for Pete's sake. Nonetheless, my mind drifts further away with each roll of the van. I have no way of curbing my mind as it ebbs away like an evening tide. It's going out and it won't be stopped. Maybe because I don't want it to... maybe I need to think of something other than what has happened.

Oh, Jesus, I forgot to call Gabby. Certainly she'll figure I'm involved somehow. Nevertheless, I should have called her. I bet there isn't a line open anywhere in the city so what's the use of worrying. She'll be okay...she'll figure it out.

The siren and honking snap me back again. I look around. My troops all have a thousand yard stare. Everyone is lost in his own thoughts. Their looks and my feelings just keep the tide going out, and with it my thoughts.

What the hell caused this to happen?

God damn, this is America. How can an assassination occur here? In this country? My country?

Why am I here, in the van? Is this some kind of fate thing?

It seems like just last evening I was standing at the Lanai bar at the "O" Club in Kaneohe Bay. I was leaving for duty at the Marine Barracks, 8th and "I" Streets, Washington, D.C. The Post of the Corps. It was great. Life was good. I can almost smell the salt air pushing across the golf course...

CHAPTER 2

LEANING ON THE BAR AT the Officers' Club in Kaneohe Bay, Oahu, Hawaii, the thought finally sinks in. It's my last Happy Hour here. April '62 and my tour of duty is over. Orders in hand, toasts made, goodbye said. I'm headed for Marine Barracks, Washington, D. C. Eighth and "I", Post of the Corps.

Only my old pal, Captain Tony "Big Stoop" Paletta, remains from our initial clan at the bar. The six-foot, four, 240-pound silver-haired Lithuanian is stayin''till the end. When he speaks about his Slavic heritage, I always retort, "You mean slobic, don't you?" That always incites a howl of laughter, then a discourse on the rank structure, and a thump on my arm. We go back a long way. Korea. In One-Five together.

It's about time to shoot the Pali...meaning driving over the steep, winding two-lane blacktop road across the mountains, through the Pali and down into Honolulu. Once there, check into Fort DeRussy and then into town for my last liberty before boarding a service-chartered commercial flight back to the states. The good news is that it's free, not a military aircraft dripping hydraulic fluid and oil in your lap, and serving stale baloney sandwiches. The bad news is the stews are a female version of the over-the-hill gang. The additional bad news is it will probably be full of dependents with shrieking children. However, it will have liquor on board to help drown out the squealing of the kids and blur the wrinkles of the stews.

I just sip my bourbon and Seven and gaze blankly over the bar. I had been ordered to The Barracks once before, as a Sergeant; seven years ago in 1955. However, two of my mentors, Lieutenant Colonels Regan Fulmer and Carleton J. Daly, got my orders changed and sent me to Fort Benning, Georgia to Jump School, Jumpmaster School, and Pathfinder School. It was the first time I experienced mentors, well-meaning senior officers doing what they think best for me. Nonetheless, from there I went back to MCTU #1, the Test Unit, and then Force Recon as a Pathfinder Team Leader. *Wouldn't trade those two tours for gold or frankincense.*

From there ol' Barney was accepted in a Meritorious Commissioning Program. Went to Quantico, Virginia, attended OCS and The Basic School, and came out of the chute branded, a shiny new Second Lieutenant...with a little bit of rust on the gold bars and some crust on the personality.

Once again, one of my newly found mentors, Colonel Regan Fulmer, stepped in and finagled me to the 1st Marine Brigade, here at Kaneohe Bay. When I arrived, the fine southern gentleman, Colonel (CJ) Carleton J. Daly was here and pulling strings for me again.

He put me in Amphib Recon Company. All the best of training in rubber boats, operating off Subs, free and buoyant underwater ascents, and SCUBA diving. Stoop interrupts my thoughts, "Stoneface, one more for the road, and the good times?"

"Sure. You buyin' you cheap Slobic hacker?" Stoop has been my golfin' buddy for the three years here.

"Why not? It's your money. Hey, Crazy Horse, you look like you're a thousand miles away. You get a hold of some more of that tough-skin you drank on the big island when you were goin' up Mauna Loa and Mauna Kea. Doin' all that rock climbing, rappelling and Recon crap that you love?"

"Yeah, I guess I was."

"Well, you might be able to use your ski training...it snows a few inches more there than here." He laughs and motions for the bartender. Then adds, "But you're goin' to have to stow all that other recon shit when you put on the Dress Blues. They'll probably send you to charm school first before they turn you loose on civilized people."

"I'm goin' to miss all that stuff, Stoop, but not as much as you, you ugly galoot."

"Watch it, Lieutenant. You're speakin' to a Marine Captain. I was in the Corps when you were wearin' diapers."

"I'm speaking to a four handicap golfer passing himself off as an eleven, and stealing money from junior officers. Besides, you started as a Private and regardless of what rank they gave you, you're still a Snuffy... and a Magpie, just a large one."

He howls in laughter again as only he can, and does at all of our vocal jousting. The drinks arrive, he winks, and we take a long and needed slug. I return to my thoughts again.

Lots of hard work in Recon Company but for fun and adventure in a job you can't beat frolicking in the surf, hammerhead sharks or not.

What a great time! Now, I'm leaving. Finally getting to The Oldest Post of the Corps. Better late than never! I take another swig of my drink, glance out over the pool and the magnificent base golf course. We called it the poor man's Pebble Beach. Gonna' miss it all. The surf, the beach, the bikinis, but most of all the training and the Marines I served with.

I nudge Tony on the arm with my elbow and say, "Gonna miss you, Stoop." We raise glasses, I bellow, "RECON, OOUH-RAH." We clink our glasses and down our drinks.

Tony's eyes water, he thumps me on the arm, and slides down a few stools to harass a young second lieutenant staring at us. Stoop puts his arm around the young Marine's shoulder and probably is laying on some "Stoopisms."

I walk out of the Lanai Bar, not looking back.

* * *

I pull up to the main gate at Marine Barracks, 8th and "I", SE, in my brand spankin' new and whistle clean 1962 Corvette convertible. Top down since it's a beautiful May day. All white, red leather interior...spiffy indeed. Traded my '57 Ford Fairlane in Hawaii and had this waiting at a sister dealership in Santa Ana, California.

I look up at the sentry in Seagoing Blues. Nothin' but creases. Blue trousers, khaki shirt with tie, white barracks cap, white gloves, and white web pistol belt with a Cal.45, in a shined holster. His shoes are highly spit-shined as is his cap visor. He's lookin' tuff. He whips up a smart hand salute since I'm in uniform. I return it and say, "Lance

9

Corporal, I'm First Lieutenant Quinn, reporting for duty. Where do I park, and where do I check in since its Saturday?"

"Sir, you can park in that sixth slot on your starboard side. Then, take off your Vette, sir, and walk up the arcade in front of where you park to the last hatch. The Officer of the Day, Lieutenant Van Dell, will take care of the Lieutenant, sir."

"Thank you, Marine. What's your name?"

"Lance Corporal Burke, sir."

"Incidentally, Lance Corporal Burke, what is that small fenced in area next to this first house?"

"Sir, the house is Center House. The bachelor officers' quarters. The pen is the dog house, for Chesty, our friggin' mascot, sir."

"Dog house, hmmm. Hope I don't wind up in there."

"Would hope not, sir, it's nasty."

"The dog, Chesty?"

"No, sir. He's afraid of his own shadow. He does smell nasty though. He's ugly, slobbers, and has a kinky tail. And he farts all the time, like all English Bulls I guess...Sir."

"Well, that sounds like a lot of Marines I know. Thanks again, Lance Corporal." I pull through the gate and into slot six, which is marked and easily seen with its freshly painted yellow lines, figure six, and visitor on the curb. The Marine Corps paints everything nailed down, and even some things not, like rocks around tents in the field. If you're ever around when Marines are painting, move, quickly and at least several times.

I squeeze out and up from my Vette, or take it off as Burke suggested, straighten my uniform, grab my orders and go to the OD's office. I see the Sergeant of the Guard and say, "Sergeant, I'm Lieutenant Quinn. Need to check in with the OD."

"Yes, sir. The sentry called. The OD, Lieutenant Van Dell will be back in a few minutes, sir. He's out checkin' posts."

"Thanks, Sergeant."

* * *

In the Van.
Heading to Gawlers Funeral Home
Friday evening
22 Nov 1963

The van jolts to a halt. I come back to the present and realize I'm a bit tired from the early start this morning, and I guess just the mental stress of dealing with the assassination. I slowly turn and look out the windshield again. Good grief, this is a madman's paradise. We could make better time by getting out and walking along the top of the cars.

The police car's siren is going full bore now and its light is flashing. The van driver has stopped honking. It's meaningless, since everyone is honking and some offering hand signals. Angry, more likely confused and frustrated folks. Hell, we're not even on Wisconsin Avenue yet. Damn, this might take the better part of an hour. No sense saying anything, Corporal Fennell is doing the best he can.

I turn to check the troops. They look a little edgy. I give them a hand signal, like an umpire signaling safe, meaning everything's okay and stay "cool". I slowly turn back to my original position, staring at the inside panel of the van. I switch hands on the strap and my mind fades back to my first moments here at The Barracks.

What an overture that was.

CHAPTER 3

I STAND IN THE DOOR of the OD shack taking in the early May sunshine and the aura of the Post of the Corps. A first lieutenant in Seagoing Blues is approaching from the gate area. Apparently, he was out checking posts. When he nears me I say, "Good afternoon, Lieutenant. I'm Lieutenant Barney Quinn, reporting for duty."

"Hey, good to meet you. The sentry told me you had arrived. I'm Jeff Van Dell, welcome aboard."

He's about five foot ten or eleven; dark hair and eyes with a muscular build and a barrel chest accentuated by his trim waist. His uniform is impeccable, all military creases and no wrinkles. As he motions me into an inner office, he says, "Come on in." He takes off his sword, cap and gloves.

"Okay, thanks." I pause until he sits, then hand him my orders.

"Great, I'll take care of them and see that they get turned over to Personnel. Check in there at 0730, Monday. Incidentally, after you check in, the Commanding Officer, Colonel C.J. Daly, wants to see you at 0805. Right after colors."

"Colonel Carleton J. Daly is the CO?"

"Yep, why?"

"Jesus, he's here? I know him. Served under him twice before."

"Is that a problem or something?"

"Oh no. Not at all. He's a great guy. It's just that he...never mind, it's not important. Not a problem."

"Okay, good. You'll be billeted in Center House. A room is available. I'll take you over, introduce you to the House Mother, and--"

"House Mother?"

"Yeah, we have a House Mother. The senior officer living there is the Muv. It's Captain Marsh B. McKay...Mush Mouth is his nickname, but of course he's Captain or Sir when you speak to him.

"This is getting better by the minute."

"Yep, and you ain't seen nothin' yet my friend. In fact you might get to witness ole' Mush Mouth in action tonight. They're having a party. Could get wild with the cast of characters coming. I'll take you over and make the introductions and point out some things about this place as we go."

"Okay, let's go."

He hooks his sword to his belt again, puts on his white barracks cover and gloves, and checks himself in the full-length mirror at the door. We step out of the guard office onto the covered arcade. He stops and points across the asphalt parking lot and says, "That's the parade deck. Friday night parades from May until October. Some Thursday nighters on special occasions, like for the President. He's coming here in a few weeks."

"President Kennedy, coming here?"

"Yep. First time."

* * *

Heading to Gawlers
Snarled in traffic
Friday evening
22 Nov 1963

The thought of the President and the short shrill whoop-whoop-whoop of the police siren snap me back to the present. Now our driver is leaning on the horn. I peer out the windshield again. We're having difficulty getting through a traffic-lighted intersection. Traffic is still snarled, and to make matters worse, it's starting to spit...mist, not quite a rain. It makes everything more ghostly looking. Inside the bread truck, there's no shuffling around by the troops, just them hanging on the overhead straps, swaying with the van's movement. No one's talking, probably lost in their thoughts.

I look outside again. We're moving, inching along. We're nothing but a van on a treadmill. I check my watch. *This is going to take forever. I don't know what time we're suppose to be at Gawlers. Don't know what time the President's remains will be there. I'm in touch with no one, and I can't influence much here.* I say to the driver, "Get right up on that cop car's bumper. Don't kiss him, just hug him."

"Yes, sir."

"Hey, look, don't let that car get between us."

I go to lazily swaying on the overhead strap and remembering that first Saturday, the 5th, May, 1962.

* * *

Van Dell says, "Speaking of the President, up at the north end of the quadrangle is the Commandant's house, General Dixon M. Shelton, the Medal of Honor winner. He specifically invited him to come here."

"I know about his MOH, and I sort of figured you didn't invite the President, Jeff."

"Yeah, well, around here the Commandant snacks on lieutenants, and anyone else he finds wandering around. The OD has to check the KY-1 phone each night, after midnight, and insert the new code card. It's in the cellar. Not fun if you happen to run into the General."

"What's he doin' down there after midnight?"

"Checking his Sake jars, I guess."

"Sake jars?"

"Yeah, his hobby. He collects them. Just beware."

"Okay, got it."

Jeff continues his tour. "Anyway, on the right, in the red brick buildings are The Barracks offices. The top side is barracks for the troops of H&S and MCI Companies. Behind us are the gym, band hall, and Staff NCO Club. Ceremonial Guard Company is located down at the Navy Yard in Building 58. That's where I am."

"Where's the Institute?"

"Also in the Navy Yard, down at the west end. The Yard is at the end of 8th Street, on "M"...out the gate and left. The first brick house, inside the gate, on the left, is Center House. The other four are for generals except the middle one, that's Colonel Daly's quarters." He points it out. "Oh yeah, I forgot, his and the XO's offices are up at the far end of the office building I mentioned earlier. This reminds me, the

Executive Officer is Lieutenant Colonel William Donnelly. You want to give him a wide berth. He's hard on Lieutenants and fools, and it seems he thinks they're the same."

Lieutenants and fools. Nice. Wonder if that's listed in Rodale's Synonym Finder?

We've been strolling along the arcade, back toward the main gate. The Barracks is an enclosed quadrangle. Everything that's brass, shines. All the wood looks freshly painted. The grass is lush, and concrete swept clean. All this in the middle of a run-down, poverty-stricken, black neighborhood. Helluva sight.

Jeff points to Chesty's pen and says, "The guard of the day has to take care of that filthy SOB. As OD, make sure that mutt is locked up before colors or he'll be hangin' on the halyards."

"That really happen?"

"Yeah, more than once. The dog's screwed-up. Everyone has a Chesty story. You will too before you leave." He points to Center House and says, "Lets go in. You'll like it here." We cross through the enclosed porch, which overlooks the entire barracks quadrangle, and into the vestibule. Jeff continues, "We have our own bar. Nice living room with TV," as he waves a hand in that direction.

I see a piano in the living room and point to it saying, "A piano. Who plays, anyone?"

"Yeah, the Muv, but only Baptist hymns so he doesn't get many requests. Why, do you play?"

"Yeah, some, for my own enjoyment and occasionally for lecherous reasons."

"Well, be careful, the House Mother is sensitive, or at least pretends to be. Anyway, we also have a formal dining room with stewards, and great chow. Let's meet Captain McKay. Are you all set?"

"Do I need to be? Does he bite?"

"Yes, you do. No, he doesn't, just snarls, mumbles and sometimes snaps."

Straight ahead of us is the bar. As we enter, Jeff points to one gent and silently mouths, "Muv." Captain McKay is sitting with two of his, I guess, sidekicks. Each has a buzz cut with white sidewalls and all are in casual civilian attire. Mush Mouth is hunched over his drink, whispering I think, and the other two are nodding, in either approval or agreement. If not, boredom I guess.

Jeff says, "Captain McKay, sir. This is First Lieutenant Barney Quinn. He's just checked in, sir, and as the Captain knows is to be billeted in the available room on the third deck."

There is a murmur; some type of hushed, indistinguishable mumbling of what I presume is some form of the English language laden with syrup or grits from the Muv. I say, "Sir, the Lieutenant didn't hear the Captain."

Captain Marsh B. McKay spins his six-foot frame about on his barstool, and in a much louder voice, more so than needed, and a sly smile, says, "Loooooootenant Quinn, welcome. Have a drink first so I can brief you on a few house rules, like listening when the House Muuthaa speaks. And also, before you go charging off around this Post of the Corps making a damn fool of yourself, Mister Quinn." This is all said in sarcastic jest with the thickest North Carolina accent I have ever heard.

My good friend in Hawaii, Clint Rush, is from Mississippi and you could cut his accent, but not this. This is a language all its own. Not only that, but his eyes seem half-closed, or he has a constant genetic squint. Maybe the grin is also genetic because it seems to stay on his face when he speaks, mumbles or sips his drink.

Looking at the bartender, he says, "Gunny, get the Lieutenant a drink, and put it on my chit."

The gunny glances at me and says, "Sir, I'm Gunny Sergeant Mark Richards. I work at the Institute, and tend bar here. A second job. Not the bartending, it's a hobby. Caring for wayward lieutenants and haggling captains is my second job. What'll you have, Lieutenant?"

"Bourbon and Seven, Gunny." He nods. I look back to McKay and say, "Thanks, Captain...Sir."

Mush Mouth emits a gagging sound indicating his displeasure in my choice of drink as he mutters, "Soda pop." He looks at his two cohorts for confirmation. He gets it as they, too, make gagging sounds and nod their agreement. Then he says, "Let me introduce you. This is Captain Jack Kruger, better known as Julius, but Captain Julius to you." I nod and smile, Kruger and I know each other from the Brigade in Hawaii. He's six foot, dark hair and seemingly always smirking and wide-eyed. He has a low voice, like a raspy growl. He and Clint were in Anti-Tank Company in the Brigade.

The Muv continues, "And this is Captain Justin G. Milsap. He's from Yale so he's smarter than the rest of us, his granddaddy is famous, and beware, he has a hollow leg." The Eli is shorter than the other two, by a few inches and a good four inches shorter than I am. He too is broad shouldered; however, he's a little stockier than the House Mother and Julius. He looks like, if there is such a person, a sophisticated beer truck driver, who's still in shape.

I step forward and shake hands with each, saying, "Captain Milsap, my pleasure, sir. Captain Kruger, good to see you again, sir." They nod, smile, offer me the stool next to Mush Mouth. Jack Kruger winks, laughs quietly, and nods his head sideways, pointing toward the housemother, raising his eyebrows. He's alerting me.

Captain McKay says, "So, you two know each other. Good. I'll let Julius show you around the house, and to your room, and he can cover all the details...and I will hold him personally...personally responsible for your conduct in the house."

"Sir, I don't--"

"Don't interrupt me lieutenant when I'm monologing."

"Sir, is that a word?"

"What? Damn straight. If I said it, it's a word, Mister." His sly smile goes to a broad grin now, almost into a laugh.

"Yes, sir." I take a hearty slug from my drink. I think I'm going to need it before Mush Mouth continues his monologue. Without some alcohol, I may not understand much of what he says. I bet there isn't much worthwhile understanding anyway.

He leans over his drink once again, and starts with, "Looooootenant," and he continues to mumble. Three factors seem to dictate the shortened speech. First, I'm sure that Jack Kruger has informed him that I'm not a baby-faced lieutenant. Second, I'm still in uniform and wearing two and a half rows of ribbons, jump wings, AO wings, a string of Expert Pistol and Rifle Shooting Badges. He has to know I've done something beside go to The Basic School and command a platoon.

The last reason, however, is the best. He's apparently been at the bar for some time and is slipping away while waiting for his date to arrive.

During his North Carolinian mumbling monologue, the Muv's current squeeze ambles into the bar. She stops, eyes the gathering, and then squints as her eyes they settle on McKay. She's expected, but is here early. First Jack Kruger mutters, "Oh-oh." Then he quickly follows with, "Marsh, Rina is here." He winces as he looks at me and says, "Ahhh, Barney, this is Rina Palaggio."

I turn full around on my barstool. She is a showstopper. She looks like one of those gals painted on the nose of the WWII B-17's. The Blonde Bomber, with black roots and eyebrows, mischievous smile and a huge set of SCUBA gear showing a cleavage deeper than the Grand Canyon.

She turns her gaze from the Muv to me and says, "Hello, who the hell are you? A new pervert?"

Jesus, what a salty mouth, but great tits.

Before I can reply, Mush Mouth gets off his stool, stumbles slightly as he reaches for her arm and says, "Rina darlin', lets skip all the preliminary stuff tonight and just go to your place."

Loud enough for all to hear, inside and out, she says, "Not on your life. Marsh, your problem is that you are an over-sexed, under-deodorized, son of a bitch."

I take the moment of stunned silence that follows her remark to announce, "Gentlemen, and, ahhh...lady. I'm going to take this opportunity to get my gear, take it topside, unpack, and get this perverted body settled."

She swings at me and misses as the House Mother yanks her out of the bar. *I'll bet she's a deliciously bad young woman.*

Lieutenant Van Dell leaves to go back to the solitude, he hopes, of the OD shack. Captains Julius and J.G. giggle and return to their drinks. My new uncle, Julius, tells me my room is the empty one on the third deck. Then adds, "I'll be up in a little while Barney to explain some house rules, expectations and such. Don't worry, the House Mother likes you already. I told him of some of your shooting the Pali exploits."

"Oh, geez. Real nice. Okay, clue me in whenever, sir."

"After you get settled, we'd be pleased if you joined us...that is if you have the stomach for it."

"Thanks, sir. I take it that was only the opening act?"

"You got it."

I leave to get my gear.

My kind of place!

CHAPTER 4

Still on the way
Downtown, D. C.
Dusk for sure
Fri., 22 Nov 1963

I MOMENTARILY ROCK BACK TO the present as the van swings onto Wisconsin Avenue, heads to Bethesda, and Gawlers Funeral Home. Even with the occasional siren and the honking, it's quiet in the van, like some kind of twilight zone. Traffic is still a nightmare. We're crawling along in the confusion of the day's events and the now not-so-normal Bethesda going home traffic.

Just stand here and think of something to keep my mind occupied. I don't want to think about what's happened. The swaying lulls me back into thinking about my early days here.

* * *

I spend my first weekend in my room on the third deck getting settled. It's small, with a sloping ceiling like most attic or loft type areas. It has a single bed, built-in drawer and closet space, writing desk, window air conditioner, and a sink with mirror. There are three rooms up here and we three lieutenants share a common head. My attic mates are both lieutenants, Jeff Van Dell and Charles Eltringheist. The latter is called Chink because he was a basketball player in college and that's the sound the ball makes when it gets only net. He's tall, six foot four, and looks like his German ancestors with his blond hair, blue eyes, and

20

heavy-boned structure. He too has white sidewalls like all the others, but since he's pure blond, he appears almost bald.

The three captains, the Muv and his two sidekicks, live on the second deck. The Muv in two rooms, a bedroom and a sitting room. The others, one room each. All of these rooms are larger than those topside and furnished about the same. The Muv's sitting room does have a couch where I understand a married officer or two has slept off a happy hour. When someone is transferred, musical chairs take place for the rooms. It's all based on seniority.

I meet Chink and visit the partygoers later on Saturday evening. It is somewhat subdued since the House Mother has returned, alone, and is sulking. There are other gals present, highlighted by an apparent house favorite or regular, Beth Fong. She is a stew, and for whatever reason, loves Marine Captains from the parade deck and is fawning over Uncle Julius at present. Another regular, and favorite, is Donna Vazzonno. She is a legend. Her claim to fame is that she can drink more Black Russian cocktails than anyone at Center House. Actually, probably more than any living male. Nonetheless, I'm not in their sight picture, and thankful for that. Makes no difference since my Pali shooting days are over. I've set new goals. No more wenching around. Want to find someone nice with maybe more long-term possibilities.

Center House has a closed mess, meaning it's open to officers of The Barracks only, and no cash, only chits. Since I live here I'm billed for meals and don't receive my quarter's allowance. Uncle Sam directly pockets it. Any drinks at the bar are on a chit system, and billed at the end of the month. All others sign chits for meals and drinks, and are billed monthly. It is, I'm told, a mark of distinction to be a married officer and attain a "century" bar bill.

* * *

Still heading for Gawlers
Still snarled in Traffic
Still Friday evening
Still 22 Nov 1963

"God damn women drivers. Friggin' civilians." It's the driver shouting at I guess some poor woman also caught in this look-alike bumper car ride. Now he's glaring at her out his driver's side window.

21

I bark, "Hey, Atherton, keep it cool. She's probably saying something worse about you and your horn honking."

"Yeah, I know, sir, but this crap is gettin' old. They're not heeding the siren and lights."

"Keep cool, we're getting there. Do you actually know where Gawlers is or are we just following the cop car?"

"Both, sir."

"Okay, good. Keep it cool, Atherton." He nods, and shortly after I sort of nod off myself, back to Center House.

* * *

The bar is called the Drum Room because of its collection of old Marine Corps snare drums, swords, plaques and other memorabilia on the walls. There's a ship's bell as in almost every Marine bar. It's on the wall at the west end of the bar, next to a window overlooking 8ᵗʰ Street. There are two traditions involved with the bell. First, no matter where in the Corps, if you enter the bar covered, someone rings the bell, and you buy drinks for the house.

Second, here, if a person rings the bell, excluding the first circumstance, the bell ringer or fool, buys a round of drinks for all at the bar. I understand from one of the warning monologues delivered to me, it is a good practice when drinking, to sit away from the bell thereby taking no chances in the event of a weak moment, or mind, or unexplained muscular contractions.

* * *

On Monday, I'm up early, anxious to report for duty. I head for the breakfast table and there get another surprise. The XO, Lieutenant Colonel Donnelly is at the table and, although seated, it is apparent he's tall, about my height, only distinguished looking, wiry, more like steel cables. He immediately begins grilling me. The other Center House bachelors wait for me to slip up or make a fool of myself, thereby putting me on Donnelly's Fools, Transfer or Execution List. After obtaining my name and when I arrived, he asks, "Give me a thumbnail sketch of your background, Mister Quinn."

I put down my glass of orange juice and respond, "Sir, I'm ex-enlisted, joined in 1951, later served in B Company, 1ˢᵗ Battalion, 5ᵗʰ Marines in Korea, then from there--"

"You were in One-Five?"

"Yes, sir."

"Did you know that I was in One-Five in World War II?"

"No, sir."

"Well, I was. My favorite outfit! We have something in common. Great."

Great, hell I hope.

"Go ahead and finish, Lieutenant."

I have at least advanced from Mister to Lieutenant. He's not the type to ever use first names, but a leg up is a leg up. Not quite the top step, but better on the curb than in the gutter. I continue, he doesn't interrupt, and when finished, he says, "Impressive. Welcome on board."

The others are silent, from astonishment I think. I not only survived, but made points.

* * *

I'll watch colors go this morning...great sight, particularly here, then go over to Personnel to check in and get started, first Monday, the seventh... lucky number. No Chesty, didn't make colors today, good. I walk over to the far side of the immaculate, rich, green grass parade deck by going up Generals' Walk along the fine old brick homes, and cross over Center Walk, past the flagpole and yet another ship's bell, and into the Personnel Office.

I check in with Warrant Officer Tex Farrier, who with his gray hair, broad shoulders and only slightly over-indulged waistline looks like a horseshoer, his namesake. He says in a noticeable western drawl, "I got your orders and have processed them already. The CO, Colonel Daly is waitin' to see ya. He'll let you know about your initial assignment. You two must be friends. He don't often get this excited about Lieutenants comin' on board."

"We've served together before, Gunner."

"So I gathered. Let's go."

We head up the passageway, skirting the various offices. I see Captain Milsap in Operations, the S-3 office; he's the Three-Alpha. We also pass the XO's office. Farrier says, "I understand you've already met the XO."

"Yes, at chow this morning. The word seems to travel fast around here."

"Good, and nothin' bad happened. You're way ahead of the herd. And, yeah it does. Not too many secrets, especially when it comes to the Lieutenants, and some Captains."

Jesus, Donnelly must be a holy terror. Rumors and stories travel faster than the weather changes in Texas. Gotta watch my P's and Q's here.

We enter Colonel Daly's office. Before Farrier can speak, the Colonel is up and bolts around his desk. He shoves out his hand, says, "Great seeing you again, Barney." Looks at Farrier and says, "Thanks, Mister Farrier. That will be all. I'll send Barney back in a little bit." Then, "Barney, sit down, let's chat."

We do, about Test Unit #1, old friends from there, about the 4th Marines and the Brigade in Hawaii, about mutual acquaintances, and like him, some have also played mentor to me. *I can't seem to shake the mentors. A few are good I suppose, but as many as I'm picking up is not. Too many fingers in the stew, or whatever.*

He reminds me of the importance of this tour, at this, the oldest Post of the Corps. It was established in 1801, square 927, the block surrounded by 8th and I, and 9th and G Streets, S.E. Been the residence of the Commandant of the Marine Corps since 1806. When the British burned Washington during the War of 1812, they spared 8th and "I" as a mark of respect to Marines, whom they had faced in the Battle of Bladensburg. Or at least that's the Corps' story, and we're sticking to it. The history I know, however the ol' southern gentleman, Colonel CJ, is using it to impress upon me the importance of the duty here. He adds, "The Commandant lives right here, and watches our every step."

"Must be nice, sir."

"Well, yes, for the steps, and no, for the mis-steps. Anyway, I'm glad you're here, Barney. In addition, I want to get you on the parade deck as soon as possible. Since the parade season is ready to start, you'll have to practice and rehearse first, then replace one of the Lieutenants in MCI Company as soon as you're deemed ready."

"Sir, that's great. I'm anxious to get going."

"CGC, Ceremonial Guard Company, is filled right now. So, your first billet will be as the Registrar of the Institute. You'll be reporting to the Director, and in MCI Company for parade purposes. I'll get you to Guard Company later. I assume you'd like that."

"Yes, sir. Look forward to it."

The Institute is the Marine Corps correspondence school for military subjects. The Registrar's Office obviously keeps the enrollment and grade records, and so forth...paper clips, perforators, papers, and people. A pogey bait job.

"Okay, then. Get on back to Mister Farrier, and down to MCI. Damn, it's good to have you here, and to see you again, Barney. And oh yes, if you have time later on, after you are settled, come up and play volleyball. We play at noon in the gym. You remember our games at the Test Unit, right?"

"Yes, sir. All officers and me, a Sergeant...and jungle rules as I recall."

"Yes, well, we're more sophisticated here. We don't play jungle rules. Shame, it was fun."

"Yes, sir, if you were senior."

"That's right, but as I recall, you were noticeably irreverent and did your share of hammering officers whenever possible."

"Sir, but certainly never you."

"I don't recall you being even that selective." He laughs and walks me to his office door, pats me on the back and warmly guides me on my way.

* * *

In the van
Wisconsin Avenue
Getting dark
Fri., 22 Nov 1963

I open my eyes. Still crawling along. Might as well just go back to where I was. *That meeting with the Colonel really was my first fateful step. It guaranteed I would be here with the Death Watch detail. Destiny or fate? One or the other. Beats me. Sounds corny, but here I am.*

* * *

Back at the Personnel Office, Warrant Officer Farrier tells me I'm all set. He says, "On your way out, stop and see Captain Ryan Beard... Smokey Beard. He's the CO of MCI Company. He wants to meet you, and he's been told to start getting you ready for the parade deck. He's right down the passageway."

"Okay, will do."

"Then off to MCI in the Navy Yard and report to the Director. Know how to get there?"

"Yes."

"Have you ever worked with Women Marines before?"

"Worked with them?"

"Yes."

"No. Been around them some in my past. Never worked directly with them, or near them. Spent most of my time in recon and infantry units."

"Oh, well then, it should be interesting. The Registrar Section has about forty-five of them. Good luck!"

I head out the hatch, and toward Captain Beard's office. *Wonder what he means, good luck.*

* * *

Captain Smokey Beard is a big man, and loud. Every bit of six-three and two hundred plus pounds. When he comes around his desk, he sort of lumbers, or prowls like a bear. Doesn't look like a natural parade deck glider. Be more at home in the woods, eatin' honey and fishin' for salmon. He welcomes me with his gruff voice and manner. Tells me where to go to get all of my parade accoutrements, such as Sam Browne belt, buffed medals, white trou and such, and where to turn in my brass buttons on my blues to be buffed.

Then he spends time emphasizing the traditions here and warning me about all the pitfalls for new Lieutenants at The Barracks, in particular, Lieutenant Colonel William Donnelly. *Geez, again. No matter, I'm lovin' the place already.* I inform Captain Beard, "I've already met the XO. At breakfast. We got along fine. We both served in One-Five. No problems."

He raises his eyebrows at my comments, and continues with his monologue. All the Captains here seem to have monologues, and are prone to deliver them. Must be a requirement. *I'm good at monologues myself...it's a snug fit...just need to make Captain first.*

He gets up from his desk again and asks if I have any questions. "Probably, sir, but I can't think of any just now. I suppose I need to get on my way to the Institute, or Tute as Captain Kruger calls it, and just strap everything on."

"Good. I will see you on the parade deck at 0730 each morning for sword drill, starting tomorrow. And, I want you up here and at Iwo observing parade rehearsal starting tomorrow morning. Understand?"

"Aye aye, sir."

With that, we shake, and I leave to get in my Vette and get along to the Tute, and find out what that "good luck" remark was all about. *Hmmm, a room full of WM's, forty-five of 'em...probably will need some luck, and I better clean up my language...and mind.*

* * *

Wisconsin Avenue
Moving better
Evening
Fri, 22 Nov 1963

We're still moving along Wisconsin, and making a tad better progress. I look around. The troops are getting restless and grumbling a bit. Good, Marines are happy only when bitching. It's the hurry-up and wait syndrome only this time we're crawlin' and lookin' for a place to wait.

They stare at me, eyes asking me to do something. I say, "Hey, guys. Stay loose. We've got a long, long night ahead of us. Think of something else, something pleasant for awhile."

Somebody pipes up, "We've been doin' that Lieutenant, and she ain't hacking it."

"Who's that talking?"

"Me, sir."

"Well, me sir, do it some more. Besides you're probably the one that took that cheap shot at me today during the game."

"Not me, Lieutenant, but I wish it were."

I smile, and then break out laughing. *Snuffies, gotta love 'em.* "Okay, okay. Hang in there."

I do just that, hang on the strap and sway with the best of them.

CHAPTER 5

I FIND MY WAY TO the Tute in the Navy Yard, and report to the Director, Lieutenant Colonel Patrick Maloney. He introduces me immediately to the Assistant Director, Major Bill Flanagan, an aviator type. Also to his civilian counterpart, Mr. Ed Benedict, who is a professional educator and is the constant thread here. They welcome me. Then it's back to the colonel's office where he delivers a monologue about the Institute, its history and the important role the Tute Marines play in educating the men of the Corps. He adds, "Also, the parades on Friday night at The Barracks, and on Tuesday evening the sunset parade at the Iwo Monument. Plus some ceremonies, like street parades on holidays and funerals at Arlington."

"Yes, sir. Understand."

"I expect you do, because it's a part of life here. We're in the public eye frequently. Mistakes are not taken kindly."

"Understand, sir."

"I sincerely hope so because The Barracks reminds me of a saying I once heard or read. Don't remember where or by whom...probably another one of those anonymous Marines."

"What's that, sir?"

"Paraphrased, it's, 'To err is human. To forgive is divine. Neither is the policy of The Barracks.' Forewarned is--"

"Sir, I know. I know, it--"

"Don't interrupt, Barney. Forearmed."

"Well, sir. That's about as succinct as I've had it explained...over the course of a dozen warnings."

"Good."

"I guess the message is, don't fuck up, sir. Right?"

"Yes, that's right. I was told you were irreverent."

The Director goes on to explain that both the Friday night and Iwo parades are open to the public, popular attractions, and always crowded. He grins and says, "If you're counting, that's two parades and two rehearsals a week. Ceremony time piles up quickly for these MCI troops and that not including the others I mentioned."

"Yes, sir. Plays to my strength...sir."

"Good, and don't forget your day job, Lieutenant."

I nod a 'sir' this time.

He then takes me on a walking tour of MCI, where I meet all of the officers at the Tute, to include Captains McKay and Kruger, Chink, and Lieutenants Word, Howell and Havre. These last three are almost the same height, a tad over six feet, are lean, sharp and once again, short hair. The three of them are on the parade deck for MCI Company at present. *Ah, a matching team of horses. Good, I'll be in the traces soon.*

Finally, Lieutenant Colonel Maloney brings me into the harem, the Registrar's office. It's all true, there are forty some WM's and two lonely but apparently happy, and hopefully not satisfied, male Lance Corporals working in here. Also an older gentleman, a civilian, GS-12 Gov type. The director says, "Joe, this is the new Registrar, Lieutenant Quinn. He just arrived, and he will be in training immediately for the parades. Help him get started in here. Mister Quinn, meet Mister Joe Milbread."

Old grey haired Joe is balding in front and on top, is wearing a suit with vest and watch chain, and is ever so slightly stooped shouldered. He responds warmly, but meekly, "Certainly sir, it'll be my pleasure. Welcome, Lieutenant Quinn."

"Thank you, Joe. Just call me, Barney. Makes me feel wanted. How long have you been here?"

"Oh about, twenty or so years."

"Ah, good. Probably have it down pat." The colonel grimaces at my comment. I grin at my own humor. Maloney erases my smile with a quick shake of his head, and a frown.

Ol' Joe says, "Yep."

It's obvious that ol' Joe is here as the Assistant Registrar, but in reality, he is the Registrar. I'll be in the position in name only. It's a place to put an officer in the Tute so he can spend time on ceremonies, plus the Corps wouldn't want to put a civilian directly in charge of Marines. The billet goes hand in white glove, so to ceremonially speak.

Colonel Maloney says, "Well, Lieutenant Quinn, I'll leave you in the able hands of Mister Milbread. If you have any questions, or problems, feel free to come to me. Here you can make a mistake. But not on--"

"I know, sir. I know."

"And I guess I'll see you on the parade deck in the morning. I, too, am being schooled, for a parade commander spot, some day soon."

"Yes, sir. Thank you. I guess everyone goes to parade and sword school around here."

"Everyone. Absolutely."

He leaves and Mr. Milbread shows me to my desk, next to his, at the center and head of this single large bullpen, or hencoop, like area. At first impression, he seems like a nice, old gentleman, sort of a Casper Milquetoast type. That would certainly fit his name. I also notice that all forty-five sets of female eyes are on me, and the two male Lance Corporals are glancing around and are quietly smiling, slyly I think, as they observe. I wonder, who is anticipating what? I stare 'em all down for a several seconds with my best hard-ass, Randy Recon, Stoneface glare.

* * *

Still on Wisconsin
Still on the way
Nightfall
Fri, 22 Nov 1963

"I knew this was going to happen. Just knew it."

"What's that Atherton?"

"Look out the windshield, Lieutenant. It's a wreck up in front of us."

I look, see what appears to be a minor fender bender, and say, "That it is, Atherton, but that's okay."

"Why is it okay, sir?"

"Cause it's not us, so keep your mind on the road, follow the police car, and just get us to Gawlers in one piece, please."

"Oh we'll make it okay, Lieutenant, and in one piece, just maybe not today."

"Atherton, don't even joke about that. I've already been in this bread truck too long. Oh, and crack your window, the carbon monoxide is going to kill us before we get there. We'll be customers, not guards."

He vents the driver side window, reaches over to the door lever, and cracks it just a tad. All this does is let in the fumes from the street. *Screw it. Not too many things goin' right. I'll just go back to where I was.*

* * *

The remainder of this short morning at the Institute goes well. Noon arrives and Captains McKay and Kruger come by and say, "Let's go to lunch, Loooootenenant Quinn. You can drive me in your nice, new, shiny little ol' Corvette."

"Yazza, sir, Cap'n Butler, I mean McKay, sir."

Captain Kruger gags, and then bursts into boisterous laughter.

"You be still, Julius. Mister Quinn, I can see that you're goin' to be a pokin' some fun type Lieutenant. I've got a lot of monologues prepared for the likes of you. Come on, let's get moving."

"Yazza, sir."

He emits a mumbling sound that progresses to, "By the way, Julius, as you can see, Mista Quinn here, has a Vette. Three won't fit; you'll have to drive yourself to the mess. Take my car," flipping Julius the keys. "I want to ride in the Vette. You may return in our new toy after noon chow. Isn't that correct, Mister Quinn?"

"Yazza, sir."

Julius laughs. I do as well.

"Shush ya'll, don't be poking fun at your House Mother."

* * *

The table in the Center House dining room easily seats twelve, and is packed for lunch today. The XO is holding court, along with several other field grade officers. With the Yaliee Captain, is his boss, the Ops Officer, Major Jeff Smythe and Majors Bruce Black and Hank Cronin from the Institute. Met them earlier. Also, the Adjutant, Captain Buzzy Rollin, who was out when I passed through all those hatches and portals early this morning. A few other officers from The Barracks staff are present. The volleyball game must be suffering today. *Well, it looks like everyone came out of the woodwork to size up the new guy. Hell, I haven't done anything yet. Must be just to see the teachers pet.*

Lieutenant Colonel Donnelly immediately informs everyone that he and I were old teammates at One-Five, although certainly from different times. The Muv chokes on the terminology of teammates. The XO glares at him. McKay feigns some more gagging, pointing to his throat as if he were garroted while eating his salad. He turns scarlet. The XO's glare makes some folks uncomfortable, however he continues with his history monologue. The meal is only prickly for people who do not like to dance on center stage in the spotlight. I don't mind Donnelly grilling me some more. I love to perform. Give me a man with an organ grinder and a leash, and...never mind. I just like to act and feel very much at ease except for the feeling of another possible mentor finger in the stew.

* * *

My first afternoon starts innocently enough. Mr. Milbread is briefing me, showing me, telling me about every single function, rule, regulation, duty, task and so forth in the Registrar section. Finally I say, "Joe, you don't mind if I call you Joe, do you?"

"No, that's fine with me. And I'll call you Lieutenant Quinn. Is that okay?"

"Sure, whatever. How about I just call you Mister Milkbread, so as not to tighten your vest." *He got my message. He's no longer pasty white. Maybe my not-so-subtle mispronunciation of his name skewered his liver. I really wanted to call him Casper.* He snickers, politely, what else. We'll get along fine; he's a good man and will chew on my humor, and maybe adjust to it. If not, he'll just have to swallow and digest it like a plate of cold, day old sauerkraut.

I begin reading through the seemingly massive pile of papers and folders he has spread before me...have to dig into this job. I'm not one to be second fiddle, regardless of the situation.

After about an hour, I hear a rustling in the room, also an extremely low murmuring...the Magpie kind. I sense someone close behind me, and to my right. A warm breath panting in my ear. A strong scent of lilacs or flowers or something seductive is floating around my head and neck, and up into my nostrils. I feel a large, soft lump on my right shoulder. *Now that feels familiar, but normally not on my shoulder.* I turn to find a young, somewhat plump yet seductive looking WM leaning over or rather on my shoulder.

She says, "Sir, my name is Lance Corporal Teresa Casilonnia. Can I ask you a question, Bar---oops, I mean Lieutenant Quinn?" This is followed with a winsome giggle.

"Sure, Lance Corporal. First however, why don't you take your tit off my shoulder, and get your butt around to the front of my desk, and at attention until I put you at ease."

Poor Milbread chokes, squeaks and sputters like a rusty ranch pump. The murmur in the room stops. All the troops and troopettes are wide-eyed. And, unfortunately I suppose, Lance Corporal Casilonnia emits a loud yelp, followed with a sobbing scream of some sort, runs off from my desk in tears with her hands to her face. She wiggles, squirms and weaves her way around the multitude of desks and out of the hencoop. I look at her leaving, and then turn to ol' Joe and say, "Guess the question wasn't all that important."

"Well, um...ah...guess not."

"Or, she got an answer only it wasn't the one she was hoping for." I laugh, pleased with myself. I glance around the room and see forty-four astonished faces and two snickering lance corporals. *Mission accomplished. No more shenanigans. Now I feel good.*

"You know, Lieutenant Quinn, you have to be less gruff and more careful than perhaps you're accustomed. These ladies are very young and impressionable."

"Yeah. Right. And so, so innocent, too."

I look away and give the group a hard stare. Order is restored. Lance Corporal Casilonnia doesn't return. However, within three-quarters of an hour, I get a call from the Director. "Lieutenant Quinn, Colonel Maloney here. Could you step up to my office, please?"

Here again is another common phrase in the military. Maybe important, maybe not. Why is it that one steps up to the colonel's office, and down to the lieutenant's? Why not step in? Oh well, it's probably just my leprechaunish and peculiar Irish mind at work.

"Yes, sir. Should the lieutenant bring anything down with him, sir? The colonel has a question or something, sir?"

"No, just get up here, now."

"Yes, sir."

I guess it's up, not down or in, and this doesn't sound good. I hurry down, or rather up, the passageway, arrive, and knock on the Director's hatch.

"Come in, Mister Quinn."

Now then, here's another one of those phrases that is commonplace in rank and power structured environments. When a senior officer addresses you, and he has good things to say or tell you, he will always use your first name. If not, it's your rank, title, or worse. This doesn't sound good, and my intuition tells me the thoughts I had on the way are about to be vindicated.

"Sir, Lieutenant Quinn reporting as--"

"Shut up, and sit down, Barney."

Ah, Barney, good. It's not going to be as bad as I first envisioned. This will be one of those fatherly monologues, with a moral and a lesson included. Sort of a leadership fable. Good. Easy listening.

He continues, "I just got a call from the Commanding Officer of the WM Company. One of her girls called her, in tears, hysterical, saying that you were rude and gruff, and used foul language to her this afternoon in your office. Is that true?"

"Sir, did the Captain tell the Colonel what the Lance Corporal did, or only what the Lieutenant said?"

"It's Major. Yes, she said you told the girl to get her, her, um, breast off your shoulder and her ass in front of your desk. I'm quoting her. She's really upset. As is poor Lance Corporal Basi...Rasi--"

"Casilonnia, sir. And she ain't--"

"Casilonnia, whatever, Quinn. Good Christ, Lieutenant, you've only been here a few hours."

Jesus, now it's just Quinn. "Sir, if the Lieutenant may. Yes, the Lieutenant did tell Lance Corporal Casilonnia to get her tit off my shoulder and her butt, not ass, out in front of my desk."

"Fat ass, to be accurate, Mister."

"No, sir. Butt, not ass, and not fat. It was cute. Anyway--"

"Lieutenant."

"Yes, sir. Yes, sir. Anyway, the Lieutenant now sees the error of his ways, sir. However, in the Lieutenant's defense, sir, the WM in question had crept around behind the lieutenant while he sat, innocent and busy at his desk...and placed her left breast on the lieutenant's right shoulder, and whispered in his ear. I mean, right in the ear. Her goddamn tongue was flicking the lieutenant's earlobe for Pete's sake. Even started to use my first name.   So, sir, the Lieutenant did what he--"

"For Christ sake, Barney, stop this third person crap."

"Okay, sir. The lieu...I mean, I was just trying to stop the nonsense, sir. Quick."

"Well, you're driving me nuts. Go ahead."

"Yes, sir. I told her exactly that. The whole damn hencoop or bullpen or room, whatever you want to call it was watching and waiting. So, I put this type of crap to rest, first time out of the chute, sir. And sir, I think you should tell the good Major, to get her 'ladies' in line, and their minds focused on their jobs, and out of my skivvies. Especially while in the Registrar's office. My office, sir."

"Barney, I suppose you're right in some respects. I will do that. I'm going to back you on this, but I will tell her I have cautioned you about your gruffness. And I am. Clean up your act. I must admit, I like it. I like characters. However, be a gentleman, and use courteous tones. Okay? And oh yes, you may have been busy, but I doubt you are innocent."

"Yes, sir. Is the lieutenant excused, sir?"

"Oh Goddamnit, yes, the lieutenant is excused. See you in the morning on the parade deck. Cripes, this will be all over The Barracks by this time tomorrow."

"Yes, sir. By your leave, sir."

"Go."

As I leave, I bump into Captains McKay and Kruger in the passageway. Julius is laughing as the Muv says, "Distinguished yourself already, Lieutenant? Wonderful. Let's see, first, Rina swings at you. Then she calls you a pervert. And now, in a matter of hours you've attacked a young, innocent WM. What did ol' Melon Head have to say?"

"Who's Melon Head, sir?"

"The Director. Our name for him. Can't you see the resemblance?"

"Actually I do, or did, but these past few moments were not the time to be thinking about it. He basically agreed with my leadership, but not my style, technique or graphic language. And for the record, Captain, I didn't attack any WM, and I seriously doubt that she is innocent. Moreover, sir, Rina was taking a poke at you, sir. Not me. In addition, the pervert bit, although directed at me, was referring to ya'll based on previous conduct and performances. Incidentally, sir, how did you two hear about this already?"

Captain Julius chimes in, "Marsh, that constituted a monologue, and lieutenants are not authorized to deliver them, much less to the House Mother."

"You're right, Julius. Mister Quinn, did you hear that?"

"Yes, sir."

"Then you will refrain from such reprehensible conduct?"

"Yes, sir."

"And further, Mister Quinn, around here news travels faster than Superman or lightening bolts. Take heed. I suspect your buddies, the CO and XO, are already aware, and it is drifting down the hallowed passageways of the headquarters as we speak."

"My buddies, wonderful, just friggin' wonderful. They're not my buddies. And, sir, I'm just warmin' up."

"Barney."

"Sir?"

"Well done, damn well done! I love your style. I'll buy you a drink tonight. Maybe two or three, it was that good. This story will last a long time, and get better."

"I'm honored."

"Lieutenant, I've finished speaking."

"Yes, sir."

"Lieutenant!"

"Sir?"

"Forget it. I can't win this."

"Yes, Muv, sir, Cap'n."

* * *

I return to my office. All is quiet. I call the senior WM in the group up to my desk. Sergeant Alicia Black is a knockout. She should be on recruiting posters, or better yet, a centerfold. She must have more calls at the WM barracks at night than the Pentagon switchboard. She arrives, positions herself front and center on my desk, and says, "Sir, you beckoned?"

Based on her stunning beauty, the use of 'beckoned' sends an arousing pulse beat racing through my mind. It triggers evil thoughts, however I say coldly, "Sergeant Black, tell your young ladies, and I use that term loosely, that I wasn't chewed out; I'm still here; will be here for a long while; and not to be pulling any of this crap again. Understand?"

"Yes, sir. Fully. And I want the Lieutenant to know I don't condone any of that, and it won't happen again."

"Good, Sergeant. I'm glad we're on the same page. We're going to get along fine, and by the way, I didn't beckon. I ordered."

Her face flushes as she faces about smartly, and moves off. *I wonder how they do that with heels on...damn, she's cute, and a great ass, sergeant or otherwise.*

She gathers the group of women in the far end of the hencoop, and delivers a monologue, or ass chewin'. The language is, well, direct. A lot of shocked and red faces. *I wish her CO could hear her now.*

* * *

The day is over. I return to Center House. Go to the bar and join my house cohorts to collect my freebies. The word is out; the story has been told; and unfortunately, it already has been enhanced and sounds only vaguely similar to the event. Well, that's what makes history, legends, and such.

CHAPTER 6

Closing on Gawlers
Van is rockin' along
Friday night
22 Nov 1963

"HEY, LIEUTENANT. YOU OKAY? WHERE are we? I can't see anything from back here."

It's Gunny Elms, shouting from the back of the van. His gruff, Drill Instructor like voice wakes me like a long ago, but not forgotten, boot camp reveille. *Whoa, must have really slipped away. Jesus, I'm tired already.* I finally croak out, "What's that, Gunny?"

"Where are we? Better yet, where were you?"

"My mind was drifting, Gunny. Let me check and see if I can... damn, it's bad out there. Well, we're still on Wisconsin, and movin' a little better. Still crawling our way toward Gawlers. Can't be too far now."

"Okay, that's good news. At least we're around that accident. I'm lookin' out the back and it's a mess. We're gettin' tired swingin' on these straps...and getting seasick in this piece of shit. This is worse than being below deck on an APA in heavy seas."

"Yeah, tell me about it. Well, hang tough. Can't be much longer. Want some Dramamine?"

"Dramamine! How 'bout a beer?"

"I wish."

With that, I resume my trance-like state, only now I use two hands to hang on this damn strap and stare at the inside panel of the van. In just a few seconds, it comes to life in my mind's eye, like a movie screen, and I see those early days at the post.

* * *

I haven't had any more serious problems with the WM's in the Registrar Section. A few attempts to sneak around behind me but I stop their forays before culmination and wave them away with a few flicks of the wrist and my index finger pointing to the front of the desk. Sometimes I add a growl. Lance Corporal Casilonnia is back at work. She has not participated in the subsequent ambush attempts. However, she still sashays in front of my desk suggestively looking at me offering a polite, singsong, sultry, "Good mornin', Lieutenant." Otherwise, life at The Barracks has become routine in many ways, or at least in, "Barrack's ways."

The XO, LtCol Donnelly has become somewhat agitated over the lack of entries in the OD log. It started this June morning. The colors were raised upside-down. Both the off-going and on-coming OD's were there in his office, changing the watch, so he couldn't blame them. This, along with the lack of comments caused him to first change the time of the turnover of duties to 0815, after colors. And, he delivered a monologue to the off-going and on-coming OD's about the lack of adequate details in the log.

The two OD's immediately pass word of mouth alerts to all of us bottom feeders, the lieutenants, to beef up the log entries. This is followed by an order, in the form of a proclamation of sorts from Donnelly that was inserted in the log. As fine Marine lieutenants, we respond in typical fashion. We record every move, and every detail of activity to the point of absurdity. For example, a series of entries appear as:

0800 – Colors raised properly. All is well.

0805 – Went to the head.

0807 – Returned from the head.

0810 – Departed for XO's office for relief.

Then the oncoming OD would start out his tour with:

0815 – Assumed the duties of OOD. No new orders.

0820 – Checked parking lot; all secure, but did notice one cigarette butt in the far northeast corner, 17 inches from the northern edge, and 13 inches from the eastern edge. Dispatched supernumerary of the guard to pick up the butt. All secure.

0845 – Got cup of coffee.

0848 – Returned with coffee.

These absurd entries continue, to include every inconsequential discrepancy we find while checking The Barracks area in general which would cause the Commanding Officer of Headquarters and Service Company, Major Dan Roberts, no end of problems. He thought we were on a vendetta against him since he was a field grade officer. When he pleads with us to let up, we tell him we're just following orders from the XO. He apparently doesn't want to approach or confront the XO, and Donnelly never says a word about the entries to any of us. Only lieutenants stand OD, so the trend will stop when we decide to relent, or the XO orders. It will have to be the latter...collectively we're stubborn... and roguish. It's also much too much fun baiting and harassing the Major. He's too good a target.

* * *

Each day, before shuffling papers at the Tute, I attend sword training and parade preparation. I watch, practice, and do whatever the good Captain Smokey Beard desires. Every Friday I watch parade rehearsal. I feel like a place kicker waiting on the sidelines for my big chance. Finally, at the end of June '62, I'm told, "You're off the bench and going in the game." I get to participate as the Platoon Commander of the 1st MCI Platoon during parade rehearsal. Both at The Barracks and Iwo. I'm deemed ready, perhaps even over-trained. Lieutenant Howell, the officer I am to replace, is pushing for immediate replacement. I think he's tired of parades. He is not a career officer and is a bit of an intellectual, which is a dodgy trait for a lieutenant around here. Nice gent, but too smart to be an infantry officer. Should be a professor or something.

Nonetheless, it's decided that I will participate in the Iwo parade on Tuesday evenings, but not the Friday night show until after the parade here for President Kennedy in July. So be it; it's the beginning.

* * *

One Friday morning in late June, some additional lore is added to the history of the parade deck. As normal, it is all set up for the parade tonight; bleachers, fifteen rows or so high are erected along the west side of the quadrangle, on each side of Center Walk. Also, all cars are removed from the parking lot at the south end, and more of the same type bleachers are set up there as well. The troops are present on the parade field, as well as their officers. The Ops Officer, Major Smythe is in charge; his assistant, Captain Milsap, our Yalie, is aiding him. The Barracks CO is out and about watching; dozens of other officers are in attendance, watching the rehearsal. Most prominent however is the XO, Lieutenant Colonel Wild Bill Donnelly. He is covering the parade deck like a pinball hitting every bumper. Watching, listening, commenting, going from one location to another, critiquing on the go...you name it, he's got his fingers entwined in the fabric of the parade rehearsal.

I'm standing on the west side, next to the bleachers, observing yet again. First Lieutenant Charles B. Goen, who reported in this very morning, strolls over to where I'm standing. He probably thinks I'm a veteran of all this, knowledgeable, and perhaps even someone important. That's absurd. Lieutenants are generally not thought of as important. He says, too loudly, "Good mornin', I'm Charley Goen. Call me Doc. Just checked in this morning."

"Good morning. Yeah, I heard. Welcome aboard. Think you're goin' to like it here? Kind of exciting with all the activity, the President coming. Patriotic stuff, huh?"

"Yeah, I guess."

"Why, Doc?"

"Started med school; decided not to continue."

"Great. Thought you might be a psychiatrist. We probably can use one around here, at least in Center House."

"Who's that up there behind us at the top of the bleachers doing all the pointing and shouting?"

I turn, and look up. "The XO. Lieutenant Colonel Donnelly. Probably want to ride a wide trail around him for a while. He's kind of a no bullshit, hardass kind of guy." *Should tell him the lieutenants and fools line...naw, this is clear enough.*

The XO is now enhancing my whispered description by shouting some critique points across the parade field. It ends with, "How many times do I have to say this before it sinks in." It's louder than intended because he started when the Marine Band was playing, and when they stopped abruptly, he continued at the same decibel level.

Goen says, "Well, it's apparent he wants everyone to know he's in charge."

"We all know. Like I said, you would do--"

"Yeah, yeah."

We stand, chatting for several more minutes. He offers a few thoughts, all derogatory, about his initial observations. He starts to make another disparaging statement about the rehearsal and parades in general. I say, "Listen, if I were you Lieutenant, I'd cool it. And quiet down some. This is serious business around here, and besides that, it's better for us lieutenants to be seen infrequently, and heard less."

He becomes louder, "Oh bull crap. Bull shit. It doesn't take a mental giant to march around a parade field, and it for sure doesn't take a genius to run one, much less be screaming at everyone. After all, it's just a Goddamn parade."

Suddenly, a familiar voice, says, "Lieutenant Goen, isn't it? I want you to leave the parade deck immediately; go sit in my office until I finish here. I want to speak to you." Donnelly is standing close behind us. *Oh, shit!*

Goen turns a charcoal ember red, then slowly fades to a burned-out grey, as he stammers, and not so loudly now, "Yes, sir."

The XO says, "Now. Right now, Mister."

His tone and abruptness is one clue but the Mister is a final one clearly indicating the situation is ominous. I can see the black cloud over Geon's head with the lightening bolt streaking down.

Lieutenant Goen salutes, faces about, and departs hurriedly in the direction of the colonel's office, to which Donnelly offers, "Not across the middle of the parade deck, Lieutenant. Go around the south end. That's to your right, and that's the foot with the big toe on the left side." A smattering of polite snickers emanate from observers, all of who are moving away from the impact area.

Well, I was wrong. This last remark is the final clue. The bolt hit him.

Goen, now an ashen color utters, "Ye...Ye...Yes, sir." He moves quickly now.

Lieutenant Colonel Donnelly looks at me and says, "Did you hear what he said, Lieutenant Quinn?"

"Which statement is the colonel referring to, sir?"

"You know very well which one, or two. The one about what's going on out here and about me."

"Yes, sir."

"Good, I may want you as a witness."

"Aye aye, sir. But, I'm not sure I really heard much. I wasn't really paying attention, sir."

"You heard something or you wouldn't have answered him, and you'll remember, correct?"

"Oh yes, sir. Yes, sir." *Two bags full.*

With that, he moves off, and goes about his parade rehearsal business. *To err is...oh, boy. This is goin' to be worse than a dose of the clap.* A few minutes later, Captain Milsap sidles up to me and says, "What was that all about?"

I tell him. His only comment is, "Oh, shit!" He leaves, and I notice all others are avoiding me like the plague. Everyone watching the rehearsal is standing as far from me as possible. At The Barracks, Donnellyism, a known virus to us, is thought to be highly contagious, and there is no vaccine available. Lieutenant Doc Goen will have no friends. It reminds me of an anonymous saying, "The reason a dog has so many friends is that he wags his tail instead of his tongue." If he doesn't already, Goen will understand this shortly.

The remainder of the rehearsal goes well, as does the morning. I return to my figurehead job so I can shuffle some papers, thump the stapler several times, and move folders and forms from one desk basket to another, In to Out. And of course, I keep a sharp lookout for Casilonnia-like forays and tactics.

* * *

At the lunch table today, the XO is not present. He is playing volleyball, as he does often, and is probably terrorizing any junior officers in the game. He's only at the table when he has an agenda. He changes clothes in the third floor head here at Center House, leaving his uniform hanging on the inside of the door. Some lieutenant, like the tomb in Arlington, unknown, goes in and turns on all the hot water taps, steaming the room.

The plan, I suppose, is to get the XO's uniform to lose all its creases in hopes he will be forced to go around the remainder of the day looking like a damp clothing bag. Donnelly never says anything so the practice continues, and only the assailant has the last laugh. For the rest of us, it's better not to know the phantom. The House Muv might know, but he is remaining mute. Not even a mumble.

Captain Buzzy Rollin is present at the table, and informs the rest of us, that Lieutenant Charley Goen is going, actually, gone. He has been transferred, this morning, to some small post out in the middle of the desert in New Mexico or Lost Balls, Arizona, or some such place. The Barracks Adjutant, beyond being a primary source of all information for Captains and Lieutenants because he knows all, also has to do the alls, the dirty laundry. This isn't a pleasant duty, such as cut the orders, inform poor Goen and get him out of The Barracks, quickly... very quickly...and quietly.

Someone at the table asks me, "What happened? I understand you were standing right next to him."

"The XO happened to be behind Lieutenant Goen and me, just as poor Charley was making judgments as to what he thought of our parade rehearsals, parades in general and the XO. The colonel overheard him and ordered him to his office. That's all I know, and all I care to know. I warned him. I didn't witness the execution, only the crime."

Someone else chimes in with, "What exactly did he say?"

Now I look up from my steaming chicken noodle soup, and not sure who asked, glance around the table. Captain Gerry Dugan, the XO of H&S Company, is staring at me, waiting for an answer. I say, "Cap'n, I said all I'm going to say. I know nothing, and frankly, don't want to know. I'm alive, and thankful. I could have been hit by a stray round or shrapnel." He's not been here that long and just made Captain. Having just come from the ranks of the bottom feeders, he's sympathetic.

Captain Milsap offers, "Maybe we should issue flak jackets for observers at parade rehearsal."

"Yeah, either that or have the new guys wear an orange hazardous material vest."

Nothing more is said at the table about Goen, goin', gone. He becomes nothing more than another ghost, and good sea story. I'm sure it will be incorporated in the House Mother's opening monologue to newly reporting lieutenants.

CHAPTER 7

THE PARADES AT THE IWO Memorial are underway, and I'm involved. The crowds are smaller than the Friday night parade at The Barracks but are a livelier group. Folks out on a summer evening, casual dress, sitting on lawn chairs and on the ground, blankets spread on the gentle sloping hill across from the Monument. Also, unlike The Barracks, the Drum and Bugle Corps not only provides the music for the parade, but also does its march and music routine. It is more than competitive with any of the great D&B Corps in the country. That, and the performance of the Silent Drill Team, makes for a great show. It's red, white and blue throughout. Like Friday night, a person leaves here lovin' America. I'm excited about being part of it and can't wait to get on the parade deck at The Barracks, which will be soon. I need to get in these things. That's why I'm here, at least in my mind.

* * *

The parade on 12 July for President Kennedy, and his special guests, goes extremely well. It's not open to the public. The Barracks is all a dither, and rightfully so. He's the first President to visit The Barracks since Thomas Jefferson. As history tells us, Jefferson rode out with Commandant Burroughs on 31 March, 1801 to select the site. Thus, The Barracks was founded. For tonight, the CMC, General Dixon M. Shelton, invites JFK on the pretext that he will be inspecting to see that Jefferson's order, that The Barracks be situated "near the Navy Yard and within easy marching distance of the Capitol", has been carried out. In remarks during the parade, President Kennedy acknowledges that Jefferson's wishes have indeed been honored. He also states that he has recently learned that the only troops in DOD under his direct command were the members of the U. S. Marine Band...and that he and the Band intend to hold the White House against all challengers for years to come.

The Secret Service demanded, and got, canvas screening strung all along the west side of The Barracks wrought iron fencing between the houses to prevent any problems with snipers and such.

The troops are magnificent and the night is a huge success. For me, it's great seeing and hearing the President in person. Moreover, now that this parade is over, I get to be in both the Friday and Tuesday night ceremonies. I made it, the parade deck, and that's important to me. If I'm goin' to be at the show, I want to dance on the stage.

* * *

Still on Wisconsin
It's takin' forever
Early night
Fri, 22 Nov 1963

Thinking of President Kennedy and that night brings me back to the present. I peek out and see that we're still crawling up Wisconsin. We've stopped the honking, and the police are using the siren only on occasion. The flashing lights are doin' the job for now. Time seems to be flashing by, but we're goin' nowhere. I check my watch. *Damn, it's taken us a long time to get here. We've gotta move it.* I check the troops. They're in a daze, minds elsewhere. I join them allowing my mind to slip back to the days following the parade for the President.

* * *

Life is going along well for me. The days in the Registrar office are quiet and uneventful. Parades are going great, particularly since I'm now participating in both the Tuesday and Friday night events. The other potential area of barracks life danger for lieutenants is the OD tours. So far, I haven't had any hiccups on the parade deck and none on watch as the Officer of the Day.

It's a bright, sunny, Saturday morning at The Barracks. I have the OD today. I'm a little fuzzy since I stayed at the bar for a lengthy period of time after the ceremony last night. Today starts well; I mean colors are up, and properly at that. Chesty is under control. He's locked up in his pen, and I have warned the Sergeant of the Guard to ensure he stays there unless walked on a leash. Granted Chesty has a pedigree, but his antenna doesn't pick up all channels. He's a disaster on four paws waiting to happen.

The Corporal of the Guard comes into the OD's office. He's excited about something. "What's up, Corporal?"

"Sir, the Chief of Staff, Lieutenant General Brown, is on the phone for the Lieutenant, sir."

"What the devil does he want? Did he say?"

"Yes, sir. He said he's got a flat tire and wants it fixed immediately but he wants to talk to you, sir."

Lieutenant General William Brown is way up the food chain. He's the Chief of Staff of the Corps, just a few slots down from the Commandant, and lives here at The Barracks, next to Center House. I pick up the phone, "Sir, Lieutenant Quinn. How can I assist the General, sir?"

"Come over here and see me, Lieutenant."

"At the General's home, sir?"

"Yes, of course." An abrupt answer and a crashing click.

I raise my eyebrows, shake my head, grimace and mutter, "Oh, crap. My turn in the barrel."

Corporal Harkins says, "What's that, sir?"

"Nothing, Corporal, just talkin' to myself."

"Not a good sign, Lieutenant. My grandfather did that and they put him in a home."

"I'm not that old, Harkins."

"You're older than all the other lieutenants, sir."

"Not much. I just look older. Like Will Rogers once said, 'I've traveled a long way and some of the roads weren't paved.' So give me a break, Corporal."

"Whatever you say, sir, but--"

"Harkins, stow it. Just remember, a Corporal of the Guard is like plastic. Indispensable one day; and into the garbage pail the next."

"Yes, sir. You win, sir."

"Always, Corporal. Always. That's one of the blessings of rank."

47

I straighten up my uniform, put on my sword, which is the side arm for the OD here at The Barracks. Scares the hell out of the natives outside The Barracks on 8th Street, however, other than that and ceremonies, it doesn't serve much of a useful purpose and will bounce off butter.

I head out the door, and up Generals' Walk, past Center House to the next one, the General's. His is sandwiched in between Center House and the CO's. It's the same as all the others. A three-story, red brick house with an enclosed porch that overlooks the parade deck. The other side faces 8th Street and the noise of the neighborhood.

I climb up the several steps leading to the porch. The first floor is about a half level up from street level. A basement sits beneath. I knock, and a steward has me enter and follow him to the living room where the General is sitting in an easy chair. I report in properly, saluting since I'm under arms. He nods and says, "Lieutenant, I want you to have my flat tire fixed immediately, and also conduct an investigation as to its cause. Is that understood?"

"Yes, sir. Not a problem. Will get on it ASAP, sir."

"A thorough investigation."

"Yes, sir. Is that all, sir?"

"Yes. Report back to me when you're finished." He smiles, gets up, pats me on the back, and adds, "I've seen you on the parade deck, Lieutenant Quinn. You don't bounce at all, just glide. Mrs. Brown tells me Mrs. Haney thinks you march beautifully. Very impressive."

"Thank you, sir." *What is that all about?*

"Now glide over and find out what's happened."

Cheap shot. That was harsh. I salute, and execute a ceremonial about-face without staggering which isn't easy on the thick carpeting. I depart, post haste.

I look at the tire. Get some off duty guard troops to take it off the car, and we take it down the street to a battered and rundown local garage to get it fixed. The tire is bald. I noticed that all of the General's tires are the same. Hardly a tread, not a groove to be seen.. At the garage, the mechanic, an old gray haired black man, informs me, "The tire ain't worth fixin', L'tenant. Whoever the joker is that owns the car, needs him to buy some new tires."

I ignore the comment and say, "Just fix it or patch it." All I want is to have it fixed, keep air in it, and get off the OD watch in one piece. Self-preservation at The Barracks is key. Do not want to be a Goen-like legend.

As the garage mechanic goes about patching the tire, he looks up and says, "Hey, L'tenant. That blade you carryin' sharp?"

"Like a Samurai's sword. Hardest steel made. Cut glass." *So it's not true. Need to keep up the image on the streets outside The Barracks. Natives think of it as knife-like..*

"Whoa, my man." He smiles, and then shows me a very small nail or tack that has caused the leak, and subsequent flat. I figure the investigation is over. The flat's fixed and the cause discovered, so I head back to the General's quarters to report the good news.

I repeat the process of entering as the steward repeats his duties. The General, still seated, smiles, "Well, Lieutenant Quinn, what did you find?"

"Sir, the tire is fixed. It was a small tack or nail the General must have picked up somewhere. The tire is badly worn, sir, and the mechanic suggests the General might want to consider purchasing some new tires. All of them are bald."

His smile disappears. He stands, moves closer to me, directly under my chin. He's much shorter than me, and most people as a matter of fact. He also has bad breath, sort of the denture odor type. However, he's in uniform and has those three stars glinting at me, which I might add makes his breath tolerable. The General says, "Mister Quinn."

Mister. Oh, oh. He continues, "My tires are fine, Lieutenant." *Lieutenant, well, it's getting' better.* "I appreciate you having the tire fixed, however..." *Oh, Jesus. Here it comes.* "I believe that someone, one of the Marines here at The Barracks, let the air out of my tire. Or put the nail in on purpose, or as a prank. I want you to investigate this thoroughly, and I want a twenty-four hour watch placed on my car, my tires. You report back, again, with the result of a more detailed investigation. Do you understand, Mister Quinn?"

"Sir, I saw the tack, and the condition of the General's tires, sir, and I think--"

"Lieutenant, I want this investigated, and I want to ensure it doesn't happen again, do you understand?"

"Sir, perhaps the General--"

"Do you understand?"

"Yes, sir. Thoroughly, sir. Is there anything else, sir?"

With this, he smiles warmly again and guides me out onto the enclosed porch overlooking the parade deck. He ushers me out the front door with gentle pats on the back. Not exactly the bum's rush, but close, and smiling all the way. This whole calamity is ruining my Saturday morning, and more importantly, soiling my already mottled record. That is if one considers the Casilonnia ambush a blemish. It won't, however, interrupt the Bullwinkle show at Center House, nothing does. Nonetheless, the news will be leaked to the House Mother soon after through the stewards network.

I return to the guard office and call the CO, Colonel Daly, reporting to him what has transpired. He says, "Do you think anyone did this? Did he ask you to inform me?"

"No, sir. To both questions, sir. The car is sitting right out here in the parking lot. It probably picked up the tack from the street when it was moved for the parade last night, or maybe this morning when coming back in. Besides, all of the tires are badly worn, bald. It's a wonder he hasn't had a blow-out or something."

"Okay, well, investigate, and also set up a watch on the car."

"Investigate what, sir? And we can see the car from the door here."

"Investigate what he believes, and set up a watch as he ordered, and report back to him. After you do that, call me, but with only good news, Mister Quinn." *Jesus, even my mentor is calling me Mister.*

"Yes, sir."

Well, there are two sayings that are appropriate. First is, "Do something, Lieutenant, even if it's wrong." The second is, "Seek the initiative and accept the responsibility for your actions." That's my two-step plan, which happens to be my only option. Makes planning easy.

I set up a watch. Have the Corporal of the Guard check the tire every thirty minutes, log in its condition in the logbook, and report that to me. Then consistent with the Donnelly Proclamation, I will log it in as well. The Sergeant of the Guard gets a tire gauge from some damn place, and it will be used to check the tire, every thirty minutes. Next, I will wait several hours, until late afternoon, and then inform the General that I have conducted an investigation, and although he may well be correct, I can find no evidence, or no one, that can conclusively prove any malicious actions by any Marine of The Barracks.

For the remainder of my watch, the entries among the others will have:

"1300 – Cpl of Grd checked C/S's tire. 34 lbs pressure this time/ date. All's well." A *Gunga Din* type entry without the watch towers.

Every thirty minutes this occurs. Good, this will be forty-eight entries over the normal twenty-four hour watch in addition to all of the other entries. This might change the XO's mind about his edict. It's possible we could go through a logbook in record time with this number of entries. *Well, if you're goin' to do something, Barney ol' boy, it might as well set a record.*

At 1600 hours, I reluctantly walk to General Brown's house and report the results of my investigation. He says only, "Thanks, Mister Quinn. I still believe someone is letting the air out of my tires. Keep a close watch on the car."

"Yes, sir." I depart with no more scars.

I reluctantly call the CO and report the latest. He's fine with the results. It's obvious he doesn't want to know too much about it. Keep me out of it; fix it; let me keep my head in the sand. He says, "Thanks, Barney. Have a good evening." Click. I look at the buzzing handset. *Ah, at least we're friends again!*

I can't wait until my relief comes on duty tomorrow, Sunday morning. It will be the normal informal relief since the XO isn't involved on weekends. Just the two OD's. My buddy, Lieutenant Word is going to go into shock. The checks will continue every thirty minutes throughout the day and night, all weekend... perhaps forever, but that's not likely. Surely, someone will put an end to this foolishness.

Another OD story; more lore to be added to that already accumulated. There will be others I'm sure. The trick is, try not to be involved. However, that's nothing more than a crapshoot, particularly with the KY-1 phone and Sake jars lurking in the Commandant's basement.

Morning comes; Jim Word arrives. He's stunned, but howls. My watch is over and I retreat to the sanctuary of my third story room to freshen up and change into casual clothes.

When I arrive at the breakfast table, my Center House brethren are already seated and have ordered. The steward asks me if I want the specialty this morning.

"What is it?"

"Shit on the shingle, sir."

"SOS, fantastic. Better on the shingle than where it was all day yesterday."

The steward doesn't look or even act puzzled. I guess everyone has heard. I add, "And some orange juice and coffee."

"Yes, sir." He smiles and retreats to the kitchen.

Captain McKay says, "I understand you managed to distinguish yourself once again, Mister Quinn."

"How's that, sir?"

"Didn't you and General Brown have a not-so-pleasant meeting yesterday?"

"How did you know?"

"I told you once before, Mister Quinn, news travels fast around here. A steward told me as well as the gate sentry."

"Great, damn Magpies. How come they don't report any of your shenanigans?" Magpies is also a term of endearment. They are Snuffies that mumble and grumble in the ranks, and spread rumors elsewhere. Love Snuffies and can't exist without the Magpies.

"Because, I is the House Muv, and can do no wrong or evil."

"What? Sir."

"Exalted and protected, Lieutenant. Exalted and protected!"

"I see, sir."

The food arrives, saving us all from a monologue and me from explaining the incident in detail.

The SOS is great. I'm safe from the idiosyncrasies of the Center House since the three Captains are busy planning a foray uptown.

Quiet reigns. All's well in my world...for now.

CHAPTER 8

Gawlers Funeral Home
People gathering
Friday evening
22 Nov 1963

I'M BACK IN REAL TIME again. We're here. I mutter aloud, "Good God, look at all the people. Thousands on the street in front of Gawlers." *What in the name of hell are they doing out here in front of Gawlers.*

The Gunny says, "What's that, Lieutenant?"

"Take a look outside if you can. Huge crowd."

"Can't see anything from back here, sir."

"Well, take a look when I get out."

Man, reverence can be loud. When this many people are in one spot, and even when they speak in hushed or normal conversational tones, it's loud. Can be heard over the normal sounds of the city. I look around to the Gunny and say, "Hey, Gunny, I'll get out and go inside to find out the scoop. Keep everyone inside the vehicle until I get back with some word. We may not be popular."

"Aye aye, sir."

I find an Army major inside Gawlers, a rep from MDW. He welcomes me and tells me we're the first of the Death Watch detail to arrive.

"That's a surprise, sir. I didn't think we would ever get here. The traffic is a nightmare. It's crazy out there. What about the crowd outside? What are they doing here?"

53

The major says, "I'm told it's about 5,000 or so strong. Curiosity seekers...want to see the President arrive, if he does. Maybe the first thing you and your troops can do is provide crowd control until the DC police get some more officers out there."

"Major, my troops are in Dress Blues and are here for the Death Watch. They have been announcing on TV for hours that Lee Harvey Oswald, the shooter, was a former Marine. Hells bells, if we go out there, we'll probably incite a ruckus of some sort. Begging the Major's pardon, I'm not taking my troops out there, sir. Tell the police to hurry, and do their damn job."

"Lieutenant,--"

"Sir, we're in dress blues, it's rainin', we have no raincoats and like I say, those folks could get ugly. I know you don't want a mess on your hands. Do you?"

At first he was shocked. Maybe thought I was insubordinate. Now he changes his expression and says, "You're right. Sorry. Bad idea. Just bring your men in here and wait for the others, and orders, or whatever."

"Yes, sir...and, Major, you said earlier, if they bring the President here. Are they or aren't they? If not, we're in the wrong place and it will be hell getting to the right one."

"That's the word I have at present but I think it may change. I'll keep checking."

"Okay, sir. Please do. I don't want to be a wrong-way Harrigan or Corrigan, or whatever his name was...not today." "Got the message, Lieutenant."

I'm buggin' him. He's heard about me. I'd bet on it.

Once inside and settled, the major introduces me to the Director of the funeral home and an assistant, and then he directs me to make a security check of the home.

"Sir, what for? I don't think anyone in here is leaving." I start laughing at my own joke. Hell, a person could wait a lifetime for a chance at a straight line like that. *The major doesn't think it's funny. He's glaring at me. I'm right, he has heard about me.* Nonetheless, I can't stop laughing. After a few seconds, I get myself under control.

The major cracks a slight grin, and then says, "You're a piece of work. Just walk throughout and make certain that only one entrance is unlocked, and then post someone at that entry."

"Yes, sir." I'm still smiling over my one-liner. Even the assistant is smiling. He liked it…will probably use it, first opportunity.

The assistant honcho, a mortician I would imagine, and I depart. Maybe it's my imagination but they always smell like formaldehyde. *I wonder how they ever get a date, and Jesus, they can't talk about work.*

He takes me everywhere, even the preparation rooms. We ensure every door is locked. Workers are in two of the prep rooms preparing bodies for viewing and it is not a pretty sight. One is a scraggily, old woman and ugly, but then I suppose it would be difficult to look good under her circumstances. I leave the room feeling queasy.

It's one thing seeing dead folks, entirely another when someone is nonchalantly working and hovering over them. I'd rather be a fencepost in Texas than a mortician. This duty is becoming not so glamorous. Nonetheless, the walkabout is completed. I have all doors locked. *I still think it was a great line.* I tell employees not to allow anyone to enter, except at the front door. The Gunny will post a sentry. The exception will be the hearse with the President. I have to assume he's being brought here for preparation at this point.

We're given a vacant viewing room to use for a rest area. Here we take off our blue dress coats and carefully sit down on the front edges of chairs to relax, or at least try, until we get some definite scoop.

The major arranges for some chow, sandwiches. Barbecued beef… smells good but looks bad to me after my tour. We've not had anything to eat since just before the flag football game.

On top of being starved, the big toe on my right foot is throbbing. It feels like it's broken…someone stomped on it during the game. I hope it will ease up soon. If not, so be it. Will be suck-it-up-time for ol' Barney. Also, I have a kink or muscle spasm in my back from someone's elbow shot. That was on the opening kickoff. Sort of a wake up call to let me know the troops were going to take their shots at the lieutenant.

Before the major leaves, I ask, "Sir, got any aspirin, or something to relieve pain?"

"No, what's the problem?"

"Aches and pains. Young rank, old body, sir. Thanks anyway." He leaves the room at a hurried and worried walk. *He's not sure what's goin' on. Hope he finds out shortly.*

As I sit in the corner of this viewing room, with its musky odor and scent of flowers engrained in the chairs, drapes, and carpet, my mind slowly spins back once again to my early days at The Barracks. It's uncanny. I wonder. Is it fate that has me here, at this time? Or Destiny? I vaguely remember there is a difference. Oh well, I'm going to have to chew on that for a while. My thoughts drift away and I see my barracks life as if I'm standing outside a store window, looking in, watching mannequins play it out...even the voices and sounds are vivid...

* * *

One of the little known benefits of the Friday night parade for the Center House bachelors is that single women call into The Barracks wanting to speak with, and meet, the officers in the parade. Notably, captains and lieutenants. When they attend the event, they get a program, which lists the sequence of events in the parade, and the names of the parade staff and company level officers. I guess it's something about the moment and the blue-white dress uniforms that prime the hormonal pump of these gals or it could be their gatherer instincts being cast aside and taking on those of a hunter.

Whatever the motivation, it is the duty of the officer taking the call to use his hunting instincts and Marine training to gather information. The age-old patrol report format of SALUTE works wonders...Size, Activity, Location, Unit, Time and Equipment. Just get the size of the party; is it dancing or costume or something else; address; is some organization involved...God forbid something like the Daughters of the American Revolution; get the time; and is it BYO, the rest of the equipment we will bring. Make some judgments based on voice tone and vocabulary. Never offer an invitation to come here first; it holds too much danger of embarrassment on home grounds. Run a patrol first; sacrifice a bachelor for the good of the house.

The parade is a spectacular, patriotic event conducted under the lights each Friday night during the summer. The crowds are far from bowl game size, but several thousand attend each week. It's the place to be on a weekend night of '62 in D.C. The atmosphere is electric. The parade deck is a lush, green grass plot about football field in size. If a spot or two is worn, or slightly burned out, it's sprayed with green vegetable dye. It's going to be a luxuriant, shamrock green come hell or high water. It's a rectangle in the middle of The Barracks. The long axis runs north and south. It is bounded by sidewalks on all four sides. At the north end is Commandant's Walk; on the west side is Generals' Walk; on the east, Troop Walk, and beyond it is a row of thick hedges that are next to the offices and barracks building. Along this building is the roofed arcade. At the south end is a battery of cannon, decorative only. Beyond is the parking lot.

Bleachers are installed each week. The unreserved seating is in the parking area, the end zone. The reserved seating is along the west side of the field. Barracks officers and senior NCO's in blue-white dress, not in the parade, function as seating escorts. Behind these bleachers are Generals' Walk and the five brick homes to include Center House. The walk that crosses the parade deck is Center Walk, which leads into the arcade. The Barracks is a quadrangle and a perfect setting for a parade... Broadway or Hollywood couldn't create a better set or stage.

For the parade, the U. S. Marine Band is in their traditional red tunics with some black and white trim and braiding along with the white cotton trousers. The Drum and Bugle Corps is in their distinctive but different red-white dress uniforms. Their tunics are pure red without all the salad dressing, and they too wear the heavily starched, white cotton trousers. Both wear white barracks cap and white gloves. In the spectators eyes they both look colorful and military. To the critical eye of those on the inside, the D&B is much sharper in dress and manner. The bandsman are musicians first, the guys in D&B are Marines first.

The troops are in blue-white dress uniforms. Dark, Navy blue high neck tunics, heavily starched and creased white trousers, and white caps and gloves. All brass on the unnies is gleaming. All shoes, Sam Brown belts, and visors are spit-shined to look like patent leather. Everything, grounds and men are pristine looking but reeking of tradition. All glistening under the flood lit parade deck. That alone will make you gasp upon first seeing it.

The parade itself is a kaleidoscope of music, color, military commands and precision movements. It teems with patriotism. The audience reaction spans the range of awe stricken...from hushed, reverent silence, to strident mouthing of approval, to loud oohs and aahs with bursts of applause and whistles, and often glassy eyes. If one isn't a patriot when they arrive, they will be when they leave...everyone.

It begins with a Marine in parade uniform coming from under the arcade. Slams to a halt, leather heels audibly clicking and with a trace of sparks from his metal cleats on the cement. He rings the ship's bell, DING-DING, two bells indicating its 2100 and the parade is about to start. The bell ringing is an old custom...based on a four-hour cycle, six times daily. Nine-thirty would be three rings, sounding like, DING-DING...DING.

Then the handler walks Chesty out on a leash and across Center Walk stopping in front of the bleachers. Jerks on his chain and Chesty half leaps in the air, pawing. That's the only trick the dog knows and he screws that up most of the time. Then he is led off to sit at the side of the reviewing area. Chesty is not in blue white dress, but he does have a uniform. A scarlet and gold dog coat with his name and rank sewn on the side. The drooling beast is a corporal.

Next is Officer's Call, sounded by a bugler from D&B standing, spotlighted, at Center Walk in front of the flagpole and bell. The eight company officers march in a column of twos from behind the bleachers, across Center Walk, past the flagpole and bell, and to their units hidden from sight in the arcade.

Then the troop march-on. The band sounds Attention. Company Commanders bring the two companies to attention, and to right shoulder arms out of view and under the cover of the troop arcade. The parade deck is dark. Then the Band and D&B sound Adjutants' Call, followed with the march-on music, always some stirring Sousa march. This brings the troops marching, actually bursting out of the darkness at each end of the arcade, and onto Troop Walk along the parade deck, toward the flagpole, and one another. The lights pop on just as the units hit troop walk. At this moment, the adrenaline is raging in both the boys in blue white dress and the crowd. I never tire of the rush...proud, of the Corps and the US of A.

When the two units are on the parade deck and formed facing the front, the Parade Adjutant commands, "Fix, Bayonets." The bayonet portion of the command rolls off the tongue with a musical lilt. Captains Rollins and McKay are the two best at this. I think it has to do with their native accents. Rollins from Texas, and the latter from North Carolina. The troops fix their glistening chrome bayonets to their rifles, to the music and a silent six count.

The lights are vanquished once again. The Adjutant commands, "March on the Colors." The colors are marched on...again from the darkness of the arcade at the north end with a single spot light draping itself over this four-man unit. The U.S. Flag and the Colors of the Marine Corps with all its battle streamers fluttering in the slight breeze. The Color Guard maintains a brisk pace to ensure the colors are streaming out behind them. Once front and center, a taped narration of the battle color is played to the crowd over the address system. It presents information regarding the well over forty streamers for the various battles, campaigns, service and citations.

The colors are posted to the Troop Walk, between the two parade units of MCI and Ceremonial Guard Company. The Marine Band and the D&B march the length of the parade deck and back, in Sound Off. They play military marches and the music booms and reverberates off the old brick walls of The Barracks. Both reform at the north end.

The parade is formed and the Commander orders the manual of arms by the troops. The rifles CRACK and POP as the Marines move them through each command..."Left shoulder, Arms." THWACK. "Port, Arms." CRACK. "Order, Arms." CRACK, POP, and CRASH as the rifle butts strike the concrete. One crack, one pop, one crash...144 rifles. Nothing but sound and precision. This is followed by the publishing of the orders of the day, and by Officers Center. The company commanders and platoon commanders upon order, march to the center, form, march forward to the Parade Commander and all give a simultaneous, flowing, precision like sword salute. They are posted by the Commander, and return to their former positions with their respective company.

Darkness covers the rectangle again. A moment of silence, then BOOM. Out of the arcade comes the Drum and Bugle Corps, under spotlights, snare drums rat-a-tat-tatting the military beat and forming around the flagpole. Then a brief moment of silence, and WHAM. They burst into music with all their bugles, horns, drums and cymbals. In their red-white dress uniforms, they contrast sharply with the troops in blue-white dress on either side of them on troop walk. They play a two-piece concert routine and return into the arcade in much the same manner as they entered. The crowd responds loudly with extended applause, and some yelps and whoops.

As soon as they disappear, The Barracks goes dark again. Then, lights on again and the Drill Team marches forward and to the center where it performs a silent drill routine of over 400 counts including rifle exchanges and spins, all with bayonets fixed, ending in a long line of twenty-four facing the bleachers. There they do several manual of arms movements with the rifle including a more sophisticated version of the age old Queen Ann salute, each in a rippling effect up and down this long line.

Then, a Sergeant, the rifle inspector, conducts a ceremonial rifle inspection, twirling and spinning the regulation 9.5-pound, M1 rifle culminating the inspection with a throw from behind his back and over his shoulder back to the Marine in line. He does this at each end of the line. They reform in three ranks of eight and return to the troop line. The essence of precision. They don't march, they slide and glide as one. The audience is at first silent, in awe. Then begin responding with oohs and aahs, hushed at first, and then exploding into much louder exclamations accompanied with clapping. Like the D&B, the DT also gets some yelps and whoops, mostly from the peanut gallery in the end zone. A few "HOO-AHS" also come from this less sophisticated grouping. If the truth were known, we perform for the guests in the reserved seating; we play to the end zone. Doesn't mean the West side bleacher section isn't appreciative; they are, just more restrained, especially where the guest of honor is seated.

At this time, appropriate honors are rendered to the guest. This is followed by the passing in review of the battalion. When they return to Troop Walk, the company officers are dismissed, coming off the parade deck in the same manner as they first entered. The Parade Sergeant Major and the NCO's take charge, and conduct a march-off, by the center and into the arcade. Lights dim, except at the flagpole. Taps is played, and then echo taps is sounded from a far corner of the post. The parade is over. Several thousand folks leave this summer night outing glassy eyed and with goose bumps regardless of the temperature. They go home better Americans.

Participating in this makes me stand taller, and love this country a little more each time. It never gets old and never seems routine, at least to me. It's why I'm here. Why I wanted on the parade deck so desperately. Vain perhaps, but I gotta' be on stage; gotta' be in the spotlights.

Regardless of the sometime antics and shenanigans off the parade deck, these men, these boys in blue white dress, are good. The absolute best.

Good Lord, I love it...I love it so.

* * *

Gawlers Funeral Home
No one else here
Waiting for word
Fri, 22 Nov 1963

The pungent odor of this room brings me back to the moment. That, and maybe my thinking about the parades, the patriotism and my country. I kinda' wish I could get my hands on that little twerp, Oswald, myself. I look around, the troops seem okay. Some smoking, some not. Most just staring straight ahead. They're tired. The day has been long for them also, actually longer. They always get up earlier.

My toe is still throbbing, back still aches, and my brain-housing group is starting to pound, trying to determine what the devil is happening or not happening. *Everyone in here is lost in their own thoughts. Might as well go back to daydreaming.*

CHAPTER 9

AFTER EACH PARADE MOST OF the officers gather in the Drum Room of Center House, the bar, with their guests and the guest of honor. The troops return to The Barracks and many go to Tuns Tavern, the enlisted club in building #58 in the Navy Yard. They also have a large female following and they attract some good lookin' honeys. Can spot them in the end zone bleachers just before making the column left at the end of the parade deck after passing in review.

The Staff NCO's adjourn to their club in the south end barracks wing. I like all this because the Corps was founded in a bar, Tuns Tavern in Philadelphia. We still cluster together in pubs, bars and slop chutes to tell sea stories and get the hot scoop.

Tonight's parade, although it's a hot and muggy August night made worse by the lights, should go well. It starts as normal at two bells. The crowd rustles and murmurs in eagerness, then hushes.

From my pre-parade position behind the reviewing area, I watch the handler bring the uniformed Chesty out on his leash. The crowd stirs once again. As the handler in his blue white dress marches smartly across Center Walk, Chesty on his leash is ambling along in the bowed-legged waddling walk of a bulldog. Chesty doesn't prance or strut. At this point, all is going A-okay or C-okay as it were. The handler stops on his mark in front of the reviewing area between the bleachers. He tugs on the leash, which is the signal for Chesty to half sit-up and half leap in the air, pawing. A supposedly cute trick to show off the mutt and amuse the crowd.

It is, except Chesty is aroused for some reason and displays himself to the crowd. His tongue is also hanging out, a string of drool is dangling, unlike him, flaccid, from his mouth to center walk.

Colonel Daly, the CO reddens to a beet color and drops his head in momentary despair. The guest of honor also flushes. However, he's choking back a laugh. He quickly gathers himself and takes on a look of anguish to match the CO's. The wives of each, half turn facing one another, hand to the mouth and blush. Then their color drains and both take on the ashen gray color that has come over Colonel Daly who is now frowning and vigorously rubbing his mouth and jaw with his right hand as he shakes his head. He's pissed but can do nothing. A not so pleasant experience for any Marine.

The handler jerks Chesty back down on all fours. He walks off with an uncomfortable Chesty at his heel. They retreat to his accustomed spot on the grass adjacent to the reviewing area, close to the barrack's officers' wives reserved seating section of the bleachers where Chesty is suppose to sit, quietly. Upon arrival, instead of sitting, Chesty squats and unloads a record setting dump. The odor hangs heavy in the muggy air while Chesty, as dogs are prone to do, takes a sniff of his handiwork. Then he nonchalantly attempts to cover the pile.

The handler, who has retained his brilliant scarlet color, jerks the leash, and drags our wonderful mascot away from the bleachers and to his dog pen. Chesty is unceremoniously relieved of duties. He could care less; he already relieved himself, and looks pleased. Personally, I believe it is a premeditative act on his part. He didn't want to sit and watch the entire parade. I could be wrong, but I swear he has a smile on his face on the way to his pen. He even looked back, mouthed an "expletive" in bulldogese in the form of a snort.

Chesty's subsequent parade exposure will be limited, I'm sure. Certainly, no more cute tricks, and he won't be sitting next to the bleachers. At best it will be on and off quickly. If he weren't the official Marine Corps mascot, he'd be with Doc Goen.

Nonetheless, Officers Call is sounded and the parade goes on this evening as if nothing has happened. That's always the case when there is a small mistake or flaw. We actually practice recoveries from mistakes so they either go unnoticed by the crowd, or appear to be part of the show. The crowd is again full of oohs, aahs, and applause for almost every move on the parade deck. A ceremonial Marine from the guard of the day has quietly and unceremoniously removed the pile. We hadn't rehearsed this recovery, it wasn't anticipated. If it were, how would you explain what you were about to do to the troops. Oh well, like in *Gunga Din*, "All is Well." Our CO, Colonel Daly, the fine, soft-spoken southern gentleman recovers with a clearing of his throat and a forced grin. The show goes on and Chesty is forgotten.

After the Officers Dismissed portion of the parade, I hang around the bleachers behind the reviewing area. I don't have a purpose, just still on my usual high after participating in the parade. I chat with a few of the officers that had the host duty tonight. I feel a tap on my shoulder, pick up the scent of a lovely and seductive perfume, and hear a soft voice say, "Hello, Barney Quinn. Small world."

I spin around and there stands a gorgeous red head, actually more of a soft light auburn and coppery color. Her somewhat more than shoulder length hair springs and rebounds with the slightest of head movement. She shows a few freckles that seem to accentuate her sexiness. My quick but obvious eyeball reconnaissance takes in all of this five-foot, seven or so, well-endowed gal with appetizing utilitarian hips and long, shapely triple threat legs. She is wearing a lightweight, dark blue jacket and skirt with a pale blue frilly, sheer blouse. Her green eyes glimmer like shallow ocean water in the Bahamas. *Jesus, she's stunning. Whoa! Goddamn!*

It seems like an eternity but it's only a moment before I say, "Hi. Do we know each other? Ahhh...Wait a minute, I do...can't place--"

"I'm Gabrielle Monjeau. We went to high school together; were classmates."

"Oh, yeah. Right. Right! Gabby. Damn, how are you? Geez, you look sensational. What brings you to town, and here to the parade no less?"

"First, thanks...for the compliment. I work here in town. At AT&T. Live out near Bailey's Crossroad. This is my first parade. My boss and his wife have been here and told me this was a must-see...a have-to-experience type event. They were right, it is. And incidentally, only those that I love call me Gabby."

"Well, okay. I can handle that. It's nice you're here... great to see you again. I was just transferred here several months ago. Live right here on the post," pointing to Center House.

Gabrielle waves the program at me and says, "I couldn't believe it when I saw your name. I got so excited I told my two girlfriends from work, and I guess all those around me, that I knew you. We were classmates. Barney, you look delicious."

"Uhm...well, thanks, I guess. Where are they?"

"Who?"

Good. She's distracted. Interested. "Your friends."

"Oh! Yes, right here, I mean there." She points to a pair of lovelies a few feet away, near the corner of the bleachers.

I lead her by the arm, and we take the few steps over to her friends. She says, "Harriet, Sally, this is Barney Quinn."

They nod and smile simultaneously. The taller of the two says, "Hi. Gabby's been raving about you all night, or at least since she realized it was you out there."

"Raving? Really? Finally."

Gabby. They must be close friends...tight as ticks. Anyway, I'd like to have heard that. Did you ever notice that when women travel in threes, one of only two situations exist? Either one is gorgeous and two ugly, or all three are the same. Never, ever, two tens and one coyote. This trio is drop-dead gorgeous. My wandering mind and roving eyes quickly return to focus on Gabrielle.

She moves closer, coyly grins, and says, "What does that mean... finally?"

"Well, you never gave me a tumble in school."

"You weren't that inviting."

"Ouch."

"Now you are, so stop whimpering."

I can't keep my eyes off her. The longer I stare; the more she talks, and the more I remember of this gal. She was a looker in school as well, played the violin in the orchestra, and was popular...went steady with some guy with a car and a few coins as I recall. A light bulb comes on and the "gentleman" bell chimes within my head. I say, "Would you ladies like to join me in Center House and have a drink or two as my guests? Let the crowds thin out some. Where did you park, at the Navy Yard?"

Gabrielle says, "Let's see, a few questions. Yes, we would love to have a drink or two. Harriet's car is parked at the Navy Yard. And, lets go, right girls?"

Harriet and Sally nod in unison, "Great." Harriet is slightly taller than Gabrielle, leggy, well endowed and proportioned. She has either a great tan or Mediterranean ancestry, along with dark, dark hair. Her face accommodates full lips and huge, dark eyes. She can snatch your breath away. Sally is shorter by several inches, soft looking with a cute face and heart-shaped lips, nice legs and is deliciously top heavy. Seems like the bubbly type, a breath of fresh air. The three are proof of my theory. If Gabrielle hadn't had such a vise-like grip on my heart, I could gawk at these two longer. Better I don't.

I take Gabrielle by the arm and lead her and the other two beauties toward Center House. Once inside, I order drinks for the three, and Gunny Richards hands me my bourbon and Seven without me ordering. There is something obscene about that. Gabrielle sees this, looks at me, says, "Creature of habit, or just a regular at the bar?"

"Both, and thirsty at the moment."

Captains McKay, Kruger and Milsap are lurking at the far end of the bar, watching me, whispering, and ogling the two strays. I could introduce them, but choose to let a couple of lecherous lieutenants slide in and introduce themselves. I love it, the captains plan, the lieutenants act... worry about the consequences later. It's the old "do something lieutenant, even if it's wrong" syndrome at work, or at play as it were. I keep all of them away from Gabrielle with more nifty moves than Gene Kelly. Sometimes, fate is kind, or is it destiny? Whatever, when it is, don't do anything to tempt it, just accept it.

We chat over a few more drinks. Harriet and Sally are fending for themselves, and doing fine...might be trolling. Gabrielle and I try to talk about old times and the in-between- times but the Drum Room, although steeped in tradition, is also crowded. The din of voices, make it hard to hear any soft conversation. Her two friends slide over, and whisper to Gabrielle they've got to leave. She nods, tells them to wait a sec, and turns to me, "Barney, are you free tomorrow?"

I start to make a sarcastic remark about being free, but think better of it and say, "Yep. Nothin' goin' on here."

"Why don't you come over to my place? We can chat comfortably, I'll feed you lunch, and then we can take a dip, sit by the pool and enjoy ourselves. Get reacquainted."

"It's a date. What time, and where?"

She smiles coyly. *Probably thinks I'm easy. Hell, I am.* Actually, I'm somewhat defenseless against her. She gives me the time and directions to her apartment near Bailey's Crossroads, across the Potomac in Virginia.

She's still smiling, eyeing me, then whispers, "Promise to come."

I just nod. The woman has me slightly unhinged.

As the four of us enter the vestibule outside the bar, Gabrielle leans toward me, our bodies touch as she puts her hand to the side of my face, brushes it along my cheek ever so softly, and kisses me on the opposite cheek, resting her head by my ear and murmurs, "Don't be late." She oozes sensuousness, and smells sexy and fresh. Then she tilts her head back a tad, looks at me with those shallow water eyes, and gives me a soft peck and brush on my lips. She says, "Good night, sleep tight, and I'll see you tomorrow, Barney."

Sleep tight. I don't think so. Unhinged is an understated thought. I probably need to be put in the pen with Chesty and only let out on a leash. Nonetheless, I whisper, "Goodnight." I kiss her on the cheek and continue, "It's late. I'll walk you to the shuttle bus."

We all go outside the main gate where the bus is parked at the curb. The three of them get aboard and head for the safety of the Navy Yard and Harriet's car. I go back inside, and the Gunny slides a drink toward me as I approach the bar. Julius asks, "Who was that?"

"A friend. A dream come true. Finally, something, or rather someone, from my past that's good."

I glance around. The bar has emptied out with the exception of the six of us, the house dwellers. I ring the bell. Look at the Gunny and say, "Give my housemates a drink on me. Life is good tonight."

We drink; I mentally toast Gabrielle, and tomorrow.

* * *

Gawlers
Waiting
Evening
Fri, 22 Nov 1963

I'm out of my daydreaming mode again...and it is open-eyed daydreaming. I don't want to close my eyes in this place. Might wind up with that scraggily old woman in the prep room.

Nothing going on yet and the night seems to be advancing no faster than a long, creeping freight train. We're still sitting around the viewing room. Thinking of creeping, this place gives me a case of those. I look over to the Gunny and say, "Hey, Guns, did you change our man at the front door?"

"Already relieved him, Lieutenant. Go back to dreaming... and stop smiling. You're not supposed to have a happy face here." He laughs.

I smile. Say nothing.

With this I resume the wait, and return to my fog. It's like sitting in a car at a country railroad crossing, mesmerized by the clickity-clack of the wheels as the sound rocks you away somewhere pleasant. For me, it's thinking of Gabrielle.

CHAPTER 10

SATURDAY MORNING BREAKS CLEAR AND sunny. This is good because it's an important day for me. My fateful surprise meeting with Gabrielle Monjeau last evening still has me unhinged, nervous, but anxious to see her.

The Center House crew of bachelors eats breakfast and after a few minor household and hygienic chores, we adjourn to the living room for the Saturday morning ritual. I know, you're thinking it must be something important and serious for these fine, young, parade ground captains and lieutenants to meet on a day off. Perhaps a discussion on infantry tactics? Maybe a political discourse led by our in-house White House Aide, Lieutenant Van Dell? Possibly an always-delightful, long, syrupy monologue from our House Mother, Captain McKay, ol' Mush Mouth.

Well, it's none of the above. This select, top one percent of the Corps company grade officers settles in to watch *The Bullwinkle Show* on TV. Yep, it's a can't-miss event every Saturday. Perhaps today, it will take my mind off Gabrielle. Rocky and Bullwinkle live in Frostbite Falls, Minnesota. Rocky is a flying squirrel. Bullwinkle's also the President of Moosylvania. Boris and Natasha are two evil doers whose dastardly plans are thwarted by Rocky and Bullwinkle, and they never, ever, win out over the Moose and Squirrel.

Apart from what you might think, we enjoy ourselves and laugh until the tears flow. Good fun and it starts our weekends on a happy note. Regardless, it doesn't erase Gabrielle from my mind. For me, this

69

is much more than a happy start. I'm on my way to capture a dream, or be in one.

I leave, motor down to M Street, hang a right, go the several blocks past Hogates Restaurant, and continue on to the 14th Street Bridge. I zip over the bridge, past the Pentagon, through the mix master and onto Columbia Pike. Out the Pike several miles and just before getting to Bailey's Crossroads is her apartment building. It's off to my left, up on the hillside, overlooking a park-like area populated by huge elms, several maples and some smaller dogwoods. I pull in and locate her apartment on the second floor, overlooking the green area. The pool, already bustling with beauties, is in the center of the horseshoe type building arrangement.

She buzzes me in. When I arrive, Gabrielle is in the doorway waiting. Damn, she looks even better in the daylight. Although none of my past flings have been the last geranium, there have been times when my late night choices didn't look quite as good in the morning sun. However, she is beautiful and stacked. She's already in a one-piece black bathing suit with a jacket-like pool thingy. The suit, one-piece or not, leaves very little to my imagination. Those damn faint freckles. A few around her nose and cheek, then some much paler ones have matriculated down to her breasts. Something sexy about that, at least to me.

Gabrielle looks me up and down and says, "Where's your swim trunks, Bernarr Leslie?"

"Bernarr Leslie. You remembered."

"No. Looked it up in my yearbook. Master of the Mats! Anyway, sorry to let the air out of your balloon."

"Master of the--"

"Trunks. Trunks would be good. You are going to the pool with me, aren't you?"

"Got 'em right here, rolled up in my towel."

"Why didn't you just--"

"Had the top down on my way here. I didn't want to be swarmed by any ladies along the way, so I dressed rather than wear them. Still got some serious looks though."

"Yeah, right. You wish...top down? You have a convertible?"

"Yeah, a Vette."

"My, my, my. Boys and their toys. Maybe we can go to my favorite weekend hide-a-way sometime soon and cruise the boardwalk, like old times. Ocean City...Maryland, that is."

"I couldn't cruise back then, didn't have a car. Didn't figure it was Jersey, although that was popular with you and your elitist friends in school...who could, and did cruise."

"Nasty. We weren't, either. I'm going to forgive you for that remark because I know you were teasing. Right?"

"Yep, just kidding. Nonetheless, the Ocean City idea sounds good. But, no cruising."

"Okay, great. We'll talk about it later. Now that you're in, let me give you a quick tour. Then you can change. We'll eat, and head for the pool."

"Sounds like a plan."

Her apartment is a two-bedroom and two-bath layout, new. Has a small kitchen, a nice cozy dining area with a glass top table. A living room larger than most, with a fireplace. It's furnished in what I classify as homey, warm, comfortable, lived-in-looking furniture. Over-stuffed chairs and couch. Everything is in varying shades of greens and blues. *Colors must have something to do with her hair.*

Scented candles and other knick-knacks, some in black, here and there. Watercolors on the walls, no prints, most are seascapes.

The living room opens onto a balcony that overlooks the hillside park area. The trees near her balcony rise above it, providing a shady sitting area. On it are padded, white wicker chairs and a matching two-person, tiled-topped table with a glass-enclosed candle. Nice. Probably romantic at night, or if alone, comfy.

She says, "Well, say something."

"Beautiful, cozy."

"That's it?"

"Ahhh, let's see. Warm, comfortable and no pictures of men. Must have stuffed them in drawers."

"Harriet and Sally were right. You're a piece of work. Going to be hard to...never mind." She cocks her head to the side, raises her eyebrows and shakes her head a few times.

"Hard to handle...damn straight. Okay, I'll try a realtor's approach. Near to stores for convenience, an easy drive to work, several quaint family style restaurants nearby and no children here."

"You're a real smart...you know what. Good Lord, where do I find them?"

"At parades. Give me a break. You and that outfit have me a little unglued."

"Good, now you're making progress and scoring points. However, the drive to work is not good. The mix master is a bear, but it's worth the hassle. This is a pretty area. I like the Virginia countryside. Almost as much as the Maryland shore."

"Well, gal, at least it's an easy drive on Saturdays, even with all the folks out and about in the good weather."

"Let's have some lunch. On the patio." Pointing she adds, "Open that bottle of wine, please. You do drink wine?"

"Wine! I prefer grog, or maybe some barbed-wire juice squeezed by hand...and perhaps a nail sandwich. Of course I drink wine. I'm not an animal."

"That's a shame. Oh well. Take these glasses out for me. We're having pasta salad, some good garlic bread, a nice wine and lots of questions from me."

"Another great plan. Should I change now, or later?"

"Open the wine, take out the glasses, then change. By that time I'll have everything ready and on the table."

She points to her bedroom, "Use mine, not the guest." I do as ordered. Check out the bed. It seems like a nice playground. Softer blues and greens in here except for that huge stuffed white sheep dog on the bed. Damn thing looks real. "Woof, grrrrrr." Nope.

I toss my stuff on the bed and start to change. I hear, "Close the door, Barney. What are you, an exhibitionist?"

"No. Just trying to peak your interest."

"Close it."

"Yeah, okay."

I do so and quickly change into my faded black Makaha surfing shorts left over from my time on Oahu, a sun faded red Kaneohe Bay golf shirt and my well-traveled Korean Eedewa shoes, vintage '53, made from jeep tires...thongs in this world. Nine years and the tread is still good. Will see if the Ocean City girl is as glib about these shorts and stuff as she is about everything else.

She's waiting on the balcony, seated, lunch on the table, and wine poured. "Well, well, a left-over surfing bum, I see."

"Yep, saw right through me." *You're quick, that's for sure. This could be a championship match.*

She laughs and says, "I hope you're not that superficial."

"Close. Just kidding. I'm not, but in most respects, fairly simple, straight-forward with a tint of sarcasm." I sit. "This looks great." I take a bite of salad. "This is really good, Gabrielle. And the setting is beautiful." She nods and smiles. I take a sip of the wine. "Hmmm, much better than grog."

"And barbed-wire juice."

"Oh yeah. This is smooth. Doesn't scratch the throat."

"Good. I know my wine and the rest is pretty much my repertoire. I'm an eat-out type gal, and that's a warning because now that I found you again, I'm not planning on letting you escape any time soon."

"Okay, another good plan although it sure sounds ominous." We continue to eat, chat about where we've been, and what we've done during these intervening eleven years. Damn, it seems like just yesterday I was infatuated with her. Maybe it was! I try to maintain eye contact but it's difficult. Although she's wearing a sheer, jacket type, whatsemabobit thingy over the bathing suit, her fair skinned, twenty-eight-year-old body is poured into the suit. It's shapely and toned. *Hell, she may injure me.*

As she talks about her past, a ray of sunlight works its way through the branches and leaves, and settles on her head. It fascinates me, I stare. My trance is broken by her slightly raised voice, "Barney, are you listening to me. What's wrong? You seem lost."

"No. No, I heard every word. It's the way the sun is striking you. There's not many things prettier than your hair in the midday sun. It makes noon look like a sunset."

"Wha...my God, Barney! What a lovely and poetic thing to say. I never--"

"Ah, come on, please. That's my, aw shucks line. It was a thought, the moment. Anyway, you were saying something about college."

"I'll try to get back to it but you took my breath away. Anyway..." She continues the conversation by telling me she went to Western Maryland College majoring in French with initial desires to work as an interpreter, maybe in the import-export business. For one reason or another, she didn't finish but stayed in the general area, D.C., to work. Has been with AT&T since school, now manages a marketing group. She is attending George Washington in the evenings, majoring in education. Wants to teach someday.

Then, out of leftfield, she throws out, "I'm just out of a serious relationship that went south. Actually, a little more than a year ago. You?"

"Me, what?"

"Anything serious going on, or went on?"

"No, just the Corps. Maybe a few flings."

"Flings?"

"Yeah, passing fancies. Dates. Nothing serious."

"Why nothing serious?"

"Hard to net. No, just kidding. Gabrielle, I was an enlisted Marine for seven and a half years. One doesn't get too serious about anything on a hundred and fifty bucks a month. Then after I was commissioned four years ago, I was in Quantico only temporarily... for just a year, training. Then PCS'd to Hawaii."

"PCS'd?"

"Permanent change of station. Transferred."

"Oh."

"There I was in amphib recon and I spent most of my time out in the boondocks training or on operations. When I wasn't, I was playing handball and golf with my buds or playin' at the beach. Chasing waves... some board and body surfing. None of those are conducive to finding or formulating long-term relationships. Besides, maybe the Corps is my mistress. You know there's an old Marine saying, 'if the Corps wanted you to have a wife, it would have issued you one.' So, there you have it."

"Ummm, that's cute, and encouraging."

"What?"

"Your last remark. The mistress and Corps thing. Depriving."

She continues by telling me again how much she likes Ocean City, and the southern coastal portion of Maryland. Both on the ocean and bay.

There are also moments of silence as we enjoy the food and the sun and fate-generated warmth. A gentle wisp of a breeze drifts through the trees. The rustling of leaves sounds like whispering on-lookers. I was right, the setting is comfy. *She's in thought. My remarks and attempts at humor may have shaken her. For sure, something's on her mind.*

After lunch, I help clean up. KP duty is not my favorite chore, but I'm on my best behavior now. This woman has my attention and by helping, standing close, I capture her scent, and it's seductive.

We finish and go to the pool. She picks out a couple of lounge chairs shaded by an umbrella, saying, "As you probably know, or perhaps recall from our Crystal Springs Pool days, I don't sun well. Fair-skinned redhead and all. Brings out my freckles."

"Yeah, well I like 'em...looks sexy."

"Good, more points. Anyway, we sit in the shade or play in the pool. So, let's set things down, get wet, and then sit." She drapes her towel over the chair and drops the tote bag alongside.

I drop my towel, and as I'm pulling off my golf shirt, I say, "Crystal Springs? Damn, were we there together? Probably not. You were goin' steady then, and I was always broke."

"I don't know, was just dragging you into the past to get a reaction. See if you really remembered me. You acted last night as if you barely did."

"Oh, I remember you all right. You played the violin. I joined the damn school orchestra just to get close. Didn't even play an instrument, had to learn the doggone kettledrums. I reaped nothing from my endeavor. A plan gone sour. You just looked at me like I was some sort of bug."

"I did not. I didn't even look. You were shorter than me then... and a wrestler. Everyone thought wrestlers were crude."

"Yeah, but cute."

"Let's get in the pool."

She dips her toe in, then sits on the edge, and shudders, "Brrr, cold." She slides in slowly.

I dive in, feeling at home from my aku amphib recon days in Hawaii. We swim some. Mostly stand in the semi-shallow end and talk. As I noticed Friday evening, she's a bit of a touchy-feely type person so we hold hands, hug and brush lips occasionally. She sits on my lap with her arms around my neck as I squat and bob in the shallow end. We talk some more in this enjoyable position, then get out, and dry off. She settles in the shade of the umbrella. I move as close as I can but in the sun, to catch some rays. I've never been this pale. It's hard to get a tan in the city and at The Barracks. We chat some more. The day is going good and the quietness following my remarks seems to have passed. I bask in the warm sun thinking of this stunning turn in my life.

She asks, "Barney, all kidding aside, how about we go to Ocean City next weekend?"

I pause for a moment, trying to shake the drowsiness brought on by the warmth of the sun. I run my schedule through my mind, and say, "Like to, but I can't. Have the duty next Saturday. How about the following one."

"Duty, what's that?"

"OD, Officer of the Day, basically guard duty at The Barracks."

"Oh. Okay, the following weekend. It's a date. We'll leave on Saturday morning since you have the parade on Friday night, and come back Sunday night sometime. I know the area so I'll make the arrangements. Okay?"

"Sure. How about coming to The Barracks Friday night? Have dinner in Center House, and then take in the parade. I'll eat with you, but then will have to leave you with one of my buds after dinner and during the ceremony."

"That's wonderful. I accept. That'll be fun."

"Okay, I'll set it up."

A coy grin creeps across her face, "Can we see each other before then? Two weeks is a long time, although I guess it really isn't after eleven years."

"Sure. I'll give you a call."

"Don't call on Tuesday or Thursday, they're school nights."

"Okay, will call on Wednesday. Maybe go sightseeing or something on Sunday. How's that sound?"

"As you say, it's a plan."

We talk some more. Get dry, and head for her apartment. I change, she doesn't. While I was getting back into my duds, she must have ordered some pizza. It arrives within minutes of my returning to the living room. She says, "Pay the man, Barney. Then have a glass of wine. I'm going to change."

She returns wearing black slacks and a dark green blouse that accentuates her green eyes and long, thick, fluffy hair that seems to float gracefully around her shoulders.

We eat, on the patio again. The sun is about to kiss the earth so she lifts the glass and lights the candle. We chat some more, hold hands on the tabletop, and sip wine. She goes from holding one hand, then my other, and then traces her finger lightly around the backside of my hand and wrist. We continue to talk quietly allowing the evening's looming darkness to engulf us. Exchanging looks, searching each other's eyes for meaning.

Time has passed all too quickly. I say, "I have to get goin'. Hate to...it's been such a fun day. A nice time...warm...good. But, it's best I get along. Have a bunch of shining to do."

"Shining?"

"Yeah, shoes, boots, Sam Browne belt and stuff."

"Oh, yes. That's right. Your mistress calls."

"Whoa, that was mean."

"You're right. It was. I was just teasin'. It has been nice, more than nice...wonderful. I haven't felt this comfortable, this...this, ah, wanted or needed or something in quite some time." She leans across the table, softly traces her fingers over my cheek, hooks her index finger under my chin and tugs me closer. She kisses me, brushing her lips slowly around my mouth. We stand, and regardless what I'm thinking, she leads me, hand in hand, to the door, the front one.

We lean into one another and our lips meet in a more meaningful and deeper kiss than the soft brushes. Then another. She murmurs or purrs something, maybe just a sound, then nibbles my ear lobe. *Damn she smells good...and tastes good.*

She gently pushes me away. I don't resist, just back off. I look at her and say, "Ahhh, Gabrielle, thanks for a great day. I'm glad we bumped into one another. Nice. Really nice. Talk to ya on Wednesday."

"Me too, and yes." She brushes my lips once again, gives me a peck on the tip of my nose, whispers, "Don't forget me...again."

"Won't. Didn't the first time. Just never got to the plate."

"Well, you are this time...and taller."

"Night."

I turn and leave, glance back as she blows me a kiss and closes the door. Hot damn! Where's the guy with the bucket of cold water, or garden hose, when an old dog needs it.

I stop abruptly. *Left my gear in there. Good!* I smile and head for the Vette.

CHAPTER 11

Gawlers Funeral Parlor
Getting late
More troops arrive
Fri, 22 Nov 1963

SOMEWHERE A DOOR SLAMS. THE noise shakes the haze from my head like a bugler's reveille. The major from MDW is standing in front of me, his voice sounds like a foghorn. Finally, it registers, "Lieutenant Quinn. Lieutenant Quinn, are you with us?"

"Sir?"

"You look as if you were gone, Lieutenant...perhaps someplace pleasant."

"Yes, sir. Guess I was. What's up, sir?"

"The Navy and Air Force units have arrived. The officers in charge tell me that they and the troops are not the same as were trained at the MDW session months ago."

"Really? That's surprising...Naw, I guess not actually. What can I do to help?"

"How about giving them some indoctrination...some before-the-job-training, then let me know what you think. Like, will they be able to perform up to standard?"

"Sure, sir. What standard? MDW's or the Marine Corps'?"

"What? I...they were right about you. You think you're the only service that...Never mind."

"Sir, it's a state of mind. The Corps, sir, is a state of mind. I meant no disrespect, sir...I just like to poke fun and jerk chains. Prod the pride as it were. I'll get on it right away, Major. Will let you know."

"Thanks, Lieutenant. Quinn, isn't it?"

"Yes, sir. Bernarr Leslie Quinn, sir. A fine, pig-shit, potato farming Irish name."

"Okay, okay, I get it. I can use some humor around me today. Yours will have to do. Actually, I could use someone like you everyday. Keeps things in perspective."

The gunny and I head for the viewing room that houses these new arrivals. They're looking sharp, for Wing Wipers and Dixie Cups. The situation is not as bad as the major depicted. Some of them were at the session, and I've seen them at MDW ceremonies before. At the White House and the Tomb.

We get to work and show them the movements required to get on and off watch around the casket. It's not at all simple, indeed, it's complex. There are no commands. Everything is based on timing, anticipation, and subtle, hardly detectable movements. Coming to attention is certainly simple in itself, but the anticipation and timing is what is important to ensure precision with solemn ceremonial smartness. And, as usual, no mistakes. There is a zero tolerance level for mistakes around here, be it at The Barracks or MDW.

I take the two officers aside and work with them. The gunny and our corporals work with the others. When I'm done with the lieutenant and ensign, they return to their own troops. The gunny and I depart, leaving our NCOs to conduct the training.

I hunt down the major and inform him that everything is under control. He's happy, or maybe just relieved. He's obviously nervous, antsy at least. It's getting late, and the Army unit from Fort Myer hasn't arrived, nor has Hooligan's Navy, the Coast Guard. The Army is always the first at MDW ceremonies since they run the show. I don't know about the Major but the simple fact that they aren't here yet leads me to believe that something's gone afoul. I'll let it go for the moment. I'll push the Major harder if some word doesn't get to us damn soon.

I return to my seat in the corner of our viewing room. I wonder if I'm beginning to smell like the room...scent of flowers or that distinct odor of funeral parlors. Nevertheless, it takes only moments for me to fade out and think of my early barracks days, which now seems eons ago. I gradually disappear into my haze while my troops are busy training the others.

* * *

Life at The Barracks and Center House is both hard work and fun this late summer of '62. Parade rehearsals, bantering at lunch, and avoiding ambushes in the Registrar's Office occupy my days. The parades, liberty runs, a drink or two in the evenings while listening to Uncle Julius and Mush Mouth, and calls to Gabrielle occupy my nights. Kruger and McKay expound on the pitfalls of barracks life, women in general, and of course Wild Bill Donnelly. JG always nods in approval but with his usual impassive mask. A human recording device. *Is probably going to be an author someday.*

We have a new Adjutant at The Barracks. Captain Buzzy Rollin has left, replaced by a diminutive and intellectual red-haired, Irish Captain. I'm not sure those traits are commonly associated with Irishmen, but Captain Jake Dennehy is just that...Dennehy, it ought to be the name of a taproom, with darts and shuffleboards...Dennehy's, on the corner of Fourth and anywhere.

The wee, balding Irishman quickly becomes the company grade officer's most vital source of information, and he seems to know everything going on at The Barracks. Already his reputation is well known and the saying is, "If Captain Jake don't know it, it ain't so or tain't happened."

Anywho, he has informed us that Donnelly is leaving, to be replaced by Lieutenant Colonel Harry Gimletti who is already aboard, but not officially the XO yet. Wild Bill will have his play-off, a long-standing barracks tradition this Thursday evening.

The normal Friday night parade and my OD watch will follow the play-off tomorrow on Saturday. Based on my call tonight, Sunday afternoon, Gabrielle and I will do some sightseeing. Take in the various memorials in the city; follow it with dinner at an upscale German restaurant, Old Europe, near Wisconsin and Calvert Streets. Nice place, not too pricey. Have a strolling violinist that plays at the tables. Since Gabrielle plays, or played, she should enjoy this. I'll ask one of the musicians in the Marine Band instead of one of my house cohorts for a selection to request. That way I'll get a sensible answer. All I know are Irish ballads and ditties like, *Roll me over in the clover* and *Ninety-nine bottles of beer on the wall*...and some other nasty beer drinking songs. I don't think any of them have arrangements for the violin...well, maybe the fiddle.

After my call to Gabrielle, I drop by the Drum Room for a quick nightcap. Just one, tomorrow evening will be a long night. Play-offs tend to let the animals out of their cages, which lead to forays uptown to disrupt the civilian population and end with a rock-hard, twenty-five cent White Tower hamburger on the way back. Oouh-Rah!

* * *

It's a Thursday afternoon and the reign of terror for Lieutenants is over. The XO, Wild Bill Donnelly's play-off is upon us. This tradition is years old, perhaps decades and is simple, yet meaningful, and done for all officers leaving The Barracks, except the Charlie Goen's of the world. In this case, Lieutenant Colonel William Donnelly will be played-off from this, The Post of the Corps.

At 1600 hours, he, as all others before him have, will go to the Commanding Officer's office for a brief visit. Here he has the opportunity to discuss with the CO whatever he chooses about his tour at The Barracks. After this formal visit, the two leave in the Class "A" uniform of the day. This means the wearing of the coat, or blouse, as it is officially referred to, with all ribbons and badges.

They stride across Commandant's Walk, toward the houses, and then turn down Generals' Walk to the middle. There they turn on to Center Walk, and stop, stand at attention, at the normal parade reviewing spot. As in TV, it's marked with a painted white dot. Nothing left to chance.

Lined up behind them on Generals' Walk, led by The Barracks Sergeant Major, are all the Staff Non-commissioned officers of The Barracks. They are on the north side of Center Walk. On the south side, I and all the officers of The Barracks arranged by rank, stand at attention. The Drum and Bugle Corps is formed across the parade deck from the CO, and XO in this case, at the juncture of Troop Walk and Center Walk, fronting the Ship's Bell and flagpole.

The D&B play two numbers of their choice, then a number selected in this case by Lieutenant Colonel Donnelly. After the music, he walks to the D&B and solemnly addresses them. *When my time comes years from now, I'm goin' to get some reaction from these guys.*

82

After doing so, the XO returns to his position, and the CO leads him first to the row of SNCO's, then to the officers, allowing all to shake hands and bid a formal farewell. As he moves down the line of officers, he stops momentarily in front of a few and comments. Mush Mouth is one, causing him to flush red, maybe he's embarrassed after all of his warning monologues. Donnelly moves rapidly through the lieutenants but pauses in front of me, smiles, and says as we shake, "Mr. Quinn, maybe we'll get to serve together in one-five again someday."

Gad, I hope not, this has been tough enough.

I mutter, "Yes, sir."

After this, the CO, XO and the officers adjourn to the Drum Room in Center House. All order a drink. The CO then addresses the assembly highlighting Donnelly's tour at The Barracks. Milsap murmurs so only those of us in the rear of the gathering can hear, "I bet he doesn't mention anything about last year's IG Inspection."

Gerry Dugan whispers, "What?"

Captain Milsap looks around to ensure we're not being noticed, "There were so many troops lined up for Request Mast with the Inspector General because of him, the line stretched the length of the troop arcade and flowed into the parking lot."

"For what?"

"For what? For being such a hard ass all the time. About every little thing."

Request Mast is a rite of passage. Can go to the top with your complaints. Not that often used so there is a message here. We're still mindful so our laughter is muffled but stops abruptly with the House Mother's admonishing stare, the now-boys type.

When finished, Colonel Daly asks, "Anybody like to offer any comments?" In this case, no one does. Just a lot of relieved looks that the reign of terror is over. The CO goes on, "Well, then, let's get to the fun part." He offers a toast.

"To fair winds and a following sea. Safe Journey."

"Here, here" is voiced by all.

Then, "To the Corps."

Again, by all, "To the Corps."

When the toast is completed, the XO is given the opportunity to join the Four Second Club, and if successful have his name inscribed on the plaque, which hangs in the Drum Room for all to see, supposedly forever. To do this, he must drink a bottle of cold beer, from a mug, in four seconds or less, with no notable spillage. Minor drooling is permitted, but no leakage at the corners of the mouth.

For those of us in the know, which are few, we understand the control Gunny Richardson, the bartender, has over this event. If he likes the departing officer based on his general demeanor around Center House, resident or not, he will provide a slightly chilled beer, designed to slip down the throat easily. If he dislikes the person, the beer will be ice cold, designed to constrict the throat and make a four second mark unattainable.

If completed successfully, all cheer and offer "Oouh-Rah's." After this, regardless of success or not, the departing officer is presented with a fine pewter beer mug with the name of The Barracks engraved on it, along with his name and his tour dates. This over, the officer addresses this clan of ceremonial warriors. A play-off monologue. These vary in length, intelligence, wit, and enlightenment.

The field grade officers in most cases seem to be unable to down the beer in four seconds, but of course some were served ice cold and others were simply throttled by a lack of practice and imagined decorum. Donnelly's was "Gunny" doctored...probably even spent time in the freezer. He doesn't make it...not even close but I suspect he doesn't care. His monologue or rather comments are short, concise, understandable, astute and perhaps perceptive but not warming.

If this were a play-off for one of the known rowdies, junior officers, the beer would be down in under the time limit, some with a belch, some glassy eyed, some with a string of drool, or any combination of these. However, so far, none neared the record of 1.5 seconds of Warrant Officer Tex Farrier.

In addition, the monologues of the lieutenants and captains are lengthy, mostly humorous, not mentally challenging, and usually bring up several tales of past bawdy behavior that answer questions the CO might have had about niggling but legendary events. Those formerly anonymous souls now no longer remain in the vanquished light of history. They're bared. However, they are long gone so they can't be made to walk the plank.

After a few drinks and socializing, the senior officers begin to scurry down the anchor chain so not to be left alone with us animals during the serious drinking. By doing so, they avoid the great sport of baiting them by us lieutenants. A few majors are more susceptible than others, and one in particular. The lure is floated in the form of a question from Chink, "Major, sir, how come you can't obtain a White House clearance?" This is a well-known hot button. Major Dave Roberts launches into a discourse. He's hooked by feigned questions of interest by others. Time flits by until he's the last senior officer present.

He is now responsible for all conduct at the bar, and any foolhardy antics and actions. Baited and trapped, his presence acts as an aphrodisiac to the remaining rowdies, the boys in blue white dress. *He's not foolin' anyone, he relishes this role. It's his way of being one of the boys again.*

The night wears on and the P-whipped, married company grade officers head for the anchor chain, except for the gamers, the century club group, which remain with the bachelors. The number isn't large, but infamous and equally as villainous as their bachelor counterparts. This play-off party goes on for hours, and will head uptown to some watering hole to terrorize the customers. Sometimes at a fashionable spot, like Basins on Pennsylvania Avenue, maybe the Farragett Inn which has a piano bar, or often to a location of lesser elegance in our surrounding neighborhood. All in good fun. Sometimes, an incident is conceived, born, and later nurtured into a legend...like karate chopping the plastic catsup and mustard holders at the White Tower, or maybe climbing the statue in Lafayette Park to sit with the French hero. Tonight's play-off will be no different, and Basins is to be blessed.

These play-offs are normally held on Thursday evening. Consequently, the Friday morning parade rehearsal is a monumental challenge for the Lieutenants on the parade deck and maybe a parade adjutant, particularly if it's Mush Mouth. On these occasions, his eyes go from his normal half-mast position to a wide-open, self-enforced stare. Milsap, you recall, has a hollow leg so if he suffers, it's in silence and never distinguishable. Uncle Julius, not a parade adjutant but a parade staff officer, and escort on occasion, never recovers well and his suffering is most noticeable by his bloodshot, watering eyes. He always blames allergies for this reaction...or a lieutenant who utters a comment.

Those that are not involved, gather at the rehearsal to enjoy the pain and suffering of those of us that have over indulged. However, it is interesting to note, to date, that basic fear of failure, of screwing up on the parade ground, prevails. Amazingly, no related catastrophes occur.

The XO, Lieutenant Colonel Donnelly, is played-off. A fine and distinguished Marine officer. Hard, but fair...sort of. He was good for The Barracks, and good on the parade deck, but rehearsals will be less tense and traumatic. Nonetheless, the snuffies and magpies are happy and the Lieutenants will now breathe easier fearing only the OD watch and trips to the Commandant's basement late at night to change the code card in the KY-1 phone.

* * *

Still at Gawlers
Still not all here
Nearing 2200 hours
Fri, 22 Nov 1963

I hear some loud chattering, and look up only to find some of my troops talking of the training session with the anchor clankers and the bus drivers. The latter is in reference to the blue and silver dress uniform of the wing wipers. They look like they work for Greyhound. I see the major, so I get up, go over to where he's standing, and ask, "Any word yet?"

"No, just called. Told me to stand fast. They think they're taking the President to Bethesda Naval Hospital, but are not sure yet. So we wait."

"Yes, sir. But, he's not coming here, a civilian place. They're goin' to do everything they need to in the confines of a military establishment."

"Think so?"

"Yep, I mean, yes, sir. With that in mind, how about letting me take that sentry off the front door and tell the folks here to just keep it locked?"

"Okay. Oh, by the way, thanks for the training help. They look good."

"No sweat, sir, and they'll be fine."

He leaves the room and I return to the corner and my self-induced version of a coastal fog. Can't see anything, but can hear the sounds.

* * *

My OD watch on this clear, quiet and pleasant late August Saturday passes uneventfully, and my Sunday afternoon with Gabrielle goes well. We visit the Jefferson and Washington Memorials. Stroll up the mall along the reflecting pond and visit with Abe. Then we sit on the top step, people watch, and talk more about each other's past.

With the sun dropping quickly bringing with it the amber sky, we mosey, hand in hand, to my Vette and head to dinner at the Old Europe. As we drive up Wisconsin, she says, "Barney, nice afternoon. Thanks."

"Yeah, it was fun. I'm looking forward to tonight. Our first dinner out, together...a real date."

"I think you'll enjoy Old Europe. If not, we'll enjoy us. Right?"

"You bet."

Normally, heavy German meals don't lend themselves to romantic circumstances. However, the ambiance does and we keep it as light as we can with only knockwurst and sauerkraut, staying away from pork, potatoes, dumplings and such. At Gabrielle's suggestion, I order a Muller-Thurgau wine. The wine steward says, "Superb choice by the beautiful lady." She smiles and nods. He bows and leaves but not before giving her a glance, a once over, and what I consider a lecherous smile. I catch his attention with a Stoneface, Randy Recon stare.

I look at her and say, "And? The wine? Tell me."

"It's a cross between a Riesling and Silvaner. It's milder than a Riesling, not much acidity and has a light flowery bouquet."

"You don't say. I'll be damned. Probably won't taste like barbed-wire juice. I need to bring you along with me to my regular watering holes."

"Barney, Barney, Barney. Always a crack. I just know my wines. Remember, I had an interest in the import business at one time."

"Well, all I know is that I've never had a bad wine; just some better than others and in some cases, straight from the bottle...but those were usually good reserve stuff found in half-gallon and gallon bottles."

"Suavé, Bernarr Leslie, suavé. I'll have to teach you."

"That and what else?"

"Down, BQ."

The strolling violinist is at our table. He asks if we have a selection. I say, "Any one of Bach's sonatas for the violin would be nice."

He shrugs, raises his eyebrows and grins. I don't know what that means. Maybe he's surprised I know something about music, or it's a ridiculous request, but nonetheless he starts playing something that sounds good, and difficult, at least to me. Gabrielle looks shocked and says, "Barney, where did you--"

"Chalk it up to a hidden talent, one of many."

She smiles, and the wine and the music, along with the candlelight entice Gabrielle into her finger-tracing mode. I submit without a whimper. She says, "Barney, I want this to continue, and I'd like to see more of you."

"That's good, I'm game. However, I hope you understand that in a few weeks, when this '62 parade season is over, I'm going to do everything I can to be transferred into Ceremonial Guard Company. My CO, Colonel Daly promised me as much."

"Okay, great, I guess. What's that got to do with it...or with us?"

"My time will be eaten up with more ceremonies. Not just the parades. All the Military District of Washington (MDW) ceremonies around town. The White House, Tomb, funerals at Arlington. Maybe, hopefully some travel. That means more training, rehearsing and such, and more shine time."

"Shine time and your mistress calling."

"Yep. No slack in this area. Got to be T – U – F - F, tuff. All the time."

"Well, what are you saying? No?"

"No, not at all. It just might be limited to weekends, and not even all of them. Plus I want to try and squeeze in some night school at the Maryland extension program at Bolling Air Force Base."

"All right. All I'm saying is that I want to see you, as much as I can, or rather you can, or whatever. As I said Sunday, I'm more comfortable than I have been in a long time. I've enjoyed our time together. Since fate intervened for us, or at least me, I just want a fair shuffle."

"Fate?"

"Yes, fate, Barney."

"Well, you've got me on my heels. I'll admit to that. But, fate, that's heavy stuff, but okay, if you believe that. We'll see where the path leads."

"You don't sound very excited."

"No, I am. Really, I am. I'm just a little nervous...or something. Fate, destiny, what if, if and...and whatever."

"Barney, what are you jabbering about?"

"Nothin'. Forget it. I feel good about this."

"Well, okay. I'm excited. And I believe in fate. So, on to Ocean City next Saturday. Early start. It's about a two and a half hour drive, or slightly more. We're going to stay at The Commander Hotel. It's right on the boardwalk. A nice, old place. Been there for years. I booked us rooms."

Rooms, plural. Interesting, fate is apparently conservative. Think I'll check the almanac and see when it's get laid month.

I say, "Sounds good to me." And leave it at that.

We share an apple strudel, which we probably don't need, but leave nary a crumb. We continue to linger. I order another bottle of old Professor Muller's wine. We sip wine, talk again about ourselves. The violinist strolls by once again, smiles and nods, and plays another number. *I wonder if it's another piece from good ol' Johann.*

Gabrielle talks less, and asks more questions about where I've been and the things I've done in the Corps. Nothing heavy. The night ends, it's late, and tomorrow is a workday. I drive her home with the top down. Her hair is swept back as the wind whips over the windshield. She leans back in the seat, head on the rest, and hums along with the music from the car's radio. Cripes, it's *Unchained Melody*. Yeah, makes me hunger, too. Occasionally she glances at me and smiles. My eyes go from her to the road and back.

We arrive at her apartment and stroll to the door. There we say goodnight with a few meaningful kisses and another peck on my nose and a blown kiss. I head back to the post, both bewitched and bewildered. Jesus, guess what's playing on the radio as I head down Columbia Pike.

Fate is beginning to needle me.

CHAPTER 12

Still at Gawlers
Still waiting
Getting later
Fri, 22 Nov 1963

THE HAZE HAS BURNED OFF. I come out of my self-induced Southern California, June-gloom, and coastal-like fog for a few moments and glance around the room. Everything is status quo. The troops have settled quietly, some with eyes closed, but not in my world this trip. I go back within myself. Gabrielle started me thinking with her fate remarks. First that our chance meeting was just that, and then her constant reminders. Then those two songs, *Unchained Melody* and *Bewitched*, playing on the radio that Sunday night, pushed my thoughts further along the path. Next, the unexpected turn of events that very next morning implanted fate deeper into my psyche garden. The idea won't go away, like a weed. Does remind me of a joke however...how do you tell the difference between a weed and a plant. Pull it out. If it comes out easily, it's a plant. Well, this won't come out so it must be a weed, but not necessarily unwanted.

* * *

Monday, the morning after my dinner date with Gabrielle, I find out from Captain Jake that my old mentor, Colonel C.J. Daly is leaving. This is odd. A CO and XO leaving this close together in time. The new CO is Colonel Edward Weaver, and guess what? He was the XO of my regiment, years ago, in Korea, when I was a Sergeant Squad Leader in

"B" Company, 1st Battalion, 5th Marines. *This is weird. Gabrielle's started something...perhaps fate is stepping in?*

I doubt Colonel Weaver knows me or has heard of me. I hope however, ol' Colonel CJ will tell him of my desire to go to Guard Company, and his commitment to make that happen. Probably not, they have more important topics to address other than Barney Quinn. Normally, I wouldn't care about these type changes...none of my business, but not this time. I want the Drill Team.

* * *

The change of command takes place at the Iwo parade Tuesday evening, killing two birds with one stone. One less ceremony, which is almost always good. Although somewhat strange, the play-off follows that Thursday. Usually it's the same day. It's a milder one since most of us haven't fully recovered from our Donnelly escapades.

The next day, Colonel Weaver surprises us with an appearance at Center House for lunch. The CO's here usually eat at home since its right here on the post, second house up in fact. Most likely hasn't moved in yet. He sits, we all introduce ourselves, although it's just a formality. Everyone was at the change ceremony. The serving of the meal goes on as normal as soon as we all scramble back to our seats. The soup of the day is a homemade vegetable, loaded with chunks of veggies in an aromatic broth. With the Saltines, almost a meal in itself. After a few spoonfuls and while others continue to devour their soup, I launch into a sea story about an old friend of mine, Tony Paletta. A few sentences into my tale, Colonel Weaver says, "Are you talking about Captain Tony 'Big Stoop' Paletta?"

"Yes, sir."

"You know him well?"

"Yes, sir. He and I are buds."

"Buds, Lieutenant?"

"Yes, sir. Close friends." I ignore the implied reference to the difference in our ranks. "We served together in Korea in One-Five. And again in Hawaii, in the Brigade. Played golf together almost every weekend in Kaneohe, save duty and field exercises. Yes, sir, I'd say Stoop and I are buds...tighter than ticks."

"You would, huh. Hmmm? Stoop? He only allowed a few of his very best friends to call him by that name."

"That was me, sir."

"I know, you said, Lieutenant. Since you were in One-Five in Korea, did you know that I was your regimental executive officer?"

"Yes, sir. Well, vaguely. I was just a Sergeant then. Didn't see you where I was, sir, and figured you didn't know me."

"Yes, well, I didn't know you. Did you know your Regimental Commander there?"

"Well, sir. Knew of him, didn't know him. Did see him once. Colonel, now Brigadier General Walter Barto. He's down at Quantico now."

"Yes, I know that. He and I are very good friends. As, Stoop, Captain Paletta and I are as well. In fact, we three stay in touch from time to time."

Oh-oh. I'm smellin' an ambush...and he sounds perturbed to boot.

I mutter a weak, "Yes, sir."

"Colonel Daly has told me all about you, and I called Stoop to learn something more of you."

It is an ambush and you walked right into it, dummy.

I put my spoon down, wipe my mouth with the napkin, take in some oxygen and say, "Colonel, sir, Stoop tends to exaggerate and I sure hope the Colonel took that into consideration. He loves to add color to every tale, and if there isn't any story, he'll make one up. I wouldn't put a lot of faith in what Stoop, I mean, Captain Paletta said about me.

"Oh?"

"On the other hand, sir, I hope Colonel Daly had good things to say."

"Any other advice or thoughts, Lieutenant Quinn?"

Shut up, Quinn, you dummy.

"No, sir."

The Colonel goes on, "They both did. Does that surprise you? I want to see you in my office sometime in the next two weeks. I'll get the Adjutant, Captain Dennehy, to set it up."

"Oh, Jesus."

My housemates have slowed down their eating process and are listening intently. In fact, Mush Mouth's spoon clatters into his bowl. They don't have any soup left, they're faking it. Mush Mouth looks like he's waiting for me to stumble so he'll have another left breast or flat tire monologue to deliver.

The silence gets the better of me so I say, "Sir?"

"I want to see you, Lieutenant Quinn. Want to talk to you. Is that okay? Do I need to get an appointment?"

"Oh, yes, sir, Colonel. No, I mean, no, sir! Certainly, sir. I'm available at the Colonel's convenience, sir." He gives his head a bewildered shake as if I may not be the same Lieutenant Quinn, Colonel Daly and Stoop described...as if maybe my skylight leaks a little.

Silence continues to reign among the junior officers at the table. Captains McKay, Milsap, and Kruger are head down, continuing to fake spooning the soup, but with eyebrows raised and eyes at the top of their sockets looking at me. Mush Mouth is shaking his head, slower than a funeral cadence, as if in total despair. Colonel Weaver, sensing the lull, looks at Captain Milsap, and asks, "John, what does the ceremony schedule look like over the next few weeks?"

Milsap responds, indicating that Iwo's are about over, what's on tap for the Friday night parades, a few special Thursday-nighters and some scheduled MDW ceremonies. After this, the normal conversation of sports, news, world events, but not Bullwinkle, returns to the table. I stay quiet, no more sea stories. My mind is overheating at 14,000 rpm's trying to determine what this meeting might be about but hoping it will include me going to the Drill Team. Whatever, I'm goin' to be lookin' tuff; standin' tall; be ready for anything; and hopefully be more tuned in than today...you know, be a little smarter than bait. In addition, if the subject doesn't come up, I'll let what appears to be another mentor know I want to go to Guard Company, and I want the Drill Team.

It appears that I have three more mentors if I add Stoop and Brigadier General Barto. That's a lot of fingers in the stew, almost a full hand. Not much room for my finger.

* * *

Gawlers
Waiting, getting concerned
And getting late
Fri, 22 Nov 1963

I hear something that brings me back. Another door slamming and what sounds like a heavily laden gurney straining down the hallway.

Maybe one of those poor folks I saw earlier. I glance around the viewing room. Nothing has changed in here...it's really only been a few minutes since my last burn-off. All's well. I'm getting comfortable here and that makes me nervous. Never want to become comfy in a funeral home.

I relax once again and my thoughts turn to Gabrielle...the night I invited her to dinner and the parade before our Ocean City trip.

* * *

Friday evening, the last in August, Gabrielle arrives for dinner. She is stunning, rather than just gorgeous in her black cocktail dress and black heels highlighting those well-toned calves. Neckline discreetly low enough to be in good taste for this setting and also to let the boys in blue white dress know she has the scuba gear. On top of everything else, the lights of the dining room chandelier give her coppery colored hair a soft, day ending glow...not as awesome as the sunlight on her patio, but eye-catching.

The cook and stewards have outdone themselves once again. First, we have Maryland crab cakes. Gabrielle glances at me with a questioning smile. She mouths the words, "Did you do this just for me?" as she points to the plate then to herself. I shrug reluctantly, shake my head no. The steward sees this and smiles. At least he knows one person for sure is pleased. We start. They are good, better than good. Appetizing.

The entrée is bacon-wrapped scallops with crusted White Sea bass over a bed of rice pilaf. Iced tea is served and a slightly chilled Chardonnay for guests and those not in the parade.

I have the House Mother escort and seat Gabrielle at the parade. This after he takes her into the bar for an after dinner drink. He will pour on his North Carolinian "chivalry and syrup", making her evening fun until the parade is over and she and I can get together. He has the time and willingness to do this since he's not the parade adjutant tonight. He also has the charm to do so when the occasion arises. Underneath his weird mumbling exterior beats the heart of a southern gentleman.

The parade goes well, is a clean performance once again. Gabrielle and I hook up behind the bleachers afterwards. I say to Captain McKay, "Thank you, sir, for escorting my date."

Gabrielle smiles and gives him a squeeze on the arm and says, "Marsh was sweet, and he told me all about you...about your first day on the job at the Institute."

"Thanks, Captain. Hopefully that ended your story telling."

"Not entirely, Barney. Isn't that right, Marsh?"

Mush Mouth starts to flush, then begins his monologue-mumbling whine.

I say, "Can't hear you, Captain."

"I was saying, my sense of humor overwhelmed my better judgment in trying to impress the lady with what an enriching character you are."

Gabrielle says, "Lady? Enriching? It started as a date with a Marine. Come on you two, let's go have a drink."

We turn, laughing, and head for Center House. It will be a short night for her and me. We're leaving from her place for Ocean City at six in the morning. We'll make the drive a little longer by stopping for breakfast along the way.

This time, I join her on the shuttle bus to the parking area. Walk with her to her car, and receive a smooch goodnight, which includes another nose peck. Then she's off. I return to the Center House where Captain McKay and crew are waiting to descend on me with questions and monologues. Mush Mouth is in love and wants to know what my intentions are. I reply, "Better than yours, sir. Your nick-name needs to be changed...flap-jaw would be more appropriate...sir."

"I only--"

"Sir, please."

Captain Julius' questions are more mundane, and along with his evil but humorous grin, border on being predatory. Captain JG is nodding once again, impassively, sipping scotch and recording I think. *He is going to be a writer, I'm sure of it.*

I sip my bourbon and Seven and laugh to myself as I think of McKay and Kruger. I sometimes think they have been dating too many Johansson's and White's Lucy's of Hadar lately...an upright walker with a relatively small brain. Genetically maybe one-step above claws. Perhaps I should do them a favor and introduce them to Harriet and Sally. Naw, that would be the same as turning two bumblers loose in a chemistry lab...Ka-boom!

Nonetheless, this upcoming weekend with Gabrielle; with her talk of fate; and my now scheduled meeting with Colonel Weaver have me strung tighter than a gut racket at Wimbledon.

CHAPTER 13

Still at Gawlers
Concerned
1945 hours, no hot scoop
Fri, 22 Nov 1963

THE COMMOTION OF MY MARINES entering the room lifts my personal haze. They're talking about the training session, and the other unit's troops. We, meaning the Drill Team, see the others as not at our speed. We think of the Army unit from Fort Myer as second stringers and the others being scout teams or red shirts. Maybe not palatable for some but that's our mind set. It's a competitive arena at the ceremonies. I'm always looking for some way to make us standout from the others. Make the Corps look good. There are always people watching these ceremonies and we're always, as the Brits would say, "on parade." Therefore, I'm going to make us look what we are, the best.

The noise level lessens. The troops relax once again. I look at my watch; it's late, nearing 2000. Geez, I wish I had called Gabrielle. I hope she's home and watching TV; maybe getting some sense where I might be. I swear I can smell her perfume, her scent. Whatever, my mind washes back in time, like a spent wave receding on a beach, returning to the sea.

* * *

O dark-thirty on the Saturday morning after our parade date, I arrive at Gabrielle's door. Labor Day weekend of '62, cooler, a far cry from last year at Waikiki. After buzzing me in, she leaves her apartment door ajar. I walk in, don't see her and call out, "Anybody home?"

"I'm in here. Come on in. You'll get a glimpse of what a mess I am in the morning."

"Okay." I saunter into her bedroom and see her at the bathroom mirror dabbing, fluffing, and inspecting herself, or from my point of view, God's handiwork. "Mornings look fine to me. Damn fine. You almost ready?"

"I am. Can you get that clothing bag for me? I'll take the tote."

"Got it."

We leave, head to my car. When there, she stops, grins and says, "Not much room for anything other than me. Is that by design?"

"A thought, but alas, unfortunately, there's plenty of room for more than a toothbrush. I'll put the tote, if you don't need to carry it, in the trunk with my stuff and lay your bag on top so it won't wrinkle anything."

"That'll work. Have my purse; don't need my tote."

I do just that, and we slither into the Vette and we're on our early morning way. We zip, traffic free, through Virginia, D.C., and the general Annapolis area before starting to look for a place to eat. We find a spot in Maryland, a wee bit south of Easton. It has more than several cars and trucks parked in front, so in my mind, it must be good. Gabrielle mutters, "This is it? My first breakfast with you?"

"Sure, why not?"

"Looks like a greasy spoon."

"Yeah, it does. Great. Nothing like some grease to start the day, along with some burnt toast dripping with a butter substitute that's probably only one molecule away from plastic."

"Yuk!"

"Snob."

"I'm just teasing. I bet the food is great...or the grease as you say."

We go inside. It's not a truck-stop greasy spoon. Rather it's a Mom's home cookin' type place with carpeting, cozy booths, heavy counter traffic, and the smell of fresh biscuits and the friendly chatter and quips of locals. We order and eat. Eggs, bacon and hash browns, greasy, hot, along with the fresh orange juice, and hot rolls with melted butter oozing out. More than Gabrielle can eat so I scavenge some. It's scrumptious, and a kick-start for the short run to the beach.

It's warmed up and become a pleasant Indian summer day so I put the top down before we leave "Alice's Kitchen." We're on our way. Clear skies, the smell of salt air, and light, enjoyable chatter highlight our trip. Did you ever notice that you can smell the ocean further away than humanly possible when headed there? Never can smell it when leaving. Maybe it's the anticipation, and believe me, anticipation is key... and speaking of that, Gabrielle smells much better than the sea air, and that gets my mind churnin' more than the ocean surf.

We arrive mid-morning and check into the Commander Hotel. It's old, nice, perhaps grand. Worn, but not worn-out. And as Gabrielle said, smack-dab on the boardwalk. Our rooms are on the fourth floor, overlooking it, the beach, and the Atlantic Ocean. I help Gabrielle with her bags, and then go to my room. Once inside, I hang my clothing bag in the closet, glance about eyeing the furnishings and notice the adjoining door between the rooms. I open a window to truly get the smell of the ocean. The salt air drifts in and with it, the saltwater taffy and buttered popcorn aromas, and the hubbub of people on the boardwalk below.

I hear a knock on the tweener door and Gabrielle saying, "Barney."

I open what turns out to be just a single door and say, "What's up?"

She pokes her head in, looks around, steps in and says, "Okay?"

"Sure, come in."

"No, I mean the room."

"Oh, yeah, nice," and pointing to my open window, add, "Catch the aromatic scent of the shore, and the clamor of the boardwalk. I hope it quiets down later. What's the schedule?"

`"Let's change. Swim suits, and beach stuff. Take a walk on the boardwalk and--"

"Do we pass Go first, or--"

"Oh hush. As I was saying, then look around. After that, get some swim and beach time. Okay with you?"

"Sure, great. But, I thought it was funny."

"Yes, clever. Cute. Now, let's change and get to it. Be back in a jiffy." She gives me that peck on the nose again, grins, turns and goes into her room, pulls the tweener behind her leaving it ajar. *Interesting. Trust or invitation? I think it's trust...I'll not RSVP.*

I put on my faded Makaha's and a tee shirt from my days in the Brigade. It's a sun and salt bleached scarlet color with "AMPHIB RECON" on the front, and "Swift, Silent, and Deadly" on the back. Both in what was gold, now a pale yellow. Classy, especially the skull and crossbones above the lettering on the back. I slip into my Korean eedewas, grab a telltale hotel towel with its green stripe and hotel name down the middle, and I'm ready.

I tap lightly on the door to hear, "Just a sec." In slightly longer than the promised jiffy, she comes through the connecting door in another, but different black one-piece bathing suit. This one with a deeper cut neckline and a higher hip cut, and she's wearing the lacy thingamabob again. Also carrying a tote bag and wearing some type of designer sandals. Pink lipstick, coppery hair now in a ponytail, fingers and toes painted a lipstick matching pink. I mumble and stammer, "Wow. Anticipation is--"

"What are you muttering about?"

"Not muttering. Thinkin' out loud and tryin' to get some air and cool down."

"You warm?"

"Could say that."

She looks me up and down, raises her eyebrows at the RECON bit, puts her fingers on my shoulder and gently moves me a half turn and mutters, "Swift, silent and deadly? Nice! Did you bring your mask, fins and knife?"

"Just wanted you to feel safe."

"From whom?"

"Damn, you're a hard-ass. But, I must admit I like the humor, the quips, particularly since you seemed to have lost the whiny, Philadelphia accent. Must have been the French classes."

She smiles, slowly shakes her head in mock disgust and says, "Nice thongs." We head out, she's giggling quietly. Me, I'm silent, momentarily bested, and for now, neither swift nor deadly.

* * *

We stroll up and down the boardwalk for more than a spell. She shows me this place and that, and relates stories about some. A few are apparently associated with her ex, the   relationship person. She awkwardly stumbles through a change of subject. I don't care. I suppose we're going to talk about these topics sometime. I'm not in a hurry for that, if ever. Too many clothing bags in my closet.

It's a few ticks and tocks after 1300 when she stops abruptly and says, "Are you hungry?"

"Yeah, I could use some chow. Better yet, a...cold-beer."

"Good. How about here?" pointing to a boardwalk deli with an outdoor cafe. "Great sandwiches and they have beer, which is a heckofa good suggestion."

We go to the hostess, get a table under the awning on the boardwalk. The aroma from the counter area smells good, especially mixed with the salt air. We look at the menus and seem ready as the waitress arrives. She smiles, flips out her pad, and says, "What can I getcha?"

I say, "Gabrielle."

"Ah, let's see. You go ahead. I need a second."

"Sure?"

"Yep, order if you're ready."

"Okay." I look up at the waitress who is young, college age, beautiful, and well endowed. I'm not just a breast man mind you, but I do love 'em. She notices my eyeball reconnaissance. Doesn't blush, just leans over a pound or two more...Salty, or sultry wench. I ask, "What's your name, darlin'?"

"Susan."

"Nice. A warm name. Susan, I'll have an ice cold Bud. First. Almost immediately. And then, I'll have the BLT, on toast, white. Okay?"

"Sure," she smiles bewitchingly, "Anything you want." Looks at Gabrielle and says, "Ma'am, you ready?"

"Yes," icicles hanging from the Y and s, "also a cold Bud, please, AND, I'll have a BLQ, oh, I'm sorry--"

"A BLQ...what's that ma'am?"

"Him, and I already have it." pointing to me. Susan reddens and sputters; I flush and grin. *Caught.*

A devilish smile spreads across Gabrielle's face, unhurried, like ripples across the water on a windless day. She quickly adds in an icy tone, "Just kidding." Then an octave or two lower, "Sort of. I'd like the BLT as well, only on whole wheat, not toasted."

Damn, she was swift, not silent, and definitely deadly.

Susan smiles, says, "Good choice, but I suspect the BLQ is better," and softly nudges me on the shoulder, giggles, and allows that to transcend into laughter as she prances away.

Jesus, that'll keep the claws out.

Gabrielle raises her eyebrows while her eyes narrow with flickers of flame in the green, shakes her head from side to side, leers and hisses, "That'll teach me to be a smartass. And you--"

"I was just bein' nice. All in good fun."

"Yeah, it always starts that way, but I don't need to help her." She giggles, "And you Bernarr Leslie are a flirt."

"Naw. Friendly, just a friendly guy."

"No, a flirt. And I love it...with me."

The cold beer arrives, Susan smiles again, and says, "BLT's in a minute, enjoy," and departs looking over her shoulder. Gabrielle mutters, "See what you started," and softly pushes me on the shoulder, and giggles again, louder, and longer.

Good, the claws are in, the fur laid flat, and the hissing and spitting has stopped.

The time at the table moves along smoothly, like a wide, lazy river in late summer. We eat, chat, gulp, almost chug, our first beer, and then sip the next at a more refined pace, and in a frosted mug this round. We talk of our past, and finally about our plans for the day. We will go to the beach next. Umbrella again for the redhead. Spend whatever time we can without frying ourselves. I've been eying the beach. There's more boobs and buns tumbling out of skimpy bikinis than I've seen in clubs in downtown Norfolk on a payday weekend.

Better keep your eyeballs in their sockets, Barney ol' boy. This is a waitress-aggravated "no can look, no can touch" situation.

At the beach, we find a spot, settle and sit a spell. Gabrielle asks me to rub some lotion on her. One slice of my anticipation is rewarded to some degree as she motions me to do her legs as well as her back. She does the same for me. On my back. Her touch is light, brings goose bumps, or maybe it's the soft bite on the back of my neck when she finishes that causes the temperature change.

We sit and talk about her work, and my service. I remark, "Marines serve, not work." It draws a frown.

After an hour or so, we go frolic in the ocean. The water is great, with a mild surf running. A spilling type, not rough and tumble, and not much undertow. The Atlantic is warmer than the Pacific on the West Coast, but not in Hawaii. We play, stay in shoulder deep water most of the time trying to keep her from burning. In the shallower, white water, she attempts several sneak attacks aimed at dunking me. It's more fun losing, so I do.

When we're back sitting on the beach under the umbrella, which feels good at this point, she says, "Well, what do you have planned?"

"This may come as a surprise to you, but I did some research, and made a call or two."

"You know, Barney, I knew you would. I've already determined that you may be many things to many people, but one thing I know for sure. You're a thoughtful person, and have more depth...deeper feelings than you let on."

"Whoa. That's pretty insightful for such a short time together."

"Depends on how you count, but anyway, the most recent has been quality time and concentrated. A lot of you and I, compacted into a small time capsule. You know, Barney, you're a softy. Now then, before you reply and get me more melancholy than I already am, what's your plan for tonight?"

"You probably already know this. They used to have a fantastic and popular old fashion clambake, at the Commander, right on the beach. Lobster, corn-on-the-cob, and clams, cooked in a huge pit, covered with kelp."

"I know, and it was magnificent."

"Oh...well then, you probably know the storm--"

"Ohhh, yes. The Ash Wednesday storm. Huge. Washed away tons of sand; parts of the boardwalk. A lot of damage."

"Yeah, well they still have the clambake, only inside, and I'm told it's as popular as ever. So, I got us a reservation for tonight, nice table in a corner, at eight. You game?"

She tears up slightly, leans forward and brushes me with her lips again, then sniffles and smiles, "See, you are a softy. Wonderful idea, you bet I'm game."

"Probably better than a BLQ."

"I doubt it, but it's going to be a marvelous evening. Let's go inside, have a drink at the bar, then clean up, change, and get on with your evening surprise."

"Sounds like--"

"I know, a plan."

We get up, brush and shake off most of the sand, pick up our gear, and head for the hotel bar, with a short stop at the boardwalk outdoor shower. From here, I easily find the bar with my internal WHRS, Watering Hole Radar System. We squeak onto the leather, seat back type bar stools.

The bartender slides a couple of cocktail napkins in front of us, along with a bowl of peanuts, and says, "What'll it be, folks?" He ogles Gabrielle as she orders a Tequila Frost. I guess it's one of those exotic, or better erotic, drinks. I watch the bartender, who doesn't ask anything nor look it up, just quickly goes about his job. Along with the tequila, he mixes in some pineapple and grapefruit juice, some other ingredients the last of which is iced milk. After a spin cycle in the blender, he pours it into a parfait glass and adds a slice of lemon and a cherry. I just have a frosty draft, Bud again. When they're served, I ask Gabrielle, "Come here often?"

"No, first time as a matter of fact."

"Hmmmm. Really? I feel better, I think. The bartender must just be good."

She missed it.

No, she's smiling.

We talk, people watch, listen to music piped in from somewhere, and steal a few pecks on the lips. We order another drink and continue to grow comfortable with one another as the room darkens with the oncoming dusk.

* * *

Consistent with the history of mankind, I'm ready first. Slacks and loafers, and no penny, so I've advanced somewhat. I wear a long sleeved shirt with a lightweight sweater vest since the temperature has dropped as expected this late in the season.

The tweener door is closed.

Hmmmm.

Makes no difference. I go out, and knock on Gabrielle's hallway door. She opens it and seems taken aback. "I went to the other door first."

"Yeah, well, not this time. This is a special evening, so I came a callin' at your front door." As I step inside, I bring three long stem roses from behind my back and say, "I got these for a beautiful gal. The red to match your hair; the pink for your complexion after a day in the sun, and the white one for the pure joy you bring me."

She slowly tears up as I speak. A single drop spills from the corner of her eye and wanders down her left cheek. She wipes it away with her pinky, taking in an audible breath, and seduces the roses from my hand, holding my fingers momentarily. She looks at the blooms, lifts them leisurely to her nose, and sniffs each, slowly inhaling the fragrance deeply. "Barney, thank you. See, I'm right. There is more to you than people know." This time, no brushing of the lips, I pull her close, give her a more meaningful kiss, and then brush my lips on each of her eyes. First comes another tear, and then the peck on the nose, with a giggle and, "Let's go, Barney, and enjoy the ambiance and specialties of the house... before this gets out of control."

She's wearing dark blue slacks, and a teal or something like that, colored sheer blouse, with a white sweater draped on her shoulders. She's not wearing a bra, which has been made more apparent by the rose moment. Her hair is down again, soft, light and swirling with every move of her head. I took in the freshness of it when I kissed her. Just being with her makes me feel good. This doesn't feel like another of my flings.

* * *

The restaurant's lights are dim. It's comfortable, warm looking. I give the reservation name, Quinn, to the maitre d', along with a folded twenty dollar bill handshake. This advice from one of the House Mother's many monologues on conduct outside of The Barracks. I say quietly, "I was promised a nice, romantic table in a corner."

"Certainly, sir. I have one being held for you and the beautiful lady. This way."

It is. He holds the chair for Gabrielle, and we sit. I say, "Thanks." She, "Nice." He nods and says, "Enjoy."

Those last two words seem to sum up our time together.

We look over the menu but both know what we're going to tackle. Gabrielle, my personal wine stewardess, suggests a Chardonnay for me to order, which I do. We decide to share an appetizer of Maryland Crab Cakes. Can't come here and not do that. See how they measure up to last night. We both order the feast of baked lobster, corn-on-the-cob, and steamed clams.

The wine is served. It's smooth, although I'm not much of a white wine person. In fact, tonight, and that Sunday night dinner were the first times since, I don't even remember when. The crab cakes are better than advertised. However, as in Blackjack, The Barracks earns a push. After a few more sips of wine, the entrée arrives. We devour everything with no room remaining for dessert. Only thing left are shells, cobs and some melted butter...oh, and sticky fingers.

The waiter returns with two finger bowls and fresh napkins. I pick up my bowl. Gabrielle blurts out, "Don't you dare, Barney."

"Gotcha."

"That you did."

"Know what we would call this out in the field?"

"No. I can guess, and don't you dare say it."

"Okay, okay. Let's have an after dinner respite." I call the waiter back and say, "Wonderful. Food was delicious. Service great and the ambiance warming. And because of the latter, we've decided to mellow out with an after-dinner drink. Do you have Apricot Brandy?"

"I think so."

"Good, if so, I'll have a double, straight up and not chilled." Turn to Gabrielle, "You?"

"I'll have a Fontainebleau Special."

The waiter says, "Excellent."

I blurt out, "Here we go again."

Gabrielle says, "What?"

"What the hell is that? Do they even make something like that in this part of the world? Is this something you learned while taking French?"

"Gad, I can't take you any place. It's brandy, anisette, and vermouth...chilled. Smooth. And yes, they make it here. No, I didn't learn this in a French class. And Barney, no, I don't come here all the time, either."

She did catch it.

The waiter leaves satisfied with her discourse, and God Dammit, her blouse, or rather its contents. Geez, he was obvious. I shake my head and mumble, "Don't serve it in the slop-shoot, and you're getting a bit testy."

"What's wrong with you? Want me to order barbed-wire juice or a ration of rum...what do you call it, grog?" She laughs.

"The waiter was ogling you. Ticked me off."

"No more than you, BQ."

"That's different."

"Well, not really, but much, much better."

She's one heck-of-a-smart-ass. A quick and sharp tongue. Nevertheless, I love her cut, and the give and take. No slack, no quarter. Can't even get the last word.

The drinks come. She offers me a sip of hers and I oblige. Can taste the licorice over everything else. It's good. I offer her a sip of my apricot brandy. She does, scrunches up her nose and mutters "Yuk! Why don't you have some pancakes with this?"

"Ah, finally. I knew it. It's not fate. We're incompatible."

She smiles, and in a singsong whisper says, "It is fate and we are compatible. And you're not going to get away that easily. Just maybe, you've met your match."

"Possibly."

"Probably."

The night trails on. We chat, hold hands across the table, and take pleasure in the evening and ourselves. She's right. I'm no better than the waiter. I can't keep my eyes off her...her blouse. I'm obvious. She just grins coyly. After another nightcap, we leave and take a stroll along the boardwalk. She slips on her sweater. It's chilly. I can feel the damp breeze chafe against my once frost bitten face and hands. Sixty-eight is cold to me. I rub my face and blow on my cupped hands.

We go a few city-length blocks, up and back. It's late, nearing seven bells. As usual, the sound of the waves crashing on the beach is thunderous at night, making one think their size greater than in fact, reality. The salt air fills our nostrils and clears the sinuses. Smells great, but it is nippy.

We return to her room, go in. She walks over, turns up the thermostat, and slips out of her sweater. I rub my still frosty hands together as I breathe on them. They have never fully recovered from the Korean winters.

We meet in the middle of her room; I put my arms around her waist. I pull her close and kiss her. She responds easily and warmly, lips parted, but nudges me toward the tweener door. I pull her closer and we kiss again, and again. We are melded tighter than a winning pinochle run. I have one arm still around her waist, the other hand cupped on her ear, interlaced with her hair. She has one arm around my neck, the other, her fingers tracing lightly down my cheek.

She leans back in my arms, hers lightly on my shoulders and says, "Barney, a wonderful evening. It was magical." As she finishes I brush her lips with mine, pull her close so our bodies are completely meshed, and I kiss her again, deeper and longer than the others. And yet again, and again. She nibbles my ear, and nips my neck. I kiss her lightly on each side of her neck, and do the same on her throat letting my tongue seek out the hollow in her neck. I gently ease her head back and lazily sweep my lips across the swell of her breasts just at the open collar line of her blouse. She gasps, murmurs, sighs slowly and eases back. She takes in a breath and says, "Barney, I--"

"What? Is something--"

"Yes. I mean, no." She inhales deeply, "Ohhh, I mean not wrong. I just need to be sure."

"Sure, of what?"

"That this is...if I'm ready for...if, damn, Barney, that this isn't just another fling to you. Maybe we're moving along too fast or I'm expecting too much."

"I knew I shouldn't have used that word, but, okay. I got it. I think. I guess I under--"

"I just want to be sure. I don't want to get hurt again, or to hurt someone, you. Want it to be right. Need to be sure about us, me. I truly believe fate brought us together for a reason."

"Fate again. Okay. Let's be as sure as we can be. I'm all right with that. Besides, I may be a little out of my natural element right now."

"Natural element?"

"Yeah, you know, bein' serious and all."

"Well, Barney, I'm serious."

"I can see that. You just stunned me, and took the wind out of my sails, so to speak. Need to have someone throw a bucket of cold water on me."

"Don't tease me about this."

"Okay, I won't. I'll be serious."

"Promise."

"Promise."

She says, "Night, Barney, and you might think about calling me Gabby, if you like," and I get another peck on the tip of my nose. She puts her finger to her lips, then presses it against mine, nudges me and slowly closes the tweener door.

Gabby, if I like. The reasoning is interesting, but I like Gabrielle. It rolls out of the mouth, off the tongue...it's seductive, like her.

Nonetheless, this whole bit is like a fade-out scene in an old movie, only I'm on this side of the screen.

Well, no click when the tweener closes. That tells me something, not sure exactly what.

I still need a cold shower and go swiftly and silently to the head... the icy water is a killer, deadly.

CHAPTER 14

I awaken Sunday morning to a knocking. After blinking away the cobwebs, I realize it's the tweener door rattling. I stagger upright and open it. Gabrielle's standing there with a tray of coffee. Nice cups and saucers, sugar bowl, matching cream pitcher and napkins.

Geez, sometimes I just miss a canteen cup over a heat tab.

She says, "Morning. Whoa! Get some clothes on BQ; you're making me forget the coffee."

I look down. My jockey shorts are a bit awry. She breezes past me. I make an adjustment as I go to the chair and slip on my slacks from last evening. Visit the head and take care of business, brush my Chiclets, swish some *Listerine* around.

Phew, that'll wake you up. I spit it in the sink, take in a deep breath and examine myself in the mirror. *Looked better in my jockey shorts.*

She looks great. She's in a sheer ankle length gown that flows out on both sides of her as she walks. She does have a shortie jobber on underneath. Neither hides anything. Her hair is down, lipstick on and foo-foo juice tingling my nose.

Jesus, she's killin' me.

She pours the coffee, fixes mine. She remembers. Damn she's good, or cares.

We sip the coffee, chitchat, and plan the day.

* * *

We start with breakfast on the boardwalk and a long chat about the night before. Netted out, she's been hurt before by some guy named Chuck, a Marine no less. Was at Quantico but was transferred to Oblivion, New Mexico or Lost Balls, Arizona, or Broken Bow, Nowhere. She doesn't know where, clueless, and that should tell her something. Maybe it has. She wants to be sure that what's happening between us is meaningful. However, she's not sure she understands a Marine's mentality and lifestyle. Ends with, "Do you understand what I'm saying?"

"I guess, maybe."

"It was the way he acted. The non-commitment. Then, bam, gone. And now, some of the things you say. Your lifestyle. Your seemingly total dedication to your job."

"It's not a job, Gabrielle. It's my career. My life--"

"Yes, I know, but--"

"Gabrielle, listen. It's a state of mind. And I'm not Chaz or Chunk or Hunk or whatever his damn name is."

"Chuck."

"Chuck, whatever. Don't give a hoot. I'm me. So get to know me. Focus on me. We'll go from there. When you're comfortable."

"Don't get angry, Barney. For goodness sake, I think I'm falling in love with you. I just want to be sure, okay?"

"It's okay. I think I'm droppin' fast myself, too, but it's early in the game. What d' you say we get on with the day."

"Wonderful. You can call me Gabby if you'd like." She leans over and kisses me on the cheek, then turns my face with her hand, repeats it on my lips.

"I know, and maybe I will on occasion but I like Gabrielle. It's... it's, never mind. I like your given name better."

"Nice. Why?"

"Like I started to say, it's melodic...seductive...like a fresh spring day."

"My goodness. You are full of surprises."

We'll continue and see where the path leads. She's too nice, too beautiful not to, but she's close to being a tease. I also think she hears her biological clock ticking, and perhaps she's frightened. I, or we, or she, needs to be sure it's not panic.

After breakfast, we sightsee in the Vette, top down, along this spit of land bounded by the Atlantic and the Isle of Wright Bay. We stop for a snack in mid-afternoon, and then walk it off along the boardwalk.

We get our stuff, find a spot nearby on the beach and spend the remainder of the day as we did yesterday. When the chill begins to drift ashore with the breeze, we go back to the same bar. We decide on Irish Coffee this time. Same bartender; same ogling; same muttering on my part. We talk about this and that, then, as is her habit, out of the blue, she mentions that maybe next summer we should rent a place for a week or so...come for a vacation. Sounds like she mentally has or is making up her mind, just not physically yet. I reply, "I won't be able to do that. Will have parades two nights a week all summer, and if my plans work out, will be standing a lot of other ceremonies."

She murmurs, "Just a thought. Forgot about your...your Mistress...Marilyn Marine."

"That was nasty."

"You're right. Sorry. I really am."

"I know. No one as beautiful and sweet as you can be nasty. Maybe a little sharp, but not nasty."

"Barney, I am sorry. No more."

"Okay."

"I'm gonna win your heart, BQ."

"Shoot, you've got one helluva grip on it already."

"Good. Let's get cleaned up and go eat."

We do just that. She takes me to a nice cozy seafood place on the bay side. Treats me to dinner, and our night ends the same as last night. Only I don't need a cold shower tonight.

      * * *

Monday morning, Labor Day, begins the same. I'm no better prepared but she's already dressed in shorts, halter-top and sandals. Bright-eyed, full of life, and smelling like a crisp, clean, clear morning after a summer rain. You know what I mean. Take a deep breath, take in the freshness and love God's world. That's her this morning.

Our morning goes the same. Breakfast, walk it off. We stop in more shops. She tries on some outfits. The first time she asks, "How do you like this, Barney? Do you like this color on me?"

Immediately my mind recalls someone's male rules. One of them is, all men see only in basic colors. Peach, for example, is a fruit. Not a color. Pumpkin is also a fruit. We have no idea what mauve is. I say, "Yes."

"Yes? That's not an answer."

Another male rule. Yes and no are perfectly acceptable answers to almost every question. Guess this isn't one of them. "Let's see, ahhh, it looks great. But...what I want to know is how you look--"

"Shssss, for goodness sakes." She anxiously looks to see if the sales clerk heard me. She didn't, thank God.

Gabrielle doesn't ask me anything in the next shop. Or the one after that. She doesn't buy anything either. Good. I believe all women have enough clothes, and too many shoes. However, I keep my mouth shut. I've played ball and know when to take a pitch.

It's now mid-afternoon so we find another seafood place on the bay for a late lunch. We have a nice white wine before and with lunch. She talks of things we need to do together...I think of things we need to do together.

Soon it's time to leave for home. We're fine. We've talked this to death. We're going to be okay. We just need to live it out. We can motor back from here, we've already checked out. I put the top up since a cool breeze has kicked up. We drive back to the real world. A lot of weekend traffic but we get home just as dusk is leaving for the night.

At the door we smooch, brush, nibble and linger, needing to stop, but not trying too hard to do so. Finally, she says, "Barney, both enough and not enough. Thanks for a wonderful weekend, and understanding."

"Yeah, I had a great time also. The best in a long, long while. Great showers."

"Barneeeyyy."

"I'm sorry. No more."

"Please, and, Barney, I think, no, I know that I'm falling in love."

"Listen, I'm with ya on this. Let's just think on it and be sure of our road and you set the speed limit."

A quick kiss, a fingertip to my nose with a slight push, a smile, and the door closes. I'm not used to this. The honeys I've been hanging around with have been grabbin' me by the neck and draggin' me inside.

I believe I know her. She's not a tease. She's like a person clamoring to get to the high dive, then at the end of the board, starts hesitating, stepping back and looking down. She won't jump, but rather gathers herself and does the perfect Jack Knife she first intended. She's a good woman. This may be going somewhere special.

Just not silently, and for damn sure not swiftly...but maybe deadly, to my freelancing.

* * *

Gawlers
2200 hours, bone weary
Friday
22 Nov 1963

One more time the major is standing in front of me. He's saying something. I look up and offer my best, "Huh? Sir."

"Lieutenant Quinn, are you with me? We've got some new word. Finally, maybe something accurate."

"Good, sir. What's the scoop?"

"The President is being taken to Bethesda Naval Hospital for an autopsy and preparation for burial. He will then be taken to the White House, which is where we are going, now."

"Aye aye, sir. We're moving."

"We'll go in convoy, with police escort. We'll leave from the back entrance and avoid the crowd which is still growing."

"Yes, sir."

"The police escort vehicles are on the way, so we'll have a short wait."

"Okay, sir. We'll get dressed and standby. Has any other unit showed up?"

"No. Someone must have passed us some bum info."

"Either that, or maybe it was straight scoop at the time, but then changed and that someone waited to make sure whatever they had was the final word."

"Yeah, that's probably it. Get loaded when you're ready, but make it quick." He moves off toward the door.

Yeah, hurry, so we can go wait somewhere else. Oh well, got to be better than hanging around a funeral parlor. Creepy.

I look at Gunny Elms. He's heard the conversation, so I just nod. He'll get the troops ready.

We're all dressed again in our traveling clothes...Dress Blues. The police escort has arrived, so we load up. Our green van is the ugliest of the group, like the last car in a funeral procession...always the wreck, owned by the black sheep nephew of the family. Nevertheless, we'll be standin' and will be lookin' tuff when we arrive. The wing wipers and Dixie cups are sitting in their nice windowed vans...wrinkling.

We get back out on Wisconsin Avenue and start moving down toward the White House. Traffic is still snarled. The police are using sirens and flashing lights. Not speeding, simply managing to navigate better than the civilian vehicles. Actually, the only place the sirens and lights do any good is at the intersections. Between those, we're gridlocked.

The troops look a little tired. I am, and it doesn't take long for my mind to wander off to The Barracks once again.

* * *

When I arrive back at Center House after my Ocean City weekend, I find Captains McKay, Milsap and Kruger at the bar. The House Mother and his sidekick, Justin G. Milsap, are at one end, whispering and laughing. Julius is at the other, by the bell and window, mumbling to himself, and on occasion, turning and pointing a wagging and mockingly threatening finger at the other two. When he isn't he sulks and stares out the window overlooking 8th Street. All three are decidedly under the weather, with Julius for sure drowning from the storm. I say, "Gunny, I'll have a bourbon and Seven, please." Then look to my left and say to Mush Mouth and Captain J.G., "What's up...sirs? What's wrong with Captain Kruger?"

The House Mother explains to me in his mumbling manner, while trying to stifle his laughter that the three of them had been to a party given by Lieutenant Buzz Satterfield and his wife. Captain Millsap's girlfriend, Gladys, had fixed Julius up with a date.

The word date brings Julius' gaze away from the window, and looking down the bar, screams, "A date. Bullshit. She looked like she played pro football."

McKay continues, saying that when they got to the party and went in, Buzz welcomed them by saying to Julius, "Nice date, one of the Redskins?"

That, along with some other opening snide remarks by other barracks officers in attendance, as Mush Mouth is telling it, set Kruger off the deep end. He decided to get drunk, and he did. Very drunk, and anti-social. Then he apparently was going to sneak out a bedroom window, but fortunately didn't since they were several stories up. So, he had several more drinks, and eventually hid under the bed in the master bedroom.

When it came time to leave, Bertha or whatever her name, couldn't find him and left, demanding cab fare from the Muv. McKay and Milsap then pulled Julius out from under the bed where he was easily discovered since he was cutting lumber noisier than a Georgia backwoods sawmill. Now a trio since Gladys also jumped ship, they came home, to Center House, here at the bar.

I have another drink and ease along the bar to where my friend from Hawaii is sitting, and say, "Uncle Julius, sir. Come on, Bertha or whatever her name is couldn't have been that bad."

"Barney, you should have seen her. JG or Gladys did it on purpose. She was built low to the ground, like a tank and had squinty eyes, stubby ears and a flattened nose."

"Sounds like a *Makapania Broomi.*"

All heads snap up, to include Gunny Richards, stationed behind the bar. Julius says, "A what?"

"A pre-historic warthog-like creature. Tends to slobber and drool when drinking at a watering hole."

"That's her, damn it. That's her. What was its name again?"

"Makapania Broomi. Broomi is Latin for Bertha." Gunny Richards breaks into laughter. Of course, it probably isn't Latin for anything, certainly not Bertha, but what do these three know at this stage. Well, the Yaliee Captain, Milsap, probably does. He's quietly intellectual and just plays insensitive. However, he always has a lure in the water.

Captain Kruger, having found an ally in me, slides onto a stool next to the House Mother and Milsap in a confrontational mood and says, "I'm not going to trust you two again. I'll rely on Lieutenant Quinn, if I must. He's a true buddy."

I say, "Captain Julius, my friend. My advice is, always be watchful. Survival for many is dependent on observation, particularly around the watering holes."

"Right."

"That's why we, man, walk upright. So we can see further than those on all fours, like Broomi." The Gunny is almost on the floor now.

Milsap bursts into laughter. Mush Mouth assumes his House Mother posture, and says, "Loooootenant, you had your moment. Hush up." That's North Carolinian for "shut up." He's still laughing at the exchanges. However, he's playing a role again. He goes on, "I'll do the instructing and advising around here. Isn't that correct, JG?"

"Yazza, Muv."

As quick as that, the beleaguered Julius turns coat, and the three are bunched together once again like a cluster of frustrated crows on a telephone cable overlooking a parched field of maize in Texas. They hang their heads over the drinks, plotting and deciding how to terrorize the lieutenants in general and me in particular. Laughing and giggling to themselves. All is forgiven. I love these guys, these boys of summer... and blue white dress.

However, they're so involved in their chortling they don't see or hear me silently slip away, go swiftly to my room, and fall dead asleep.

CHAPTER 15

Bethesda, Maryland
Heading to the White House
2215 hours
Fri, 22 Nov 1963

We've eased down Wisconsin and turned onto Massachusetts Avenue. Our driver is honking again. It can't be much further to the White House. I look out the windshield and note where we are. Close to Connecticut, probably headed to Lafayette Park...go in that way. There is an eerie, foggy amber glow. The misting rain, streetlights, car and building lights create a pale tawny world. Maybe I spent too much time in the funeral home and am beginning to see things the way those residents do.

I don't see why Atherton is honking. It makes no difference, everyone is honking again. Sounds like we're in a tunnel.

Ahhh, that's what the amber glow reminds me of, the Lincoln tunnel in New York with its lights and exhaust fumes.

"Atherton."

"Sir?"

"Knock off the honking. Not getting us there any quicker. Besides it's probably pissing people off and I think we probably filled our quota today."

"Yes, sir."

So be it, we're several minutes away from the White House. The mere thought quickly brings back why we're here. The assassination...

Jesus, in our country. By a friggin' nut-case former Marine. *Gotta relax, gotta relax, Barney ol' boy.*

Think of something else, dummy. Hanging on the strap, and swaying back and forth again lulls my mind into wandering once more. Back to the rung on fate's ladder that led me directly to the DT and here...

* * *

It's the Tuesday after Labor Day and my appointment with Colonel Weaver is this morning, right after colors. Following a nervous breakfast of juice, toast and coffee only, I clean up, and go outside Center House to observe morning colors. I love seeing the flag raised, especially here in these surroundings. I stand at attention and suck in some of this fine, crisp autumn air, with a slight scent of the Barrack's tradition.

Unfortunately, today, beside the morning air I also have the opportunity to watch a member of the guard of the day chasing Chesty around the parade deck. When colors is sounded, he is unsure whether to continue chasing the dog, or popping to attention, salute and observe colors. He chooses the latter which is militarily correct, but a bad decision, possibly leading to a disaster.

Chesty, apparently recognizing the buglers "To the Colors", heads toward the flagpole and its halyards. The bugler's eyes widen as he plays, the Sergeant of the Guard holds his salute and kicks at Chesty trying to shoo him away. The two guardsmen raising the flag go about their tasks. The other guard, realizing the oncoming catastrophe, cuts his hand salute and is back in action. He corrals the mutt, holding him by his leather collar...and no, this isn't the origin of the term "Leatherneck." The capture saves everyone the embarrassment of seeing Chesty hoisted up the pole, a halyard clinched in his vice-like jaws.

Chesty is put on a leash. His playtime curtailed, he vigorously shakes his head, splattering drool on the color detail, his acknowledgment of spit-shined shoes. I believe that damn dog grinned in satisfaction after his saliva displacement.

Nonetheless, the day is saved, and me too...Won't have to be a witness in another legendary barracks investigation. Muv would make the most of that, probably claiming I somehow caused the incident. Colors and the chase over, Chesty, in disgrace once again, is led back to his bachelor's quarters next to Center House. *Is there a hidden meaning in this fact? I suppose not...at least I hope not.*

Regardless, I head for the CO's office, splatter free.

* * *

The Colonel invites me in, offers me a seat off the corner of his desk, facing him. He starts, "Morning, Barney. Near disaster, huh?"

"Yes, sir. The Colonel saw?"

"I thought he was supposed to be accounted for, locked up, before colors."

"Yes, sir. That's correct. But that's a lot easier said than done with that fool."

"Well, it wouldn't be much fun for me if the Commandant observed him being hoisted up the flag pole, again."

"Sir, if it happens, just tell the Commandant to enjoy the moment, another Chesty story to add to the lore of The Barracks."

"Not easily done, or acceptable. However, I must admit, it's a thought. Let's get down to business, Barney."

This is going to be good. Started with Barney, added some humor, and a Barney again.

We talk briefly about several changes of personnel coming up which strikes me as strange, him doing that with a lieutenant. However, I listen quietly. Nodding on occasion. Company Commander changes, a few lieutenant changes, others leaving, both The Barracks and the Corps. Then he says, "Barney, Colonel Daly told me he planned to assign you to the Drill Team. Did he tell you that?"

"No, sir. Just said Guard Company. I was going to request the Drill Platoon."

"Well, I've asked around. Major Kendell, Guard Company's CO, and the XO, Captain Kemp, both are impressed with you, and would like to have you. Others as well think it's a good move. I took more time, and got more input than I normally would on this. The Drill Team is that important. A lot of public appearances, most of the MDW ceremonies at the White House and Tomb, and of course the out of town performances. It's extremely important, Lieutenant Quinn.

"I've said more than I should have, or needed to...or normal for me. You have the job if you want it, Barney."

"Yes, sir. I do."

"Good. It's done. Effective, immediately. However, you will finish the last parade on the MCI side of Center Walk."

"Absolutely perfect, Colonel. I won't let you down, sir, or the others. That's not a promise, sir, that's a guarantee."

"Stoop was right, you are cocky...well, maybe just confident. I like a lot of one and some of the other. All right. Okay then. Don't say anything until the orders are cut later today, and I put out the word about this and a few other changes."

"Yes, sir."

"Captain Dennehy will call you."

He gets up, shoves his hand forward. We shake, I step back and say, "Thank you, sir. Is the Lieutenant dismissed, sir?"

"You're dismissed, Barney. Give it your best. Don't let me down."

"I won't, sir." I face about, leave and head for the Tute to wait for the orders to be published later today.

Hot damn! The Drill Team.

Maybe having a mentor isn't all that bad...at least when we both want the same thing.

* * *

Later, after the orders are published, the House Mother and Julius come into the Registrar's bullpen-type office space and congratulate me. Captain Milsap calls me. Regardless of the horseplay and the antics, these three, and all others at The Barracks are the top of the Corps and can flat soldier.

After dinner, I call Gabrielle. Not an easy chore, actually. We only have one phone in Center House, and it's located in the hallway on the second floor, outside the three captains' rooms. Not a very private atmosphere and one has to be sure that no one is up there in the hallway or the rooms. The phone upstairs is only for local calls, and has to go through The Barracks' switchboard. Long-distance calls must be made from the pay phone in the arcade, outside the Band Hall, also not conducive to meaningful conversations, or long ones in bad weather.

Upstairs, a private or romantic remark could find its way to the bar in the form of a public monologue, most likely by Uncle Julius. Not that the other two wouldn't stoop to doing something like that, only that it's more in Captain Jack's laughing and evil growling style.

121

My call is short by necessity; she is on the way out the door to class. She says, "That's great, Barney. It's what you wanted, isn't it?"

"Yep, sure is."

"Does that mean I'll be seeing less of you?"

"Not necessarily, at least not in the fall and winter. Possibly so in the summer months. But, you know, what with both of our weekday schedules, we're pretty much restricted to weekends anyway. I'm not going to give you up."

"Good, nor I you, Bernarr Leslie."

"Good, that's great. This is one form of captivity I can enjoy. Listen, got to go. I'll give you a call later in the week."

"All right. Also gotta run. Bye. Love ya." Click.

Love ya. Hmmmm. How about that...not thinkin' she does. Does.

I stop staring at the receiver, hang up and head upstairs to my room for shine time. Have to be down to Building 58 in the Navy Yard, Guard Company, bright and early. Think I'll eat in the mess hall there and sniff around. See who the early birds are. Get a feel for the energy level and activity early in the mornin'...can tell a lot about an outfit this time of day. Been there before as the OD, checking chow, so it won't be all that noticeable.

* * *

I walk down 8th Street to the Navy Yard. At the "M" Street gate the sentry pops to attention, salutes and says, "Good Morning, Lieutenant Quinn. Welcome aboard."

"Good morning. How'd you know my name?"

"Rumor has it you're comin' here to the Drill Team, sir."

"Well, that's true. It's good to know that the rumor mill is well oiled by slippery tongues. I don't want to know what the rest of the BS is, just spread it thin. Have a good day, Marine."

"Yes, sir."

Magpies. Got to love 'em. They get the word spread quicker than a light switch.

Building 58 is where Ceremonial Guard Company is billeted and is directly across the street from Leutze Park, which is lined with ancient cannons. Looks to be about twenty-four of them. Leutze is on my right as I head down Admirals Row from the gate. These are Admirals quarters, big old three story houses to my left. The first one has been made into a three-story flat, with three separate apartments. A Marine lieutenant of Guard Company, the Navy Yard Guard Officer, occupies one. That's nice. Short walk to work like a few folks up at The Barracks. Married Navy junior officers stationed here at the Yard occupy the other two apartments.

I see a woman out in the yard of one of the homes. She's got a dog on a leash...one of those Yorkies. Be a snack for Chesty but knowing Chesty, he would probably try to mount her, or it...Doesn't make much difference to him.

"Good mornin', Ma'am."

"Oh, good morning young man. Beautiful day isn't it?"

"Surely is, Ma'am."

Must be the admiral's wife. Sure isn't the maid in that outfit and with those rings. I continue on my way.

The Yard is ancient. It's the Navy's oldest shore establishment, founded in the first decade of the 19th century. That is aged, at least by U.S. standards. It was originally a shipbuilding and ship fitting facility but eventually its life changed. The Anacostia River was too shallow and access to the sea limited for the ships sometime after 1812, but the Yard has a long history. The *USS Constitution* was refitted here. The famous, shallow drafted ironclad *Monitor* was repaired at the yard after her battle with the *CSS Virginia* during the Civil War.

Twenty or so years after the Civil War it became a Naval Gun Factory...has quite a history in this respect as well. The 14-inch naval railway guns used in France during WWI were manufactured here, and it was the largest naval ordnance plant in the world during WWII. Finally this part of its past faded onto history's pages and it was re-designated the Washington Navy Yard. Time and need passed it by as a port and gun factory.

I'm at the entrance of 58, stop, look over Leutze Park. Nice grassy slope. Can see that it's used for drill. Flag pole. Colors held here also each day by the guard unit down here. I take a deep breath, and enter the building and go directly to the mess hall. It's already crowded. Good.

In the NCO mess section I sit, have a bowl of corn flakes with sliced bananas and a cup of coffee. Gunnery Sergeant Robert Elms, the Platoon Sergeant of the Drill Platoon, and its Guide, Sergeant Terry

Hapgood, enter; see me sitting alone at a table. Gunny Elms walks over, says, Lieutenant Quinn, isn't it?"

"Yes, came in early."

"Heard from our First Sergeant that you were coming today, and to the Drill Team. Welcome aboard, Lieutenant."

"Thanks, Gunny. Have seen you on the parade deck."

"This is Sergeant Hapgood, our Platoon Guide."

"Sergeant, good to meet you. Have seen you as well. Both of you look sharp out there, as is your platoon...and not just the drill portion."

Both start to speak, "Thank--" Hapgood stops and looks toward Elms, who continues, "Thanks, we think so but there's always room for improvement."

"Great, always is unless you're perfect, and that's a tough goal, but possible."

"Troops have noticed you as well, Lieutenant. And, they've heard the scuttlebutt about you coming here. They think you're sharp, and maybe a hard-ass. Some of them are already touting a nickname... Mustang Barney."

"Hmmm. Well, I can do just as well with Lieutenant. As far as the parade deck, I didn't trip, fall, or stick my sword in the ground. I work hard at this stuff...not at being a hardass, that comes naturally."

Slight grins spread across their faces along with a nodding of heads. Elms is a tad under six foot, squared away, sort of stocky, thick, short hair like everyone, and he's a veteran as I am from the Korean War. Also came in the Corps in '51. Hapgood is a Sergeant E-5, taller than Elms by a couple of inches, built solid, hard looking, squared away, also a veteran of Korea, and like all others, a close buzz cut that appears shorter than it is since he's light-haired.

They get some chow and sit down across from me. We talk about the Drill Team and its troops. Mostly my questions and their answers. Their answers are in part how they hope everything will run. It's their way of letting me know what they want, and what they would like to see changed. I say nothing at this point, other than I have a few ideas.

We finish and I say, "Men, have got to go check in. See what Major Kendell and Captain Kemp have in store for me. See you two later."

In unison, they stand, say, "Yes, sir." Then Elms adds, "We're in the office on the second deck, across from the Drill Team squad bay. Near the bell on the quarterdeck...and also the company barber cage."

"Bell? Quarterdeck?"

Hapgood replies, "Yes, sir. Gotta' have a bell and quarterdeck in the Navy Yard." I smile and say, "And the cage? Is the barber dangerous or just careless with the scissors?"

"He doesn't use scissors, just electric clippers."

Elms adds, "He's only dangerous with the guidon."

I ask, "He's the company guidon bearer?"

"In training, or as they say in the kingdom...bearer in waiting."

I laugh and head toward the company offices, which are also on the second deck of this old building.

Got to love the history of this place. The Navy Yard, The Barracks, this old building with its ships bell and quarterdeck...and bearer in waiting. It's all part of the mystique of being stationed here. It gets in your blood. You become part of it, and it of you. Probably forever. I fit here. I feel like I'm already part of the brick and mortar.

Can't wait to get started. Where's it goin' to lead?

CHAPTER 16

In the van
Adjacent to Lafayette Park
Impatient and on edge
Fri, 22 Nov 1963

THE SWAYING STOPS. WE'RE BARELY moving, just inching and jerking along as Atherton rides the clutch. The ventilation in here is not the best and the smell of the clutch burning makes it worse. The honking is distant, the sirens have stopped, but there is another sound effect...like a bass section of a choir humming.

I look out the windshield; we're almost there. The lights of the White House burst out of the mist and darkness. Flashing red and blue lights out front at both ends of the driveway add to the tawny glow. A crowd has gathered...my imagined bass section I presume.

Time excruciatingly ticks slowly away. I go back to thinking about my first day in Guard Company and about Building 58 where all this started late this afternoon.

* * *

Besides all the rich history of the Navy Yard, Building 58, among other uses, was once a stable. Probably only fitting I suppose that it's used to billet the Marines of Ceremonial Guard Company although we never had a cavalry unit to my knowledge. Nonetheless, this autumn day of '62, I get to serve here and become part of its lore, I hope.

One thing for sure, if it was a palatial estate it would not have been given to the Marines. No big deal, all the services are supposed to be brethren, but it seems we've been gettin' hand-me-downs for years. Like being the youngest brother in a clan...the trouser knees are worn and the pockets have holes in them by the time you get 'em. Whatever, at least the horse dung has long since been removed from this three-story brick building now painted Navy grey with black trim.

The first deck, at street level, contains perhaps the most important part of the building in the minds of the troops... Tun's Tavern, named after the place in Philadelphia where the Marine Corps was founded some 187 years earlier. It's the enlisted beer hall, or better known as the slop chute. Also on this level is a small subsidiary of the Post Exchange and the Mess Hall. In the basement is an armory, supply storeroom, press shop and a two-lane bowling alley. Nice. All the creature comforts the troops could want.

Well, almost all. Those comforts not here are lured into the Tavern on Friday nights. You always hear of sailors having a girl in every port, which implies they always get the beauties. Not true! Myth. The Marines get the best-looking gals. Every time, every port. Don't believe me? Just go to a Marine Corps Birthday Ball sometime...take a gander. It looks like a Miss America contest. Trust me, the Snuffies do well, visit the Tavern any Friday night after a parade.

The company offices are on the second deck, along with the platoon offices, the ship's bell, the quarterdeck...and of course the barber cage.

The Company Barber is in his cage, unoccupied. He sees me and says, "Good morning, Lieutenant Quinn."

"Good morning. Don't tell me. You've heard the scuttlebutt, too. What's your name, Marine?"

"Lance Corporal Crandell, sir. They call me, Clipper."

"Clipper, huh? Good. Please don't tell me your first name is Davey?"

"No, sir, it's Richard."

He's squared away. Clean cut. About an inch shorter than me. Goin' to keep him in mind...certainly doesn't appear needing to be caged.

"Good, that's a relief. What's on the third deck Lance Corporal Richard, the Clipper, Crandell, guidon bearer in waiting?"

"You've heard, sir."

"Yes...now then, the third deck?"

"Oh, yes, sir. It has the squad bays for the three Guard Platoons. You know they rotate between here and Camp David. We provide the guard there. If the President is aboard, then the other platoons have to provide troops to fill it out because more posts are manned when he's there. The platoons, except the Drill Platoon, do two weeks there and four weeks back here, sir."

"Okay, thanks for the info, Crandell."

Everybody probably shoots the breeze in the barbershop...just like home. The place is a hub of rumors, popular with the Magpies I'm sure. I wander back to the CO's office area.

Standing outside the hatch, I eyeball the troops as they come and go. They do the same to me. The hell with the Mustang Barney bit. I let them get a good look at the Stoneface, and I look them over cover to boots. The minutes pass slowly as Mickey's hands near the twelve and the eight. My mind wanders. *This place is a historical warehouse.*

The Navy Yard itself is situated on the Anacostia River, between it and M Street, SE, and generally from 2nd to 11th Streets, SE, in our nation's capitol. Unlike the Marine Barracks, it was not spared during the war of 1812. However, the Admiral ordered it set afire so as not to allow the British to capture and use it. In 1812, there probably wasn't that much here. Interesting however, is that everything burned, except the Admiral's house. Not luck, I imagine. My guess is he didn't order his own house set afire. His wife probably told him he wasn't about to set fire to her house, nor were the damn British. So he didn't. The man wasn't a fool. Rather feel the wrath of the Red Coats than of the petticoat.

The First Sergeant pokes his head out the door and says, "Sir, the CO and XO will see you now."

"Okay, First Sergeant. Thanks."

"By the way Lieutenant, welcome aboard."

"Thanks, Top. Means a lot."

I step inside the CO's office. Their desks are side by side. I say, "Good morning, Major, Captain. Lieutenant Quinn reporting as ordered, sir."

Both stand, welcome me and shake my hand. Major Kendell and Captain Kemp sit down behind their desks and offer me a seat facing them. They waste no time and focus on what they expect from me as the

Drill Team Commander, and what I can expect in ceremonial workload. This latter is explained in detail by Captain Robert Kemp. He's tall, easily six-two or three, square-shouldered...no slope to them, and like many others here, narrow in the hip. His hair is blond, but he doesn't carry a buzz cut, however it's short and has plenty of skin showing on the sides. As we say, high and tight.

Major Kendell is quite a bit shorter, maybe five-eight with chiseled facial features and a brisk, sharp-sounding voice to match the shape of his nose. His unnie has creases as sharp as his nose, and tongue.

Captain Kemp asks, "Lieutenant Quinn, have you seen any of the ceremonies we participate in besides the Iwo and Friday night parades?"

"Yes, sir. I did a couple of funerals at Fort Myer Chapel... Arlington."

"Good. Well, Lieutenant McKean is at a White House Arrival Ceremony this morning with the Drill Team and will be doing a Wreath Laying at the Tomb of the Unknown this afternoon. Later tonight, he and the DT will be doing the White House Dinner Cordon."

"Sir, should I--"

Major Kendell interrupts, "I have to go up to see Colonel Weaver. Pleasure meeting you, Lieutenant Quinn. Good to have you here. I like your cut. See you around, but not here. I'm being moved. Will be replacing Major Symthe as the S-3. Major Cronin is coming here. Bob will brief you."

"Yes, sir. Congratulations, sir...I guess."

"Yes. Thanks."

He gets up and leaves as Captain Kemp says, "To answer the question you started, yes. You will attend and observe the latter two. Also the Departure Ceremony on Wednesday. Lieutenant McKean will brief you on those ceremonies before you go. Also on all others... ones that are conducted at the Pentagon, the airport, Leutze Park and so forth. I would listen carefully if I were you because after Wednesday, you will be doing those and others. Thereafter, Gunny Elms and Sergeant Hapgood will be your source of information. Lieutenant McKean is not only departing the company, but is leaving the Marine Corps to return to civilian life."

"Sir, when is, or are, the next ones...ceremonies?"

"There is a two-platoon funeral at Arlington on Thursday but I will assign it to the guard platoons. Give you a few days grace, but you will attend and observe. After that, you'll be doing the bulk of the MDW ceremonies here. Don't worry. I've seen you on the parade deck. You'll be fine, probably better than fine."

"Okay, is that it, sir?"

"Well, no, not exactly. We, meaning The Barracks, also provide the troops for 'H' Company, 22nd Marines. Our guard platoons provide two of the rifle platoons, MCI Company one platoon, and the D&B the Weapons Platoon. We train once a year as a combat rifle company. The DT is not part of this, however the reason I tell you now is that when Hog Company is gone, the DT takes up all of the slack on ceremonial duties and helps with the guard of the day at Camp David."

"Yes, sir. Are you getting ready to tell--"

"Yep, we, meaning H Company, will probably be put on alert. A crisis is brewing in Cuba and all the military will be on alert, and that means the reserves, which includes the 22nd Marines."

"Well, I've been keeping up with this in the papers and TV, but didn't know it had gotten this far along. I didn't have the foggiest idea Hog company would be alerted."

"Not yet, but it will be, soon. So, learn quickly Lieutenant for ye may be one of the only officers around Guard Company, other than Major Cronin, available to stand whatever ceremonies there are."

"Yes, sir."

"One factor however, is that when things like this happen, the number of ceremonies diminish rapidly. I guess when the poop hits the fan, the pomp and ceremony peter out, so to speak." He laughs, pleased with his clean-cut wit. His eyes sparkle with the laugh. This man has a dry wit, and I sense it will be dispensed frequently, if things are going well and he likes you. If not, no smile, no wit, all business and icicles dangling from his words.

I feel good about this. I belong here, I just know it. I head to see Elms and Hapgood, who are not at the arrival this morning. The troops I'll see later, and they me...probably give me the hard eye, and in time, test me...always do.

Stoneface will be ready, so will Mustang Barney.

CHAPTER 17

White House Gate
People everywhere
2300 hours
Fri, 22 Nov 1963

I'M OUT OF MY TRANCE-LIKE state. We've eased past Lafayette Park and are now at the driveway entrance to the White House. The convoy starts inside. Stops. Our van is off Pennsylvania Avenue, but not inside the gate. We're sitting on the sidewalk portion, waiting to move on through. Another delay. I've had enough delays for one night.

I open the van door to see what the hold-up is. A good size crowd has formed, several hundred, maybe a couple of thousand. The gathering is solemn, but the whispers and murmurs of individuals, in mass, now sound like the entire choir humming. I'm in full Dress Blues, spit-shined Sam Browne belt, sword affixed on the belt at my side, medals and brass glistening in the lights of the gate area. Suddenly a man in the crowd shouts, "God damn, Marines. You killed our President."

I'm taken aback by this, even though in the deep recesses of my mind I knew the information about Oswald might incite people. Still, I'm stunned and take a fleeting look to see if I can tell who had shouted. I can't but catch some movement from my right. I glance that way but too late to react. A woman has come under the police barricade, up to the door of the van, and screams, "Yeah, damn Marines," and spits at me. Splat. A direct hit, on my chest. It hits the shoulder strap of my already spit-shined Sam Browne belt.

Nothing for me to do in this circumstance. I'm angry, but just shake my head and wipe it off with my gloved hand. One of the White House policemen at the gate is out of the gatehouse in a flash, and not so gently guides the woman back into the crowd. He looks at me, shakes his head and says loudly, "Sorry, sir. People are getting a little crazy out here tonight."

"Yeah, guess so. Not your fault. No sweat."

"Well, thanks. No sense detaining her."

I nod. It's an emotional time, and the city is reflecting this everywhere. I'd bet, sometime late tonight, this woman will regret what she did...be ashamed, and hope no one she knows saw her. I've had too many positive moments with people while performing with the Drill Team to concern myself with this one distraught woman.

A few moments later, the convoy moves and we're inside the grounds and unloading. I've been on this driveway on cordons, and at this entrance so many times this past year, I feel like I'm home. We are directed into the White House and down to a subterranean part of the building. It has a large galley and living quarters, shipboard type, for dozens, perhaps hundreds of people. Fascinating, all below ground. Who'd guessed! More secrets, like Camp David.

This is to be the command post, break area, and whatever for the Death Watch detail while the President lies in repose in the East Room. We are told to stand by. I love it! This means, stand by...get set... stand by...be ready...and stand by again, for whatever happens next. Like being in the starting blocks of a race. The starter says, "Ready. Set." And then doesn't fire the pistol. You'd just be leaning and finally topple over. That's the way I feel.

It's late. We find out from the TV in the room that JFK has arrived and is at Bethesda Naval Hospital. In addition, that Lee Harvey Oswald was charged earlier for the killing of Officer Tippett in Dallas, and now for the killing of President Kennedy. That news is probably what triggered that woman outside.

We have what we need down here. All of the Death Watch detail has now assembled...all five services. There are sandwiches, milk, soft drinks, ice water, coffee and such on a large table in the room. Have to say, the White House staff puts out an outstanding spread. We have irons and ironing boards aplenty. My troops and I take the time to press our uniforms again, needed or not. Others do the same, and it is needed. We re-shine all leather and brass. Finished, we stand by...set...waiting for the word.

At least we're more comfortable than at Gawlers. No disrespect. The folks at Gawlers tried hard but I'm convinced that the only people comfortable in a funeral home are the ones not talkin'. Here there's no feeling or smell of death surrounding us as was the case in the viewing room. Solemn for sure with the knowledge of the death of the President, but not that scent that engulfed us at Gawlers. Our unnies hang beside us, freshly pressed. We sit in our skivvies, waiting, leaning.

The fatigue alone at this late hour allows my mind to topple over into the past once again.

* * *

I go from my meeting with the CO and XO to my new office. No Women Marines, no Casilonnias around here, thank God. I wait for McKean to return so we can begin the turnover. While here, I meet the other platoon commanders. Like me, two of the three are new to Guard Company. Lieutenant Van Dell is still here and has the 2nd platoon. First Lieutenant Dan Rader, a West Point graduate, who chose the Marine option, has the 1st platoon. Rader's tall, my height plus an inch, like Point guys...poured out of a mold. At first, he appears to be a bit impressed with himself. Probably not the case, but if so, one or two sessions with Mush Mouth will solve that. However, he seems like a good guy, squared away. Is a grunt, so he has to be okay.

The other is First Lieutenant Bob Reese. He just arrived at The Barracks and was assigned here immediately. He has the 3rd Herd and is about six foot, former enlisted like me, and like everyone here, squared away and in the top drawer of the Corps. Those two have their hands full. They have the H Company platoons, but since both are infantry lieutenants, and just came from a rifle company, it should be a no-brainer. Just a surprise. You know, expect to be holding only a sword and looking pretty, and you're handed a map case, helmet, pistol and flak jacket because of this Cuban Missile Crisis.

* * *

After tonight's cordon at the White House and a long first day, I return to Center House. Dinner is long over, the crew is at the bar and the chatter is about the alert, and that brings out the Hog Company war stories from Captains McKay and Kruger, both having been in H company when they first arrived. Reese and Rader are married and home. They don't get to hear Muv's horror stories from all the previous training sessions at Marine Corps Base, Quantico, Virginia, some forty or so miles south of here.

After this type of BS goes on for awhile, the House Mother looks at me and asks, "Well, Loooootenant, since you have a habit of creating a ruckus on your first day everywhere, what did you do this morning to disrupt or destroy Guard Company and the Drill Team?"

"Nothing, Muv, goin' to fit like a gluv."

The House Mother raises his eyebrows. I add, "Sir."

Kruger and Milsap burst into laughter at my attempt at poetic humor. Captain McKay raises his eyebrows and chortles, "Very funny, Mister Quinn, very funny. Based on your record to date, I'm sure you will distinguish yourself in short order. If not at Building 58 or a ceremony, maybe with General Brown once again, or better yet, the Commandant."

Captain Milsap chimes in, "You know, Lieutenant, the Commandant sometimes sits on his back porch roof in the dark on parade nights...watching...checking the cover and alignment when we pass in review. With your ears, you can't be missed." The other two laugh of course...with these three, one speaks, two laugh. It's a private vaudeville act.

I say, "The Commandant sits on the porch roof in the dark watching the parade? Why don't we just invite the poor guy. Get him a good seat in the bleachers."

"Once again, very funny, Mister Quinn. Very funny," the Muv offers.

"Yes, sir, but anywho, I'll be keepin' a low profile. Boots in the boat and oars out of the water, until I'm sure of the drift."

The Muv throws his arms up in the air and says, "Oh, God! One day at the Navy Yard and you're spewing continental era naval jargon? What next?"

"Arrrg, Matey. How 'bout some grog, and maybe a wench or two, sire?"

At this, Captain John Grider Milsap spins off his bar stool in laughter, spilling his drink on himself.

Even Mush Mouth has to laugh at this; however, he quickly looks back at me and says, "Are you trying to be funny yet again, Mis—terrr or are you asking me to buy you a drink?"

"Yazza, yazza, sir. Meaning, the Loooootenant is trying to be a wit, and would like a drink, sir."

"You're not amusing. Buy your own drink."

Captain Julius leaps into the fray by saying, "Barney, I'll buy you a drink, and while you're sipping it you can tell me about the redhead."

"Sir, I accept the drink, but you will get nothing from me regarding the redhead, except my name, rank, and service number. I fully understand my rights under the Code of Conduct. Therefore, I will--"

"Never mind the monologue. They're not authorized for lieutenants, especially you. Drink, I believe the House Mother is about to conduct an instructional session and I'm sure none of us want to miss it. Right, JG?"

The Yaliee nods. We sit quietly on our bar stools, twirling our glasses with our fingertips, occasionally taking a sip, and listening. We can't understand the mumbled, syrupy, Carolinian language, but we listen. I think it is about Hog Company again.

I should call Gabby. See what we're doing this weekend. I know we're having dinner at Harriet's Saturday night, but don't have a clue what she has planned on Sunday. Doesn't matter to me as long as we're together. I don't call; it can wait. Listening to the Muv's monologues is a form of duty around here, and duty calls...and anyway it rates only a tad below Bullwinkle on the humor scale.

* * *

The White House
Below deck
After midnight
Fri, 22 Nov 1963

I'm shocked out of my solitude by a loud voice commanding, "Listen up. Everyone get suited up. The President is on the way. We're going to form an all-service cordon from the entrance to the East Room."

We're up and scrambling. The readied uniforms are donned and we race topside. The cordon is formed. An "L" shaped one from the East Room to the Portico steps outside. I'm placed on the inside, at the juncture of the "L".

We stand at attention for twenty or so minutes. Nothing happening. No scurrying by anyone indicating something is about to happen. Something's not right. Then we're given "At Ease." This from Army Captain Graven, who's now in charge of the Death Watch detail.

We stand at ease for another twenty or so minutes, which really isn't a rest. This is at ceremonial at ease, standing still, silent, head and eyes to the front. It's just a different position than that of attention, but for all practical purposes, is the same.

I hear a murmuring behind me. Something's not right.

Captain Graves calls us back to attention, and informs us that it was a false alarm. He had gotten some incorrect word. We are dismissed, to return down below to wait again, and rest.

How can we have a false alarm...the wrong word. Jesus, you can't miss the President leaving. Not this night!

Then I realize, I bet there must be a slew of people from MDW and other government bodies running around like squawking chickens, giving orders, most of them incorrect. A madman's paradise.

I wish Captain JG were over here. He would shoulder and slither his way into the group, quietly question them, and ensure the word passed is accurate. The Yaliee is a "Steady, Eddy" type. Has a calming approach. Never panics.

Whatever, we're back, unnies hanging up again and relaxing. I drift off again. It's getting easier to do so, I'm tired. I suspect the other Marines here with me are in the same cloudbank, thinking about President Kennedy, remembrances of his time...happenings.

A lot of ceremonies, events, activities...been like marching across the pages of history without leaving a footprint.

CHAPTER 18

THE MISSILE CRISIS OF OCTOBER '62 is over. Tensions began to ease on the 28th, and shortly an agreement is reached. Seeing eye to eye or not with the means, the President warded off a nasty situation. Fortunately Hog Company was not activated so our troops stayed put. Two field grade officers, aviators, from MCI were moved to Air Wing units and flew missions. That'll be worth a few drinks at happy hour. We all love sea stories.

The Barracks goes back to clicking and snapping along its ceremonial pace and looking forward to the forthcoming annual Oyster Bowl football game between the officers of MCI and those of H&S and Guard Companies. Losers pay for the fresh oysters and a keg of beer in Center House after the game...for those still able. The game is open season on the field grade officers. The Hog Company monologues from the Muv and Kruger have ceased, but they'll create new topics with the pot-stirring Milsap peering over their shoulders.

For the Drill Team and me it's ceremonies as usual. White House arrivals and departures. Wreath layings at the Tomb, arrivals and departures at the Pentagon, White House dinner cordons, a few street parades on holidays and the always-present funerals at Arlington. In addition, we augment the guard at Camp David when the Kennedy's go there on weekends, and they do so frequently.

The Drill Team has always been referred to as the Silent Drill Team. Oddly, however, the drill does have several voice commands by the Platoon Commander. After input from Sergeant Hapgood and several troops, I decide to eliminate those and to slow the cadence just a tad to make the movements more distinct, sharper. We also decide to make a major change in the rifle inspection routine. We're going to add a double or mirror rifle inspection on the second one, or as we say, at the little end of the line. It will build on the first and is more difficult dramatically increasing the risk of a drop.

Both Sergeant Collins, the inspector, and his counterpart, Corporal Andrejewski, will do all the same movements and spins simultaneously. Both will toss the rifle back, over their shoulders, at the same time at the conclusion of the inspection...rifles passing within inches of one another in the air. It will be a crowd pleaser...and will create a pucker factor for the CO, S-3 and the home team brethren. For me, I trust my Snuffies and thrive on risks and spotlights.

This, along with doing the entire drill, some 435 counts, without any command from start to finish, is startling and momentum building. Crowds love it. It creates tension and anticipation. This means leaving troop walk during a parade, without a command, doing the drill, and ending by me coming to the front of the parade commander and crowd. Then we present arms, go back to the order. I face about, and we march off, to troop walk and the formation still without a command. Everything is done on counts and in conjunction with different manual of arms movements. All this with The Barracks as a backdrop clothed in semi-darkness and floodlights on the Drill Team only. God, I love it... and these rowdy Snuffies in blue, white dress.

Life for me at Guard Company continues to be busy. Time is zipping by faster than a racecar on the Indy straightaway. Gabrielle and I see each other as often as possible, which is mostly on weekends. That's the only time I can get away. We jealously protect and enjoy our time together. Our relationship is on the high ground and we're both still mindful of wanting to be sure we're headed in the right direction. Patience is a virtue, but damn frustrating. Christmas is coming and as expected the ceremonial business is sputtering along. Gabrielle and I plan to spend the time together at her place over the holiday period. For me, that generates notions of eggnog and a warm fireside.

* * *

The White House
Waiting again
0050 hours
Sat, 23 Nov 1963

My private thoughts are interrupted by a commotion in the room. Captain Graven has entered to low throaty growls from the troops. He orders, "Suit up, and get upstairs. The President will be arriving very shortly, and we will put the cordon in place once again."

I put on my Dress Blues and along with all of my troops and the other services, we dash topside just like battle stations aboard ship. We slide into our cordon places. Easy...been here and done this. We're at attention, waiting for the moment.

We wait, standing tall, straight and silent. And we wait some more. Minutes seem like hours as they drag by. Nothing, again. Then we are ordered to ceremonial at ease again and are at this position for another good fifteen minutes or so. Somewhere near the thirty-minute mark, Captain Graves orders us back to attention, and we stand. And wait, motionless. Mental temperatures rising. I sense some commotion, hear some people scurrying about, heels clicking on the White House flooring behind me, and I hear voices. A low, hushed argument is going on. More hushed comments followed by growls of anger.

Something's wrong. I bet it's another bum scoop alert. Dammit!

Captain Graves centers himself in the middle of the entranceway and commands, "At Ease." He's flushed.

The cordon snaps to ceremonial at ease. Red-faced he announces, "Men, it's another false alarm. The President is not yet on the way here. I'm sorry." With that he commands, "Attention. Dismissed."

We grumble and mumble our way back down to our waiting area. Take off our unnies, begin the pressing and shining routine over again. I mosey to the head facilities, shave, and take a mini-douche in the washbasin. My troops are doing the same. I return to my spot in the room, next to my hanging uniform and accoutrements, and relax. It's almost 0130 hours and this routine is becoming thorn-like. A lot of factors are starting to pile up. Early start this morning. PT test. Football game. Broken toe. Futile wait at Gawlers. Hurry up and wait. Moreover, of course, the most stressful, the assassination itself...of our President...in our country.

The result is I'm tired and have little trouble slipping into my semi-conscious, daydreaming state, thinking of Gabrielle and our first Christmas together. It was my best Noel since I saw my uncle eating the cookies I'd left on the mantel for Santa...and that was a couple decades of Decembers ago.

* * *

It's Monday, Christmas eve of '62 and I have the duty at The Barracks. There is hardly a soul around on this long weekend holiday. My OD tour is quiet. No Santa Claus and no problems as the day passes into night. At midnight, I check posts, and insert the code card in the KY-1 phone in the Commandants basement. He's not wandering around so the trip is uneventful, thank God. I half expected him to be down there to scare the B-Jesus out of the OD on Christmas Eve just out of orneriness. Later, at 0400, when I check posts again, it's snowing... hard. It's storybook-like...the scene is Christmas card perfect.

I'm up at 0600, wash up quickly, and put on my uniform. When I go to the door and peer out, the parade deck is a blanket of snow, and from the looks of the parking lot, its deep, over a foot. No two ways about it, looks as if an artist painted this picture. Unfortunately, it has to be disturbed.

I tell the Sergeant of the Guard to get the snow removal details out before the Commandant looks out the window and blows a gasket, mine. It's a way of life here. He seems to look out his window only during bad weather, or when something goes wrong with colors, or from his porch roof during a parade. Never on a perfect blue-sky day. It's Murphy's Law at The Barracks. All the walks within the quadrangle and those outside The Barracks need to be shoveled, and quick. I don't want a bah-humbugging Commandant chewin' my butt.

Everything goes like clockwork. Details are clearing the walks and parking lot. The snow has stopped. My relief, Lieutenant Van Dell, is here. We make the informal relief, and I am on my way to Center House. I'm leaving for Gabrielle's quicker than Rocky and Bullwinkle can quell Boris and Natasha. I promised to make breakfast for her as soon as I get there. It's not a surprise venture. She purchased the fixin's. Nothing fancy, just some scrambled eggs but it will be a cozy breakfast... fireplace lit, decorated tree in the corner, and a blanket of newly fallen snow outside.

I leave The Barracks after changing clothes. Gabrielle told me to shower when I arrive and not waste any time getting there. It's 0830, and you would think there would be some traffic out here but there are no tire tracks in the snow, not even a person walking or shoveling. If an old eastern city can look pristine, this is it. The curbs are covered, so driving is a matter of staying between the light poles, signs, and buildings. It's beautiful, but a slow, careful drive is the order of the day. Over a foot is deep for my Vette. Unbelievably, I don't encounter another car all the way to her apartment. The trail of tire tracks behind me is the only indication of life, except for one scraggly crow sitting on a wire along Columbia Pike...poor bugger.

She buzzes me up and is waiting at her door for me. She is in a sheer, seductive dressing gown...a thingyabob garment again. Her shadowy curves are easily discernable, alluring and tantalizing. I can feel my heart pounding. We kiss, no hug since I'm carrying a clothing bag with some changes, and I have a few gifts for her in my other arm. She says, "Come on in love, and put your things down in the bedroom. Whatsyagot in the boxes, Barney?"

"Surprises, I hope. Merry Christmas, Gabrielle."

"Merry Christmas to you, too. And put everything down so I can greet you properly."

I drop everything on the bed, and as soon as I turn around, she wraps her arms around my neck and we kiss. Whisper Merry Christmas to each again, and kiss again, holding each other tightly.

I push away slightly and ask, "Can I use your shower?...and clean up real quick? Didn't want to waste any time at The Barracks. Just changed out of my unnie, threw on some old ratty warm clothes and headed here as fast as my sleigh would carry me."

"So I see. Sure, go ahead. I'll just get things set up so you can do your breakfast thing. I can't wait." She gives me her signature peck on the nose and heads out the bedroom door. I get out of my clothes, turn on the shower letting it warm. After several seconds, I step inside and let the water hit the top of my head, my face, and run down my body as I turn around a few times capturing its warmth.

As I'm groping for a bar of soap among all the female lotions, washes, shampoos and do-dads hanging up, the shower door opens.

Gabby, is standing there, readying to take the step into the shower. No, this is Gabrielle. No doubt. I wipe the water from my eyes.

Good God. I knew she would be stunning, but...

She is a natural redhead and her ample and ever so slightly freckled breasts are firm, nipples rose pink and aroused. She says, "I'm joining you, or do you prefer to shower alone?" She slithers into the stall shower, a bewitching contrast to the sky blue tile.

"You already have, and no, this is great." My reaction is immediate.

We embrace under the warm water, allowing it to engulf us as we caress each other while locked in a deep kiss. We kiss again and again. I run my lips over both cheeks, her neck, and dwell on her nipples while I stroke and caress her. We are both more than ready. I gently lift her and allow her to settle on me as she gasps, then groans as her legs entwine around me like ivy clinging to a wall. The footing is tenuous on the tile as we make love. Our rhythm builds, reaching a zenith. She is a screamer and a groaner. She throws her head back, full face to the shower, as we peak. In this position, still clinging to me, she tightens her vaginal muscles. She does this gypsy-like contracting and expanding several times, moaning, coupled with a carnal grin. She relaxes, sighs, then kisses me softly and says, "Barney, I love you. I don't want to let you go. I love you so, Barney, I need you."

I slowly half lift and half slide her from me and say, "I love you, Gabrielle, I do...I do...ummmmmm, and...And the best Christmas I've ever had. Damn, what a shower!"

"Ahhh, a simple one-track mind. Gad, I love you."

* * *

The White House
Below decks
0213 hours
Sat, 23 Nov 1963

Commotion again. Son of a bitch! For me, crummy timing. Captain Graven is alerting us yet again. We get unnied-up and scramble topside one more time. We reform quickly into our cordon. Wearily, but still ramrod straight and looking sharp, except for the tired eyes and drawn faces. We are at attention...ceremonial mannequins.

Ten minutes goes by and Captain Graven appears in the middle of the cordon, and says in a more than pissed-off tone, "Men, it's a false alarm again. Damnit, I'm sorry. Dismissed. Go below."

We do and as he enters the room behind me, I turn, stop and say, "Captain Graven, sir, I know you're not at fault here, but how about making damn sure we don't have any more false alarms. This is bull shit. Somebody needs to calm down. Get control, and put out some straight scoop...sir."

"You're right, Lieutenant Quinn. I will. Count on it."

"Thank you, sir. I will." I turn about and go through my stand-down routine for what I hope is the last false alarm. I know in my heart he can't do anything.

He's a good guy. A Doggie, but a good person. He'll do what he can, but times like these always generate some level of panic in the herd. Need a tough trail boss right now.

I really don't need to press my uniform, but figure if we don't have any more false alarms I'll need a freshly pressed uniform for the cordon and my segment of the Death Watch, which will closely follow. So, I press, and shine, as do my troops...and of course, stand by, leaning, careful not to topple.

I sit down, take a deep breath and let my mind go blissfully back to soaps, shampoo, Gabrielle, and Christmas. One helluva holiday...I believe in Santa again.

* * *

As we begin to soap each other for a true shower, we trade kisses and nips, and we're at it again. She wraps herself around me and this time everything is slippery...me from her soaping, her from my full body shampooing, and her nature...and the damn shower floor. It is a true test of gymnastic ability but we make love again, and longer this time. When we are spent, we're near collapse, part from exhaustion and part from maneuvering on the ice rink-like surface of the shower. I think we may have done an Olympic-class sit-spin in here. She brushes my lips, murmurs or purrs, I'm not sure which, "Barney, I'm not letting you go."

"You mean I have to stay in here for the rest of my life."

"No, but hopefully with me. I love you, Barney."

Oh-oh. This is heavy. Getting serious. I feel the Vette and me racing toward station wagons and potluck dinners.

143

We soap up, rinse off, and get out of the shower. She hands me a towel, gives me another kiss, thrusts, drapes her arms out to the side, and says, "Dry please, sir."

I start toweling her off. We kiss and nip a few times, and by damn we're on the way again. This time, she pushes me away, yanks the towel out of my hands, grabs another, and says, "You are a love, but we've got to get out of here, and have some breakfast."

"Why? The best tasting treats are right here as far as I'm concerned...strawberry shampoo and all."

"I agree, but I want the breakfast you promised, then I'll have more of you."

"Okay." I let her be, and she me. We get dried, and she puts on her sheer gown that isn't going to help me focus on breakfast. She hands me a thick, white, Turkish towel-like robe. It has a stitched monogram on the front left side...Swift, Silent and Deadly. She smiles and purrs, "An early present for you, Randy Recon, I love your patrols. Let's go and enjoy our first Christmas breakfast together."

"I already have and got the scratches to prove it." I knew it wasn't a murmur.

She blushes and gives me a playful tweak of my nose.

I put on the robe and head for the kitchen.

I love friggin' Christmas!

CHAPTER 19

I NOT ONLY LOVE CHRISTMAS, I'm a fan of morning showers. It's damn hard to concentrate on fixing breakfast with Gabrielle whisking back and forth in that gown, smelling like fresh strawberries. Oh well, breakfast it is. I dice some onions, green peppers, and sweet red peppers. Sprinkle them with a pinch of dill weed and salt. Gabrielle slows the whisking, stopping behind me and bites me on the neck. "Need to stop if you want breakfast. I've got zero, zip, willpower."

"Okay, okay. You just look so good in your swift, silent and deadly robe...and smell wonderful. Like...ah—"

"Strawberries and cream probably."

"Yeah, where did you have your—"

"Stop.

"Okay."

I sauté the trappings in veggie oil. After about five minutes, I put in the eggs I've scrambled and blend everything together. My cinnamon toast is done. I pour some tomato juice. Gabrielle sets the silver coffee thermos on the table and we're set.

We sit, she pours the coffee and puts cream and sugar in mine. *This gal has me roped. Not tied yet, however, but it might take only a loop or two. She's good...at everything.*

Gabrielle pretends to be dazzled with my culinary skills. The eggs are good, different, and simple. She wasn't impressed with my insistence on cleaning everything as I went. She must be a sloppy cooker. Some folks are. Cook for two, however, if you look at the stove, sink, and counter tops it looks as if there were twelve for dinner. I use something; I clean and put it away.

After breakfast, as we finish our second cup of coffee, she says, "Surprise. I borrowed a toboggan from Sally. We're going sledding or tobogganing or whatever it's called. Go get some warm clothes on."

"Hey, sounds great. Fun. I may even show you my surfing skills. They're related, you know...I think. Will wow you."

"You've already wowed me in the shower BQ, and at the stove. Rest on your laurels. I want you safe and sound for this afternoon and evening."

"Well, I appreciate the thought, but I'm indestructible...a decent surfer and Olympic class street sledder. Did I ever tell you about the--"

"No. Spare me. Let's change."

"Geez."

We change in the bedroom, and every time I try to play, she pushes me off, "Sledding, Barney, sledding first."

We go outside on the hill beneath her balcony patio. There are some kids already out here, using sleds and galvanized garbage can covers and another couple with a toboggan. After a few trips down the steep but short slope I say, "Love bug, this was a great idea. I don't think I'll demonstrate my surfing prowess, just stay snuggled up to you on this sled. I like our crashes."

The hillside treat is becoming crowded as the morning slides by. We sled, wrestle in the snow after our crashing stops, and finally get into an old-fashioned snowball fight. She gets to hide behind a tree and I have to stand in the open. It doesn't make any difference. I intend to lose.

After a few hours, cheeks and noses red from the chill of the day and the headfirst snow crashes, we trudge up the hill, dragging the toboggan behind us.

Gabrielle slips her arm through mine, pulls me close, and says, "First thing, we need to take a shower to get warm."

"Now that's a plan. You're goin' to kill me, but it's a plan." I stop, hook the sled rope loop through my arm, and pull her close. We kiss hungrily, as if we hadn't seen each other in months, or years. The dangling sled serves as a form of a sea anchor and prevents any slippage, or drifting as it were. We part; she tugs at my arm again urging me up the hill. I let the toboggan rope slide down my arm and into my hand, and pull both it and Gabby along as fast as I can make traction in the now melting snow.

Inside, we drop clothes and head for the shower as fast and as recklessly as possible. Gad, I love Christmas, and this woman...and strawberry shampoo.

* * *

The White House
Galley area below
0300 hours
Sat, 23 Nov 1963

I snap out of my dream to shouting. It's Captain Graven again. "We're on men, for real. This is not a false alarm. The President is leaving Bethesda, in a hearse, with police escort, headed this way. We'll do the cordon, minus the first watch. That's only five men. We'll eat up the loss with our spacing. That way they'll be ready to go on as soon as we get the President's remains in the East Room."

All jump into action. I check over my uniform carefully, and get dressed once again. No more false alarms. Game time. Although we are all dragging, the occasion primes the pump and has the adrenaline raging. It's business time.

We are topside, formed into our cordon of two lines from the portico steps to the closer of the two entrances to the East Room. I'm again at the juncture of the "L" in the entranceway. We are at attention, ramrod straight, solemn, and focused for the task at hand.

I hear a slight commotion, and a shuffling of feet behind me. I sense someone close, then a chin on my left shoulder and a somewhat sour breath drifts past my ear. The attached voice whispers, "Lieutenant Quinn, I have called your barracks and asked for Marines to come and escort the President, the hearse, up the drive from the gate to the front entrance. They have told me a detail of twelve will be here ASAP. And, they said to have you form them up, and do what you deem appropriate." He comes around on my left side and into sight. It's a Navy four-striper, Captain, a Presidential aide type. He says, "Do you understand? Can you do this?"

"Yes, sir. Is someone meeting this detail?"

"Yes, they'll be brought into the White House and will come up this way...behind us."

"Aye aye, sir. Consider it done. When is the President's remains expected, sir?"

"Shortly." He looks at his watch and adds, "It's almost 0340 hours...maybe in minutes."

Good God Almighty. Lord, please let 'em be my Drill Team troops. That will make it a lot easier for me to hastily rig something and make it look as rehearsed as any other ceremonial detail.

I hear voices and some commotion. Someone shouts, "They're here. The Marines are here, the Marines are here." It sounds like something out of the movies for Pete's sake, but they're right. It's twelve of my troops from the Drill Team. If I weren't so relieved, and the situation so serious, I would ask that we do a retake. It is that good.

This smells of the Yaliee. JG knew exactly what to do and who to send. He read my mind. I owe him a drink. Well, actually more but a good Scotch will have to do.

Lance Corporal Lord reports to me. I say, "Good goin', Lord."

Is that appropriate or what.

"Thanks, sir."

"Take the men out on the driveway; form them in two ranks of six, facing the portico...at fixed bayonets and at attention. I'll be out in a second."

"Yes, sir."

Not a NCO needed. All LCpl's and Pfc's. Lord, McCloskey, Norris, Port, Ulrich, Nowak, Murphy, Slack, Cunningham, Cloninger, Timberlake, and Ski...Martyniski or somethin'...never could spell or pronounce his name. Lord has them at Port Arms and takes them calmly and militarily, heels clicking smartly, through the entrance and outside on the driveway. I have little time to react and get going, but I feel myself swell with pride. From a dead sleep in The Barracks to here, in thirty minutes, and in squared away Dress Blues. These guys are good. No, Dammit, they're superb...the best!

I check with the Naval Aide again, trying to get a feel for how much time we have. All he knows is, soon, and that they're on the way, and Jackie Kennedy is with the President. She won't leave his side.

I go outside, face my men, command, "Right, FACE. Port, ARMS. Forward, MARCH." We march in a column of twos down the driveway to the entrance, countermarch, and halt, facing back up the driveway. I give them order arms, and put them at a true at ease. TV lights and flash cameras are creating their own eerie setting on the driveway.

The troops remain motionless as I tell them what we're going to do. "We'll be at Port Arms, march up the driveway, ahead of the hearse, escorting it up to the Portico. Just past the entrance, we'll halt and allow space for the unloading of the casket. I will Order Arms, then give you a non-conventional command of Outward, Face. When I do, face, take four steps forward, halt and face about automatically. The hearse will move forward so the casket can be unloaded. I will move off the center of the drive, to curbside, and command, Present, Arms, rendering a salute to President Kennedy. The body bearers will unload the casket and take him inside. When they're inside, we'll come to the Order. Any questions?"

They have none. However, their eyes tell me to go over it again... to be sure. I hear distant sirens. We have time.

While repeating the instructions, I walk militarily amongst them, adjusting and fastening a few collars that were left undone in their haste to get here. I try to make it look like we're saying a quick prayer or something. I make eye contact with each set of two. They've got the game face look. We're ready. Standing at Ceremonial At Ease, on the driveway, by the front gate.

God, I love these guys.

Sometime after 0400 I get word that they're almost here. The wailing sirens crying out are much closer. I see the flashing red lights and the gray Navy hearse behind the police cars. I call the detail to attention. There are dozens of flash bulbs going off. TV lights are back on. News people talking and shouting instructions and who knows what else is happening around us. It's hard to see outside the edge of the drive. The flashes are blinding. I put the detail at Port Arms which I feel is appropriate. A position of guarding, protecting.

Much too late, Barney ol' boy...much too late but nothin' goin' wrong on this watch.

At nearly 0430 hours, this Saturday, November 23rd, 1963, President Kennedy, with Jackie at his side, returns home. The police cars pull up and stay outside the gate. Solemnly, at a funeral cadence we march and escort the hearse up the driveway to the entrance of the White House. Once at the portico, we do our movements. The hearse pulls up in between us and slightly beyond. The body bearer detail, made up of representatives of all five services, move as one with precision to remove the casket and take it into the East Room. I see that LCpl Cheek and Diamond have drawn the assignment from our Body Bearer section. They are lookin' sharp as always. The casket will be placed on the same catafalque that was used for President Lincoln, almost a hundred years ago.

The President will lay in repose, in the East Room, with a Death Watch detail around the casket for the entire time. Two priests will also be present, kneeling in prayer, on the backside, the wall side, of the casket.

The Death Watch will have an officer at the head of the casket. The first watch will be led by a Lieutenant from the Army's Old Guard, at Fort Myer, the senior service. The four sentries will be at the corners, one from each other service. On this first watch, it will be a Marine, Sailor, Airman, and a Coastguardsman.

The watch will be for thirty minutes, standing at attention, or ceremonial at ease. That watch, when relieved, will have two hours until they're posted again. The two hours includes getting off and back on, in formation, marching silently at a funeral cadence from our ready area to the East Room. That eats up twenty minutes at the least. The remainder is spent pressing and shining...and trying to relax.

I will have the second watch; sentries will be from the services other than the Marine Corps, since I will be representing the Corps.

These watches are to go on for approximately twenty-four hours as the President lays in repose. This is private, not open to the public, although a huge crowd has continued to gather outside the White House on Pennsylvania Avenue in some form of vigil.

After thanking and dismissing my escort troops, I return inside, and go down to our subterranean command post to get ready for my watch. I have only about fifteen minutes until I have to form up with my detail.

* * *

It's time. I inspect my detail for our 0500 watch. We go topside, form, and march solemnly at a funeral cadence down the hall, and into the East Room. We make our final approach from behind the head of the casket. I come alongside the Army Lieutenant on watch. The troops slide in and halt at their respective corners of the casket. When all are in place, the other officer and I start a slow, solemn hand salute. The slow start allows the troops to see it beginning and come to present arms seemingly at the precise same time. We end the salute, without command, in the same manner. The troops follow, coming to order arms. Then all five of the off-going watch detail step back simultaneously, face about, the troops come to Port Arms, and they march off slowly, forming as we were, in a column of two's with the officer leading. They march out of the East Room, and off to our ready area.

When the off-going detail stepped back, my detail and I side step into the formerly occupied position, at attention. We will remain at attention, motionless, head and eyes to the front, expressionless... mannequins. No blinking, or as little as humanly possible. Not blinking can become a mind game. We can move to a ceremonial at ease position. To do this, I tell my detail ahead of time that I will do it at about the ten-minute mark. When I'm ready, they sense the move. Only the ones at the foot of the casket can easily see me. I make a slow movement, imperceptible to an outsider, to start the change; they pick it up and get in synch with me, and complete the change. We'll change back to attention in another ten minutes in the same manner.

The priests are kneeling off to my left, away from the side of the casket. They're praying. Their mumbled, hushed voices sound like a droning murmur. It decidedly influences the emotion of the moment. In addition, there are four large candles on tall holders, one at each corner of the casket. They're a problem; the flame is flickering directly in the line of sight of the four sentries.

As soon as I get off, I'll have Captain Graven get them moved or lowered...do something before one of these guys drops.

The family, staff, and hangers-on have gone for the night. The room is still. The emotions raw and jagged. The men must be fatigued, as I am, and we'll be tested. This is when the training, discipline, mental toughness and pride take over. We're here, alone with the fallen president, and we will perform.

The priests and their prayers; the subdued lights; and us, the Death Watch with our private thoughts whirling through our minds. The world may be here in thought, perhaps prayer, but physically, it just us now.

I know my mind is working overtime, and I realize I will need to let it wander while on watch over the next twenty-four hours here, and at the Capitol, or I'll get caught up in the emotion of the times.

God, it's lonely in here.

CHAPTER 20

The White House
East Room
0530 hours
Sat, 23 Nov 1963

MY FIRST DEATH WATCH DETAIL is over. It was an emotionally wrenching time, but tempered by my reflections. My next watch starts at 0730 leaving an hour and a half to get pressing and shining accomplished before going on again. Unfortunately, it isn't really that much time. We have to form fifteen minutes before marching on, and when adding time to wash up, shave, and dress it leaves forty minutes and change for the P&S time, and some relaxation. A tight schedule that will go on for the remainder of the day, and beyond.

I send the night detail back to The Barracks. This includes the Gunny, and the non-rated troops, the Lance Corporals and PFC's. They will stand the night watches. The day detail, which consists of an officer and NCO sentries, normally goes on an 8:00AM to 8:00PM watch. The night detail comes on at 2000 hours until 0800 the following morning. We didn't go by the plan this first night at the White House since the President arrived so late plus the general confusion...too many chiefs syndrome, and blanketing too many wrong smoke signals. Anyway, the men leaving need the rest. We do as well, however, our adrenaline will keep us fueled for the remainder of the time in the East Room.

The troops are gone, my P & S done; I sit, breathe deep and allow my thoughts to float back to Christmas Day last year once again.

It truly was my best ever…and besides, I need some pleasing, relaxing thoughts to serve as my mental armor. The emotions of the day are more tiring than the physical effort although my legs do feel heavy. I just want to think of the pleasurable times…

* * *

Our after-sledding romp in bed is highlighted by before and after sit-spin shower performances. Straight nines from the judges, well at least the two judges present. The compulsories or foreplay was also Olympic class. When we towel off, Gabrielle says, "Barney. This could be a little embarrassing for me."

"What? Why?"

"Well, I forgot to tell you, we're going to Harriet's parents for Christmas dinner, and I'm so sore I'm not sure I can walk without showing some signs of the discomfort. Knowing Harriet, she'll figure it out quicker than a light switch."

"Sore? What are you…oh, I get it. Well hell, I may not be able to stand, let alone walk. You wore me out. But, you coerced me into a personal record."

"I don't think there was any coercing on either part, and it's not funny, Barney. I'm really sore."

"Well, chalk it up to fate. If you would have paid some attention to me sooner in life we would not have had to try and make up eleven years in one morning."

"Well, I'm happy we tried. Let's get dressed and going. It'll be Harriet and her parents, and Sally. God, she'll know too."

"Great. Should I act proud or humble, or fake ignorance?"

"Oohhh, you're incorrigible. Anyway, as I was saying, Harriet's parents live in Alexandria, and their names are Pierre, or Pete, and Margarite, or Madge…Boudreax. Sally will be alone, so it will be the six of us."

"Did I ever explain my jelly bean theory?"

"No, what's it got to do with this, or anything?"

"Well, if you put a jelly bean in a jar every time you have--"

"Get dressed, Barney."

"Okay, I'll get back to you with the jelly bean theory. It applies to us."

I manage to concentrate on getting on with the day but it is difficult when this striking natural redhead is getting dressed. Her just putting on her panty hose gets me started again but she slaps my hand and pushes me away with a playful giggle.

After dressing we drive to the Boudreaux' home. The snow is melting rapidly so the streets are clear; however, the yards and parks still show the remaining signs of a white Christmas.

We arrive and Pete and Madge greet us at the door. I play the courteous humble card. They don't seem to be aware of Gabrielle's dilemma; however, Harriet raises her eyebrows and nods along with a sly smile. Sally giggles and silently claps. They both look at me. I give them my jellybean stare...which includes the Sylvester the Cat grin.

The day moves along. The meal is wonderful. Turkey dinner with everything the food books and movies show, to include the warmth of their home and camaraderie of the group. We leave shortly after eight and head for Gabrielle's and the jellybean jar.

* * *

The White House
Galley area
0645 hours
Sat, 23 Nov 1963

It's time to suit up and go on watch again. The time between watches flies by faster than an Indy car on the straightaway. For me, the zzzziiiiiiiipppppp was a fond memory.

I give my watch detail the same instructions regarding changing positions. By this time, somebody has replaced the candleholders with shorter ones so the flame is not directly in the line of sight of the honor guard on the corners. One of the sentries on the watch following ours, got mesmerized or hypnotized by the flickering flame, and went out... down at the position of attention. He and his rifle made a loud clattering noise on the hardwood floor of the East Room.

Fortunately, he fell backwards, and since it was so early, no visitors or such was present. The supernumerary and Captain Graven remove him. The super replaces him. He did hit his head, but not first, and his injured pride probably masks any other pain. However, visualize this. When he went out, and landed on the hardwood deck, he was still at the position of attention, and holding his rifle at the Order, right there on the floor. Now that's what I call discipline. He was one of the Gawler Funeral Home Barney Quinn trained troops.

The holders are changed but I still caution my detail not to go flame hunting with their eyeballs; just pick a spot on the far wall, stand tall, relax, stay focused, and breathe.

The time is 0715 hours; we start the go-on routine, and settle into position and our watch at 0730. Quickly my mind's eye returns to Christmas Day. I have to mentally remove myself from here, with its rattling of beads and mumbling of the priests...and my feelings, my emotions.

      * * *

It's almost nine at night when we get back to Gabrielle's place. We change into our robes. Mine her gift, and hers is the same sheer seductive thingy. We settle on the sofa and are about to watch, what else, *Miracle on 34th Street*. The original version made in 1947 with John Payne, Maureen O'Hara, Edmund Gwenn, and Natalie Wood, when she was a young girl.

Before settling in, I say, "Gabrielle, Merry Christmas," as I bring my two gifts from behind my back.

She squeals in girlish delight. The joyful look on her face, along with the squeak and now a sigh is cute, warm and reward enough.

The more I'm around this woman, the deeper in the hopper I'm going. It's not just the love-making. It's her intelligence, wit, glibness, thoughtfulness, playful nature and her striking beauty...and of course the fate thing. It is always lurking in the shadows. Oh well. Mistress beware!

After her emotional peep and sigh, she reaches under the sofa cushion and hands me a small box in brilliant Christmas wrapping, and says, "For you, in case you get lost, then I can come and claim you."

We open the gifts. Hers is beautifully wrapped. Mine as if a six year old got loose with scissors, paper and ribbon. Should have had the store do it. Gabrielle's to me is an ID bracelet...my name on the top, and inscribed on the underneath side is, *Love ya, Gabrielle-12/25/62. Neat. She likes...she wants me to call her Gabrielle.* I give her a thin or dainty, solid gold, neck chain with a rough cut, or etched miniature sand dollar. The gold shell is a wonderfully crafted likeness. The other is a charm bracelet with some starting charms. One of the Lincoln Memorial and one of the Washington Monument for our day there; one of a military figure to represent our meeting at the parade; a seashell for our Ocean City weekend; another my White House lapel pin; and one a heart with Gabrielle inscribed on one side and Barney, inscribed upside down on the other.

She asks, "What happened with your name. It's not right. It's upside down."

"Yeah, on purpose. Shows that I'm head over heels, upside down, in love with you."

"Ohhhh, Barney, Barney, Barney."

We exchange kisses and hugs, as she leaks a few tears, followed by a sniffle. We put the gifts on. She whispers, "Oh, Barney, I love it, everything. The necklace feels so good. How does it look?"

"Sexy. Fits snugly in your cleavage. I--"

She quiets me with a kiss and says, "You're terrible, but cute. Let's watch the movie before we get in trouble again."

It's on TV and has already started, but we haven't missed much. We snuggle on the sofa. It doesn't take long for her fragrance and freshness to weaken what little will power and resolve I possess around her. Coupled with the sheer gown, and the moment, and her murmuring, "I know what you're thinking, and it's considerate, but I want to finish off my Christmas Day in the best manner possible." With that, she slips her arms around my neck, does her signature kiss on the nose bit, and then mockingly flutters her eyes.

"Okay, it's jelly bean time."

"What's this theory you tried to run by me earlier?"

"You put a jelly bean in a jar every time you do the deed. If you miss a night however, then make it up the next by doing it several times, you can't make up the jelly beans."

"Why not?"

"It's all math. If you miss a time, you miss. If there were nine in the jar and you miss, you've got nine. If you make it up with three times the next night, you've got twelve. If you hadn't missed, you would have had thirteen. Jelly bean theory. Can't replace them missed ones. So I try not to miss."

"So let's not miss."

We make love yet again. It starts on the sofa. We work our way on and across the coffee table, clearing it, and finish on the floor in front of the TV.

When we are completely spent we stay put, robes on again, pillows under our heads and watch the end of the movie murmuring to one another. We can add rug burns to our other physical calamities along with a few nip marks. The latter used to be marks of distinction; I don't know what they're considered to be now. I can only hope the high collar on my blue dress tunic will hide them. If not, I suppose the Magpies will be snickering.

This is more than a fling for sure, and I'm beginning to believe in fate...and jelly beans. My mistress, the Corps, had better be careful.

* * *

The White House
East Room
0800 hours
Sat, 23 Nov 1963

The moment is over and I'm back to the present. It's time to get ready to go off watch. My only remembrance of this watch has been coming on, changing position twice, and the present. It zipped by and my memories of that Christmas Day relieve all the fatigue of being on the go since yesterday morning's IG. It's now 0800 hours, so I've been up and active for over twenty-six straight hours. Getting up at O Dark Thirty, doing the PT test, then the football game, and this, these historic events, are beginning to add up. I know I can pay the piper, but the price is going to be high.

I feel the nudge on my arm of the oncoming officer, which is the Navy Lieutenant JG, and I can see the honor guardsmen coming into position next to their counterparts. A few silent, precision moves and we'll be on our way off watch.

Good, a smooth exchange and we're moving.

Be back at 1000 hours, Mr. President.

CHAPTER 21

The White House
Galley area again
0815 hours
Sat, 23 Nov 1963

WE'RE BACK DOWN BELOW, STARTING our pressing, shining, cleaning up and relaxing routine. Simply a slightly modified five S's formula. I'm tired and feel the fatigue, as if five-pound weights are attached to my chin, arms, and feet. My next watch is 1000 hours. When finished with the altered five S's I sit down and think about all the MDW ceremonies I have stood with the Drill Team involving the President. My mind seems to want to recover the memorable moments, the fun times or incidents that I will remember long after what the actual event was or for whom. I let it run its course and drift away...

* * *

It's January 1963...Tuesday the 8th, and the DT and I have already done a WH arrival yesterday morning, the cordon that night, and earlier today, a Wreath Laying at the Tomb. Nothing out of the norm, except tonight. We are going to do a special ceremony of welcome, and opening, for the Mona Lisa. Leonardo da Vinci's painting is on loan to the U.S. and will be at the National Gallery, here in Washington, D. C. The President and Mrs. Kennedy, Jackie, will be hosting. Huge cultural event with the unveiling taking place in the West Sculptor Hall where the painting will hang. A couple thousand-person party is being given.

The Drill Team and I form a two-column cordon from the entrance of the National Gallery to the elevator that will take President Kennedy and Mrs. Kennedy up to the Hall. We are in Dress Blues and are formed there for a good hour before the actual arrival time of the President. Others are entering for the event, and escorted up the stairs to the Hall. The elevator is reserved for the President, Jackie, and those close to them. I am stationed at the end of our cordon, next to the elevator.

Out of the corner of my eye, I see a little old man, at least in his mid seventies. He's in a neatly pressed dark brown elevator uniform with its gold piping on the sleeves and trousers, and of course, his nametag, JOHN SMITH...figures.

Anyway, Mr. Smith is nervously twitching about and he continually practices closing the door, taking the elevator up, and bringing it back down. It is an old one and is hand operated. This is obviously the man's biggest and brightest moment of his elevator operator career, and probably his life. I mean, why not...take the President and the First Lady up to the Hall in "his" elevator. This will earn him endless beers at the local Moose Lodge, or wherever.

The time arrives. I see the President entering. I call the cordon to Attention, then command, Present, Arms. The DT flawlessly executes the movements, and then I salute, with my sword in a silky, smooth, ceremonial tuck and drop flowing movement. The sword tip although dropping by gravity, still vibrates and shudders to a stop as I complete the move. The President and Mrs. Kennedy stroll through the cordon with an entourage of dignitaries and friends. They get to the elevator, stop, and chat with several of the people in the group.

The elevator operator is at attention, poised, for his moment. He is ash colored, lips white-tight, and eyes flitting about. The President and First Lady turn to board the lift. The operator formally welcomes them with an ever-so-slight bow and a sweeping motion of his arm. Some of the entourage enters as well. The remainder turns and head for the expansive, marble stairway rising up to meet the Hall.

I come to Order Sword, and immediately to Carry Sword. Thwack! The thicker back edge of the sword pops on the shoulder seam of my Dress Blue blouse. Then I crack out the command, Order, Arms. The troops execute. The sound of hands slapping the leather slings on the weapons and the rifle butts crashing to the marble floor reverberate throughout the museum. The President's head snaps around and he glances at me, then the two lines of my Marine cordon. We stand fast, at attention, mannequins, as the door closes.

Suddenly, the elevator door opens. The little old man is stammering and stuttering, and nervously continuing to fidget and work the elevator-engaging handle. There is a problem, the doors close, but it won't "lift off." The President, Jackie, and the entourage members with them get off. Someone asks, "What's the problem?"

President Kennedy says, "Damn thing doesn't work."

Somebody in the immediate group says, "Well, let's just go up the stairs."

Jackie adds, "Yes, we'll walk up."

Damn her perfume smells oh so good. Expensive. Moreover, she looks gorgeous tonight, as always.

The President says, "No, we'll wait. This gentleman is trying to fix it, and we should just wait. He wants to take us up."

This is all going on directly in front of me. The President and Jackie are standing not twelve inches from my nose. I'm worried that Jackie's gown is going to catch on the tip of my sword, which is down near the floor since I'm at order swords. I imperceptibly edge my sword back closer to my body. I'm envisioning a major embarrassing moment here for the First Lady and me. These type situations compel my brain into all kinds of bizarre images of possibilities, none ever favorable to me.

Jackie says, "Come on, Jack. Let's just walk up the stairs."

He says, "No, we'll wait just a bit more. Hang on. This gentleman has worked hard for this moment."

"Jack, please let's go. Everyone is waiting upstairs."

"Not yet."

"Please."

I'm inches away and a spectator to this minor family squabble. Suddenly, after she emphatically says, "Jack!" he looks directly at me again, shrugs, smiles, and says, "Don't worry, I make the big decisions." Then he turns back to Mrs. Kennedy and says, "Okay, let's take the stairs." She glances at me and has a half grin, then they turn, she on his arm, and they head for the stairway. As he departs, he gives me one last look, and mocks frustration with a quick shake of his head side to side. Then a slight grin.

They're off, the moment over. I'm stunned but still taking in the fragrance of Jackie's perfume that is lingering in my area. The elevator operator is crushed and kicks the inside panel just before he comes out. He stands with both hands on his hips, staring forlornly at the departing President.

* * *

We have two Marines standing guard at the Mona Lisa upstairs in the West Hall. One is Sergeant Hapgood, and he will coordinate the detail from here on out. The 2nd Platoon will actually provide the sentries. A Marine in Dress Blues will be posted by the Lady, twenty-four hours a day, until she is taken to the Metropolitan Museum in New York City on 3 February. In the Big Apple she will be on view from the 7th until sometime in March. The Secret Service has an agent present, and they are primarily responsible for the security. However, someone at the White House thought it advisable to have a more visible form of national commitment to Mona's safety, as well. What better symbol than a strapping Marine sentry in Dress Blues, standing guard with an M-1 rifle and gleaming bayonet.

The quick ceremony downstairs over, I collect my troops and we depart for Building 58, done for the night.

* * *

When I return to Center House, I learn from the Gate Sentry that Chesty has had a horrifying and undignified incident this evening. I glance over, and Chesty is sitting in his pen, with his nose stuck out through the fence slats, with the strangest, quizzical expression on his face. I ask the sentry what happened.

"Sir, the son of a bitch got out, and ran across 8th Street. A couple of cars damn near hit him. He saw a police officer walking down 8th, with his patrol dog, a huge damn German shepherd."

"Oh, geez. Not smart, even for Chesty."

"Yeah. I mean, yes, sir. Well, sir, when Chesty came charging at the police dog, the Shepherd grabbed Chesty by the scruff of his neck, picked him up right off the ground, and slung him in the gutter. Chesty yelped and squealed, then came scurrying across the street again and just sat here by the gate, looking back at the dog with a weird look on his face."

"How so?"

"Sir, he looked like he was saying, God damn, who the hell was that guy...Mean sucker."

I burst out laughing, say goodnight, and head into Center House.

Inside, the infamous trio of Kruger, McKay and Milsap are having a drink. I order one from Gunny Richards for myself, and mutter, "Hell of a day."

Captain McKay mumbles, "Just how is that, Lieutenant."

I tell them of the Mona Lisa incident that has them in stitches, laughing at the plight of the poor little ol' man running the non-running elevator. I ask if they had heard about Chesty. They hadn't, so I repeat the sentry's tale. Their laughter continues...I join them.

What a day. From the Mona Lisa to Chesty. Could only happen here at The Barracks.

CHAPTER 22

The White House
East Room
1000 hours
Sat, 23 Nov 1963

I snap out of my daydream.

Damn, I over...over...daydreamed, I guess. Gotta hurry now.

I GET DRESSED QUICKLY AND rush into position; check out the detail, and go.

Made it, with a heel-click to spare. We head out to the East Room. I'm slightly hassled mentally, but looking sharp and in tune.

I'll start this mid-morning watch staying at the position of attention for about ten minutes, and then I'll change to ceremonial at ease, and back again roughly ten minutes thereafter. The room is quiet except for the two priests, kneeling, and rattling their beads. They're close to the wall to my left, beside the casket on what looks like a small kneeling bench and rail. The coffin continues to be flag draped. The candles are flickering, somehow catching a wisp of a nonexistent breeze. The catafalque is not only the one used for Lincoln, but also the same one used in 1958 during the funerals for the Unknown Soldiers from World War II and the Korean Conflict.

These thoughts flicker across my mind like these candle flames as I settle into standing tall, looking rigid but relaxing the body, with my eyes straight ahead. Barney the statue, the mannequin. The quietness in the room is eerie, and the two priests mumbling make it more so. It's so quiet I realize for the first time where the saying about beads rattling comes from...I can actually hear them, clicking against themselves or the rail as the priest's finger them in prayer.

My mind drifts away to other thoughts, those of past ceremonies and personal moments. The flashes unnoticed except by me, and the President...

* * *

It's a bright, sunny, summer day of '63 and the Drill Platoon and I are doing yet another White House arrival ceremony. We, the MDW units, are formed on the White House's perfectly manicured lawn, waiting for the President and the dignitary to appear. Suddenly there is the customary commotion of the press and the stirring of the small gathered crowd. They're here. The MDW Army Lieutenant Colonel in charge, commands, Attention, then Present, Arms. Musical honors are rendered, the firing battery Howitzers boom the salute, and both national anthems played.

Next, it's time for President Kennedy and the foreign dignitary to inspect the formation. This is only a formality. They will walk to our right side of the formation and pass hastily along in front of the five different service units and the joint service color guard. After this, they'll return to the reviewing area and usually address the gathering of guests. Of course, the remarks are really for the press, and the world.

The press is spilling over everywhere as usual. Necessary, but intrusive, and to me a mass of swarming insects. We all stand at rigid attention, eyes front, not moving. It's our job; our discipline; and let's face it, who wants the press to catch you in a pose that could be published and be embarrassing. How so? Like catching you with your eyes closed or at the corner of the socket, sneaking a peek. Or worse, yawning. The press would do something like this...they have either no understanding or little feelings for the result.

Whomever the foreign dignitary is this day doesn't matter much to me. I'll get a much better look at whomever it is later. Other than having this brief flash of sharing a moment...seeing some footprints left on a page of history, it's just another ceremony. This is my umpteenth White House Arrival Ceremony, and it will be followed with a Wreath Laying this afternoon, cordon tonight, and a Departure Ceremony on

Wednesday, maybe as late as Thursday. The routine is always the same, and I'll be standing another umpteen before the year is out.

I've had eyeball contact with the President before. The Mona Lisa opening for one, several cordons, and once at Camp David, which was an unforgettable moment.

As the President and dignitary pass the Army platoon on my right, he is looking at the troop line, detached, thoughts elsewhere, to be expected. As he comes up to our platoon, where I'm standing in front as usual, he looks me in the eye... sees me, and half grins in a clear form of recognition. He holds the eye contact and broadens into a smile. A blink of an eye later he glances back, smiles again, and shakes his head ever so slightly. The look on his face silently says, "It's you again. Are you still here doing this?" I break my Stoneface stare with an ever so slight, knowing, corner-of-the-mouth grin...seen only by him.

After a few more steps he does a classic double take, still with the same expression, and yet another shake of his head. Then they continue down the troop line as normal, and back to the lectern with the Presidential Seal affixed on the front.

I'll always remember the moment. We made direct eye contact and a mental connection. His eyes spoke to me, and me alone. His grin the adjective. The break in my Stoneface an adverb.

* * *

The White House
East Room
1010 hours
Sat, 23 Nov 1963

The memory is clear as I sense his presence in the casket to my front and slightly below. We won't be making eye contact any more.

Once again, I have automatically shifted the Death Watch Honor Guard and myself from attention to ceremonial at ease, and back again. People entering the room catch my attention and shut down my daydreaming. A work detail of soldiers is putting up chairs at the foot of the casket. They form rows, several deep...and put up some form of a portable altar as well.

What the devil is going on? Something important about to happen. Oh well, probably on the next watch.

I feel a presence behind me. A voice whispers to me, and I immediately recognize it as that of Army Captain Graven, the MDW officer in charge of the Death Watch. He says, "There's going to be a private family mass. People will be arriving shortly. I'm going to extend your time so as not to interfere with the comings and goings."

I give a quick and imperceptible nod of understanding.

He shifts his position ever so slightly, to see my eyes and perhaps check my reaction. He says, almost lip-synching now, "Stay at attention. Do not make any more changes until it's over. They don't want any movement during the service. Okay?"

Again, my indiscernible acknowledgment. He silently and quickly marches away in that ridiculous, female-like, butt-wiggling walk that they have in the Old Guard.

Nice guy but always up tight. Seems harried. Is flushed again this morning. Well, so be it. A Mass! This is going to be one helluva long watch.

It will be the normal thirty minutes of our watch, plus whatever time it takes for the Kennedy family and other attendees to enter and be seated. Then the Mass itself, and I bet that won't be short. Never known a Catholic service to be short...except the weekday 6:00AM working folks Mass.

Jesus, this is going to be thorny, and I have no way to let the troops know. It's suck it up time, guys. Well, there's nothin' you can do now to help, Barney ol' boy.

We continue to stand at attention for what seems another thirty or so minutes. I sense uneasiness by the two sentries on either side of me, and I can see the other two at the foot of the casket eyeballing me. They're searching for some indication of what's happening.

Sorry, guys. Can't help.

The two next to me can see the black padded folding chairs in place. I'm sure the undetectable uneasiness I sense is their understanding. For the other two, everything, with the exception of Captain Graven's appearance, is happening behind them. Their dawn will be when the service starts. They will be able to hear but not see anything.

Finally, everyone is seated. Jackie Kennedy, Caroline and John-John come in last and sit in the front row. Directly in my line of sight.

Oh, oh.

I slowly and quietly suck in some air through my nose. Some family members are on either side of them. Other family members, relatives, close friends or White House staff, or whoever, are in the several rows behind the First Lady.

The service starts. I continue to stare straight ahead, and begin listening. This is a mistake. Big time error. I can see Mrs. Kennedy, and her reactions to the words to the moment. I feel myself emotionally sucked along like being dragged out by a strong undertow.

Barney, get disconnected, swim out of this, and quick.

I pick a spot on the far wall. I burn a hole in the East Room paneling with a laser-like stare, pull a shade down on my mind, and shut down my personal audio system.

After what seems a bone-weary eternity, the service is over. I haven't heard anything...thinkin' of Gabby and doing math problems in my head. Now I can feel the hard wood floor of the East Room pushing up through my heels, knees, hips, and spine, and into the base of my skull. This is actually good. Only bones holding me up, not muscles, which would tend to cramp and tire in one position for so long, cut off the blood flow and that'll make a ceremonial type go down.

People get up and mill about. They seem uncertain. Hesitant. Want to stay, perhaps say something. After several excruciating minutes, they meander out. The immediate family lingers, saying goodbye, and standing, unsure what's next, or proper, or expected. Searching. A seemingly uneasiness and hesitancy. I'm back to watching and listening... caught up in the moment again. Their looks say it all.

Oh, oh. I feel queasy. This is not good. I could...no way. Hang tough. I'm goin' to make this. Breathe. Again. Okay, Barney. Shipshape again.

The Death Watch is still standing motionless, few or no blinks, and giving no signs of breathing, although I'm sure we all are going deep. Perfect, ceremonial statues, however, these have feelings...is seen in their eyes. Only the eyes betray the mannequins.

Everyone has left except the family. We'll be relieved from watch pretty quick now.

Oh no, something else is going to take place.

First, the clan, the family, come to the side of the casket, kneels and whisper prayers ending with the sign of the cross. For whatever reason, I'm only aware of the brothers. I must be randomly blocking things out. I can't hear the words, only some murmurs and mutterings.

Have to hold on and ignore this if I can...can't be swept along with the undertow...the moment.

They all leave together, having waited for one another.

Oh, Jesus, Mary and Joseph, here comes Jackie.

She's at the casket, kneels at its side with Caroline and John-John. She prays. The children are there, maybe praying, or mimicking their mom. I can't tell. I can hear the First Lady's voice, not the words, just the whisper interrupted with hushed sobs. I'm hanging on like a drowning man to a lifeboat plank, and I can sense and see that the four sentries are struggling as well. This is heavy...this is a time when trying to detach myself, my mind, from the present is impossible. I just have to breathe in deep, slowly, and quietly through the nose and hang tough. I cannot let the emotion of the moment permeate my mind. Nonetheless, it does and wedges itself in the crawlspace of my senses.

After what seems like eternity, they finish and get to their feet. The two children leave, met by an escort, a family member, I think. Jackie is so close I can smell the First Lady's perfume again, like at the National Gallery. Then she motions to somebody, and a dark-suited man appears. One of the men from Gawlers, I think. He folds down the flag half way, and opens the top half of the casket. She leans over, murmurs something, the words not audible to me...only the hissing sounds of her whisper. Then she places something, or things, in the casket with the President.

My peripheral vision allows me to see the top of the President's head. I can't see anything distracting from this angle, nor do I wish to. The moment is poignant, tense and emotive...by now, I just want to be relieved and get off watch.

My security blanket is my mind, and now it's slipping from my grasp. It's like holding on to something as tight as you can...with all your strength, but it still just slowly slips through your hands and fingers. Even an anguished mind trying to hold it, to will it to remain, cannot.

It's an honor to be here...stand this particular watch, for sure. Nevertheless, it's draining, both emotionally and physically. It has nearly sapped my reservoir of strength-driving adrenaline. I am running on fumes. The First Lady's apparent strength is phenomenal. A mentally strong and resilient woman. I don't know how the phenomenon occurs.

Maybe some form of telepathic osmosis. I believe she unknowingly is assuming the grief of the country on her shoulders and in her heart. I can't imagine her feelings; only feel for her, and the two children.

Jackie takes several steps away, then she turns for what seems one last time, and takes a fleeting look back at the casket. I catch this forlorn gaze. A punch to my solar plexus could not be as paralyzing.

Breathe in Barney, slow and quiet. Easy does it...suck it up... breathe.

I get the ol' lobes full of air, and the lingering aroma of her perfume that adds to the hurt of this parting moment.

As soon as she leaves the room, workers are in here clearing out the chairs. I feel the nudge on my arm as the oncoming watch slides into position next to us.

Now I realize the full meaning of why each watch is called a relief.

We do our routine, step back, face about and march slowly away from the casket, and out of the East Room.

When we get to the designated area, I halt the detail. Face about, put them at ease and say to the troops, "Great job, men. Way to hang tough. Thanks." They let out a collective sigh. I continue, "Now, get some chow; some rest; square away; and see you for the next watch. I'll let you know when that is as soon as I check and find out what this has done to the schedule. Again, thanks, men. Great job. Dismissed."

Along with this sigh come a few muttered words. Some profane, some not...none profound.

We're all glassy-eyed. Victims of our thoughts...Captives of our emotions.

This is getting more difficult as we go...not less so, as I thought it would.

CHAPTER 23

The White House
Below decks again
1130 hours
Sat, 23 Nov 1963

FIRST THINGS FIRST. IF I sit my butt down and relax after that watch, I may not get up until the break of noon. I'm beat.

I take care of my ironing and shining...Blue blouse and trousers pressed, shoes re-spit-shined, brass, medals and sword polished. I'm beginning to feel like a live-in maid or better a valet. A batman I think they were called in the days of yore, except this is my gear.

I return my shoes and Sam Browne belt to the special wooden carrying cases I had constructed. In there, they don't collect any dust, let alone have someone inadvertently smudge them. It's not even a "can look; no touch" situation. It's a "no look, no touch," period. Next, I freshen up with a washbasin douche and a close shave, change skivvies and socks, put on some Fu-Fu juice, and I'm good to go...almost. Need some chow and mind wandering time...need to get this last watch out of my mind.

I amble over to the table and ponder the spread of chow.

Man oh man. The White House kitchen has done itself proud.

I make myself a warm roast beef sandwich, pile macaroni salad on my paper plate and grab two cartons of cold milk. Look back and notice some dill pickles so I snatch one. Mosey to the end of the table and load the sandwich up with mayonnaise, ketchup, mustard, and slap a mess of horseradish dip between the slices of prime rib. I'm hoping the dip will give me an energy boost. If not, at least heartburn to keep me mentally alert on the watches to come.

Whoa, this is a far cry from a White Tower hamburger, but then I suspect none of those guys will be working here anytime in the future.

The White House cooks, well I guess they're called chefs around here, just brought in this lunchtime spread. I eat at a long, bench-like table, chat with some of the troops and officers from the other watches. Mostly about the watch we just finished. All are interested in how we got through it, what went on and what we heard. They got some scuttlebutt so were just trying to verify or add. Everyone's emotions are still running high, but the fatigue shows when off watch. Have to look to see it, however, little clues creep through the bravado...husky voice, thick speech not yet slurred, perhaps slower. Move a bit less quickly but not as slow as sap.

After chowing down and chatting it up, I sit down in a not-so-comfortable folding chair, put my feet up on another, wiggle my toes and relax. I can't sleep; however, I close my eyes, take in a deep breath and blow it out audibly. Just dog-tired and bone-weary. I feel like an ol' hound dog after a long hunt and now with a full belly...just nestling in the leaves beneath the porch.

That ol' hound with his involuntary body tremors and soft yelps would probably be dreaming of chasing rabbits and such. For me, no whimpers, however my mind returns to The Barracks lore, which keeps me from thinking about this President...can't handle any more of that today...

* * *

The spring of '63 is on us quicker than a blink, and parade rehearsals start at both The Barracks and Iwo. Besides standing ceremonies, Gunny Elms, Sergeant Hapgood, the men, all of us in the Drill Platoon work hard to perfect our different drill routines. We have a four, eight, twelve and fifteen minute version. The fifteen ticks sequence is the parade routine.

Up until now, Gabby and I have seen each other virtually every weekend except when I've had the duty. I spent just about every Saturday night at her place. Love is in bloom I suppose. We're getting comfortable with our situation and I am no longer thinking of flings. I guess fate leads you down one path, but pushes another away, out of reach. Parade

172

season and the summer will limit our time together and that may test fate or at least Gabrielle's version. We'll see, after all, as someone once said, fate is the hunter.

At the parade rehearsals our new, totally silent drill routine and its slower cadence is unveiled. It stuns everyone at The Barracks, or at least the knowledgeable ones. On the other hand, the mirror rifle inspection knocks every one off their feet. The CO is leery, because the risk of error is greater and a dropped rifle on parade nights is not acceptable. However, I have convinced Colonel Weaver not to worry. Well, probably not completely...he'll fret some but he allows us to move forward with the changes.

As the first parade nears, I request and get a "Drill Team only" practice night on the parade deck even though the grounds maintenance folks don't like that. Too much wear and tear on the grass. However, I need to get the new troops accustomed to the lights and a sense of "been there, done that." More important is to check the overhead lights for the rifle inspector and his counterpart. During the throwbacks, the rifles get up in the lights and we need to make sure no one is looking directly at one, and if so, get it adjusted now.

* * *

We are greeted with a clear, slightly cool spring evening as we start our practice session. After about ten minutes our new barracks Executive Officer, Lieutenant Colonel Harry "Light Horse" Gimletti staggers out of Center House, drink in hand. His drink of choice, a Gimlet I suppose, what else? Mush Mouth gave him his nickname, probably with a whispering in his ear from Milsap. I think it has something to do with *The Charge of the Light Brigade* or its result. Certainly not after the revolutionary hero. Julius went along with it because he thinks there is a gin with that name, and if not, should be. Nonetheless, Light Horse has been in the Center House Drum Room too long again...and Gunny Richards doesn't craft a light drink, and this is in one of those birdbath martini glasses.

Ahhh, shoot. He's comin' out here.

He's turned toward us and onto the parade deck. He has apparently decided to offer his assistance, without an inkling of knowledge...always trouble and this could get to be a few clowns short of a circus.

I've had a problem with him before. He once used his fingernail to gouge out a long chunk of polish off the shoulder strap of my Sam Browne belt. He didn't think anything could shine like that. Probably because his belt looked like he used bearshit for polish and thought mine must be patent leather. When he realized he was wrong, he just said, "Oops," and took another drink from his friggin' Gimlet. A few minutes later, I "accidentally" nudge his elbow, spilling his gimlet down the front of his uniform. I immediately apologized, profusely, but I think he knew.

It took me more hours than I want to remember to repair the damage to my belt strap and get it back to its original luster...and all those hours were that night. I had a funeral ceremony at Arlington the next day.

Well, he's here...and with a glow that tain't a halo. Wandering around in the middle of our drill, drink sloshing and splashing, alternating going on the ground and his uniform. A toothpick from the onion in the corner of his mouth. Wonderful, just friggin' wonderful. His speech is slurred, and thick. Also loud. Drunks are always loud.

Ah, crap!

He takes a rifle from one of my troops and tries to demonstrate a spin movement. The rifle hits the deck, muzzle first, jamming some dirt and grass into the barrel. The Snuffy picks it up, plucks the chunk of sod from the end of the barrel and looks at me for help. I nod, jog over to the colonel and guide him aside as the drill routine continues.

I tactfully try to get him to leave. He not only won't, but he becomes louder, and more obnoxious. Fortunately, the drill routine has moved on, away from the two of us. He's getting louder as drunks tend to do when somebody tries reasoning as an approach. He takes a sip from his empty glass. Sputters his disapproval at this fact. This is not a circus. This is getting ugly, quick. Reprehensible behavior anywhere, but here at the Marine Barracks it is a major no-no. Only a tad short of a nuclear mishap. And Dammit, I'm involved again. Mush Mouth is going to have a field day with this.

The colonel is making a total fool of himself, and the Officer Corps. I need the time to run through the entire drill routine at least once more, maybe twice, but this is ridiculous and spiraling toward a disaster. I call the Gunny over and tell him to give the team a ten-minute break. I add, "At the far end, by the cannons, so they can't hear."

"Yes, sir, but not hearin' is only half the problem."

"Yeah, I know. What do ya want me to do, run him through with my sword?"

"It's a thought...sir."

"Go."

This retrograde movement might give me time to convince the colonel to leave. As I turn back toward Light Horse Harry, I see a silhouetted figure on the CO's porch.

Oh Jesus, Mary and Joseph. This is goin' downhill faster than a California mudslide...kinda appropriate since that's a popular drink out there.

I suck in some air. The figure is our CO, Colonel Weaver, and he's watching this circus. I wonder how much he's seen.

Only one thing to do now. I call the Gunny and motion him back. "Gunny, this could get ugly. We're——"

"It's already ugly, Lieutenant."

"Yeah, I know. Let me finish. We need to cash it in for the night. Take the troops back to 58 and secure for the evening."

"Yes, sir. Smart move, Lieutenant. I saw what you saw, and I think the shit's goin' to hit the fan. I'd rather not get splattered. By your leave, sir."

"Granted, Gunny."

"Oh, and, Lieutenant. I wouldn't stand too close to the fan if I were in your boots."

"Thanks, Gunny, but based on what I'm seeing, I think I've already been hit. Night."

He salutes, turns and marches the platoon off the parade deck into the arcade and out the back entrance on 9th Street to board the bus. I tell the maintenance man, whose eyes are as big as saucers, to turn out the lights. *Oh boy, too many folks have seen this. There's no cork strong enough to keep this in the bottle.*

As the lights flick off with that slamming noise banks of lights make, I turn to say something to Lieutenant Colonel Gimletti, however, he's already strolling unsteadily toward Center House. He is holding the birdbath martini glass by the stem, twirling it in his fingers, doing his Gimlet form of a caustic spin in the drill routine. His actions have that I-showed-them-a-thing-or-two-look.

His gait reminds me of my ol' Uncle Roy coming home from a bender. Roy at least had a reason. He was a Merchant Marine seaman in WWII, and survived two ships being sunk from under him in the North Atlantic. Also, he had to live with my Aunt Lil. When I was growing up, I often wondered why he didn't just stay on the raft; refuse rescue. Anything had to be better than livin' with Lil. Oh, well. It's not Roy, unfortunately. It's Light Horse Harry, and it's here, now.

I watch the colonel stagger away. I let him go without saying another word. That way when I enter Center House I can just go up to my room, staying clear of a confrontation. I'm sure he's headed for the bar.

I wait for him to enter Center House, and then I start across Center Walk. The silhouetted figure is still on the porch. As I get to the end of the walk, Colonel Weaver taps on his window and frantically motions me into his house. With a sigh of despair, I go up the few steps and enter. Since I'm wearing my sword, which is considered being under arms, I salute, say, "Good evening, sir. What does the—--"

"What was he doing out there? Was that a drink I saw in his hand?"

"Ahhh, yes, sir, the Lieutenant believes it was. He was observing, I guess, sir."

"Observing my foot. With a drink in his hand? Staggering all over the place? He was loud and slurring words. I could hear him from in here. Was he drunk, Barney?"

"Sir, it's not the Lieutenants place to--"

"Mister Quinn, this is not the time for your third person cra... never mind. Answer my question. Is he drunk?"

"Sir, I believe he is a little under the weather."

"Under the weather? You mean drunk."

"Ah, yes, sir."

"And being disruptive. Making a fool of himself. In front of the troops."

"He, ah...he was interfering. Yes, sir. It was embarrassing, sir."

"He took and dropped a rifle, trying to demonstrate, ah, whatever he was trying to do."

"Yes, sir. He did drop the rifle. It was embarr--"

"I'd say it was disgraceful. An embarrassment to me, to The Barracks, and The Corps. I--"

"Sir, the Lieutenant couldn't get him to leave, sir. Just cancel the remainder of the session, sir. Nothing else the Lieutenant could do, sir."

"I know. I know. And, you're doing it again. Anyway, good move. Now then, apologize to the troops for me. Don't say anything to anyone else. I will handle this. Understand?"

"Yes, sir."

"Fine. Thank you. Good night, Lieutenant Quinn."

"Good night, sir. Ahhh, sir, can I get another night on the parade deck? We didn't finish what we--"

"What?"

"Another--"

"Oh. Yes. Sure. Call Major Kendell or Captain Milsap in the morning. Now, goodnight, Barney."

"Goodnight, sir."

Well, at least we're back to Barney again.

I salute, face about, and let myself out the porch door. I walk directly to Center House, go immediately to my room avoiding any possible contact with Gimletti, or with any other officer who may be in the bar.

* * *

The following afternoon, there is an official announcement that Lieutenant Colonel Gimletti has been transferred; Lieutenant Colonel Maloney, the current Director of the Institute will be the new XO of The Barracks; and that a replacement for him at the Tute will be announced within a day or so. That was at least good news for Maloney because the scuttlebutt was he wanted out of the Tute, and up at The Barracks anyway. He couldn't have manipulated this better if he tried, or at least as quickly.

I don't think Light Horse Harry joined Lieutenant Goen in Lost Balls, Arizona or Nowhere, New Mexico, or wherever he went, but I would be willing to bet either place would look good in comparison to where he's headed.

Doesn't make much difference. No one's talkin'...well, except the Magpies in the Drill Team, and wisely probably only at their favorite watering hole, Dobkins Bar. My guess is that only four people know for sure. The Commandant, the CO, our Adjutant, Captain Jake Dennehy, and Light Horse Harry. Three aren't talking, and one isn't here to talk.

Of course, since so many people are aware of the event, word is already leaking out. Julius is creating another legend and monologue, probably...at the whispered urging of the Yaliee, JG Milsap.

For me unfortunately, I'm starting to have a personal encyclopedic file compiled of monologue material starting with the Casilonnia left breast incident, the flat tire affair, Lieutenant Geon-Lieutenant Colonel Donnelly event, and now the Light Horse Harry ride.

Hell, I may need an agent.

PHOTOS

"The 1063 Silent Drill Platoon photo shoot. The Marine Barracks in the background. The author is front and center of the unit."

"Twelve members of the '63 Drill Team under the command of the author marching toward the WH gate to meet and escort President Kennedy's casket."

"1963 Drill Team members under the command of the author escorting the Presidents remains from the gate to the White House."

"The Death Watch posted at President Kennedy's flag draped casket in the East Room of the White House. The author, then 1stLt Lee is at the head of the casket."

"The Death Watch posted at JFK's casket in the Rotunda of the U. S. Capitol. The author is at the head of the casket. Doors of the rotunda away from the foot of the casket. Note TV lights from behind 1stLt. Lee."

"Ceremonial Guard Company in the foreground passing in review at a special evening parade at the Marine Barracks. The author leads as the CO of CGC. MCI Company troops can be seen in the background. Can see the Commandants quarters on the left."

"Corporal Gary Collins conducting the rifle inspection during a parade. Collins has just completed the ceremonial inspection and has flipped the rifle over his shoulder to the Marine inspected (looking up to make the catch). Commandants quarters in the background."

"Officers Center, saluting Parade Commander (not shown) during a Friday Night Parade at Marine Barracks, 8th and "I" Streets, Washington, D. C."

"Marines of the Oldest Post of the Corps, Marine Barracks, 8th and "I" Streets, taken prior to a ceremony at the Iwo Jima Memorial in Arlington."

"The author leading a unit from the Drill Team along with two Color Guard units at an all-Marine wreath laying ceremony at the Tomb of the Unknown Soldier in Arlington."

"Members of the Drill Team and the Drum & Bugle Corps. DT members in period uniforms with historical flags for the Marine Barracks Flag Pageant presented to patriotic organizations and to schools. On the parade deck with Commandants quarters in the background, and the General Officers quarters on the left."

"The Drum & Bugle Corps, the Color Guard, and the Drill Team under the command of the author, performing a Changing of the Guard ceremony with the troops of Fort Henry, Kingston, Ontario, Canada. A SRO crowd is inside the old fort overlooking Lake Ontario."

"The Drill exiting Fort Henry, Kingston, Ontario over the lowered draw bridge. The DT is lead off by it's PltSgt, GySgt Elms with Sgt Hapgood as its Platoon Guide. Note Fort Henry sign on wall...1832, age of the fort, not the Gunny!"

*"The author speaking to members of the Marine Corps Drum
& Bugle Corps at his Playoff from the Marine Barracks. Must
be reminiscing old times together on the road at ceremonies...or
something humorous."*

CHAPTER 24

The White House
The East Room
The 1400 hours watch
Sat, 23 Nov 1963

IT'S TIME TO GO ON watch again. We suit up and move to the East Room. The execution of the movements is routine and consequently maybe the watch itself is mentally a tad easier. It's a matter of mind control now. Physically, we're all beat. Army Captain Graven looks worse than beat...he's always flushed and looks like he's ready to blow a gasket. I'd say he was stressed out.

The President will be moved tomorrow to the Capitol to lie in State. Our normal night Death Watch detail will be coming on at 2000 hours tonight. That means after this watch, I'll only have two to go...at least for today. Then I'll finally get some sleep, not just a few catnaps littered with daydreams. However, tomorrow will be more of the same in the Capitol's Rotunda, except it will be open to the public and who knows what that might entail. I know one thing for sure, it will be on that hard-ass, slick, marble floor.

We slide into position in the East Room and start our watch once again. It's quiet in here. In life, we most likely would never be alone with the President. Now we are. No bright lights; no commotion; no press; and no throngs of people cheering. Just the priests and us, each taking care of him in our own way. I still can't believe this happened in our country, in my lifetime. This is America, for Pete's sake.

Whoa, Barney ol' boy, don't get started down this road. Go elsewhere.

I do and let my mind wander. To Gabrielle, and hence fate. Maybe fate did bring me here, to this. Just as Gabby believes, our meeting again was fate. Between this, and her, I'm fast becoming a believer.

This thought leads me to wonder what Gabby is doing and thinking right now. Probably glued to the TV with the rest of the world...and maybe wondering where I am or what I'm doing. Maybe I can just wish a thought to her.

My mind skips a beat on that idea. Thoughts are going willy-nilly around in my head and now one takes me back in time. Another beat gets skipped and I'm back at The Barracks not so many months ago...

* * *

On this wet April '63 evening the six of us, the House residents, are at the bar discussing this morning's events and the newly-founded Dubious Achievement Award...created in honor of 1ˢᵗ Lieutenant Dan Rader, our only West Point K-Det, for his performance of duty on his first parade rehearsal of the season. As I recall it started with Chesty watching and listening...

This morning on The Barracks parade deck, Captain Kemp, the Guard Company XO, and its Parade Company Commander, calls his three parade platoon commanders to a meeting on the south end, suitably near Chesty's pen. He wasn't included but seemed interested. More so than Rader. Lieutenant Rader, for some reason, isn't present. He didn't listen, didn't understand, or perhaps didn't even hear Captain Kemp when he set up this last minute briefing. Makes little difference, he's not here for the meeting and Kemp is not a happy parade ground camper.

He says to no one in particular, "Where's Lieutenant Rader."

Lieutenant Van Dell and I answer in unison, "Don't know, sir." We glance around to see if he's on his way. However, no Rader is in sight, and ours doesn't pick him up.

"Well, where the devil is he? I want to go over a few details about the parade sequence." Captain Kemp always covers every detail, repeatedly, frustratingly so. Never leaves anything to chance, which is good, but after three or four times, it gets to be a bit much.

He again asks, "Where is he? This is important."

I say, "No sweat, sir. He'll be okay. I think."

Van Dell chips in, "Yeah, he'll be fine...sir."

Captain Kemp says, "What'd mean, no sweat? I'm not so sure about that. However, let me go over the parade sequence again with you two." He does so, every detail, some twice. When he finishes he says, "Any questions?"

Van Dell and I answer in unison, "No, sir." Then I add, "Captain, it's time to form up. The MCI Officers are at Center Walk and Captain Milsap is motioning us up."

"Okay, let's go. Where the devil is Mister Rader? Doggonnit."

We leave and form up on Center Walk, ready for Officer's Call. Still no Rader. Not even a blip. The veins in Captain Kemp's neck are bulging and pulsating. If he had a little steam whistle on his cap it would be shrieking louder than a gurgling teakettle. The bugler sounds Officer's Call. Captain Kemp calls us to attention. Oops, something pops up on the screen. Rader slides into place, joining us just as we step off...on time for the rehearsal, much too late for Captain Kemp's last minute briefing.

Oh boy, I sense the beginning of a Drum Room, Mush Mouth monologue. Good, I'm tired of being the prime subject.

It's just a parade rehearsal; well, actually, there is no such thing here as "just" anything. However, Rader's been talked through it in the past I would guess, and he's certainly been in many parades on the plains above the Hudson. None like this, but dozens at the Point. You wouldn't think he'd have a problem.

But, this ain't the Point, and this could be fun.

The rehearsal begins and is going well. The critique temperature is normal out here on the parade deck this dewy and sunny morning. However, Kemp's running a tad hot, based on the color of his face. If you look closely you can see some steam coming out of his ears. Good thing it is, otherwise he might blow.

Before we know it, the Pass-in-Review portion of the parade is upon us, and off we go. After the Band, Guard Company will be first to pass in review. The first platoon behind Captain Kemp will be Rader's platoon, followed by the second platoon, Van Dell's, then me with the Drill Team. After that, the Color Guard, and MCI Company. Our parade routine at The Barracks is at this point, very different from all other parades and the Point as well, I'm sure. Normally, when the troops pass in review, meaning pass the reviewing stand, they continue to march and leave the field.

Here at The Barracks, it's different. We have an end-of-parade routine: a marching-off of the colors, an officers dismissed portion, unfix bayonets and then a march off of the troops by the Parade Sergeant Major. The formation doesn't leave the parade deck until then. After the Pass-in-Review, at the south end, we execute a column left, march up the south side past the cannons, and execute another column left onto Troop Walk, and return to our original positions...Ready for the closing portion of the parade and taps. Great finish. Stunning, yet simple.

Lieutenant Rader either doesn't know this portion of the routine, or forgot, or just got caught up in the excitement of his first rehearsal. Whatever. Since he is the first platoon to pass in review, he has no other troops in front of him except the band, which always, here or elsewhere, returns to the parade field. With no one to follow, Rader marches his platoon off the parade deck, normal in most places, and into the parking lot at the south end. Van Dell and his platoon, and then me and the Drill Team, execute the column left and head for Troop Walk.

The West Pointer, realizing that he's alone in the parking lot, sees what's happening, and makes a belated column left, and tries to head for Troop Walk. First Van Dell, then me, just keep going and don't stop. We can't let him in or we'll stack up all the units behind us. Besides, this is way too much fun!

We get to Troop Walk, go left up the walk, back to our original positions. Rader sees this, and cleverly takes his platoon into the arcade behind the hedges and adjacent to Troop Walk. He executes his column movement, and marches as quickly as he can to the other end. We can see him to our right, behind the hedges hiding the arcade, scurrying along. His face is even a brighter red than Kemp's at this point and his eyes are saucer-large. Kemp's must be slits.

We all get back to our original position, just as Rader and his platoon come around the corner of the arcade at the north end. As they appear, there is a burst of laughter from those watching in the stands. We in formation are trying as hard as we can to stifle our laughter. It's a test. We can't, but manage to keep it muffled.

Captain Kemp's face is now beet red with invisible lightening bolts flashing from his eyes toward Rader. The veins are clearly showing in his neck, and he has this sick smirk on his face as only he is known for and can muster. At this point, one would think, oh well, the problem is solved. Rader's back in formation. Wrong! We, meaning the entire formation are marking time, facing north. Rader and his platoon are doing the same, only facing south. The Parade Commander commands us to Halt, then Order, Arms. All goes well. A problem still exists. Kemp is getting redder and the veins are larger and a distinct dark-blue looking. I'm trying to hide my amusement and choke off laughter. Probably everyone in the formation is doing the same. The Magpies in the ranks are snickering.

The Parade Commander orders, Left, Face, which is the normal command at this point. We all execute it...and now the circus is more apparent. Van Dell and I, our platoons, and all of MCI Company are facing front. Rader and his platoon, having also executed the left face, are now facing toward the arcade, backs to the parade field. Kemp is rocking back and forth on his feet...Face now scarlet, veins pulsating at blood vessel popping speed. The Parade Commander is perplexed, quiet...thinking I'm sure as to how to right this situation. Then Rader commands About, Face, to his troops, bringing to an end the act in the center ring. We now have everybody facing the proper direction.

Captain Kemp's coloration is for reasons more than just his anger at Lieutenant Rader. He is also in this Technicolor condition because he's embarrassed. Ceremonial Guard Company, the full-time ceremonial guys have screwed up, and MCI Company, part-time parade ground Marines didn't, and are giggling.

Beyond them, the entire crew of the parade critiquing team is almost on the ground with laughter. Milsap is leading the way and even his clipboard in front of his face can't hide the tears. McKay and Kruger, although only observing this morning, are howling. Even the workmen putting up the bleachers are laughing. Maybe only because everyone else is, or maybe they know since they do this every week. I feel for Rader but my heart can't reach him. I have a better-him-than-me mentality, as I'm sure all of us on the parade deck have.

Last, The Barracks CO and our newly appointed XO, Lieutenant Colonel Maloney, out to watch this first rehearsal of the season, are laughing. In a way, this is fortunate. They also see the humor in this. If the lieutenant's friend, our former XO, Lieutenant Colonel Donnelly were still here, Rader would have been dead-meat. He would be heading for Lost Balls, Arizona or her sister city of Nowhere, New Mexico. Anyway, all are amused, except Captain Kemp, and Lieutenant Rader, of course. Hard to tell who is wearing a deeper red coloring.

* * *

So, tonight after the rehearsal, the Center House residents have founded the Rader Award, and fondly dub it the Dubious Achievement Award. Actually, I think Kruger, with his ever-present squinty-eye, sinister grin suggested the name. Captains McKay and Milsap, the other two of the triumvirate immediately ordained it so. An informal announcement will be made, and we plan to develop a plaque that will hang in the Drum Room, next to the four-second club one. The official unveiling will be conducted at the first happy hour after the plaque is completed.

Rader is a first-class guy. He takes the ribbing good-naturedly. It was such an incredible morning, that after all was said and done, even stoic Captain Kemp managed to laugh. After he chewed out Rader of course.

The good news is that Lieutenant Rader is a legend at The Barracks, and better, he gets to stay and enjoy it. Poor Goen and Gimletti didn't, and surely, they would have been eligible for the Dubious Achievement Award. But, alas, they're gone, and nothing here is retroactive.

* * *

The White House
East Room
1425 hours - On watch
Sat, 23 Nov 1963

Back in the East Room once again, I sense my Death Watch detail is a little displeased. The two sentries at the foot of the casket are glaring at me. I got lost in my thoughts and didn't change positions. So what. My body aches in either position although the change does alter the blood flow, I think. It's not required to change, so no sweat. We just did a much longer stint at the position of attention. This one was a piece

198

of cake compared to our watch during the service. Nothing going on in here now except the mumbling of the priests and the clicking of their beads. We're alone with our thoughts, and the President.

Our watch is relieved and we return to our command post area in the bowels of the White House, near the center of the earth. I begin the between-watch iron and shine routine all over again.

Two to go...well, for today anyway. Time to relax and think of other things.

I wonder if Gabby does ironing and knows anything about spit-shining shoes?

Naw, best leave that alone.

CHAPTER 25

White House
East Room
1645 hours
Sat, 23 Nov 1963

MY DEATH WATCH GROUP AND I are ready for our evening watch. It'll be forlorn, listening to the priests and left alone with my thoughts. I'm tired and even though I have taken birdbaths, changed socks and skivvies, I still feel gamey. Splashed plenty of Fu-Fu juice on so smell okay but then ol' hound dogs never smell their own scent.

Tonight, when I get back to 58, I will ready my back-up uniform for use tomorrow. Then I'll head for Center House and have a drink, an Apricot brandy...without pancakes. It always makes me think of Gabby. Anyway, sip the brandy and talk to my buds. Then follow with a hot shower to get squeaky clean and relaxed. Then some Z's until about 0500 when it will be time to get up and do this again.

I make a last-minute check, form up, and with our solemn funeral cadence march in to relieve our predecessors at the casket.

There are White House folks, staff, aides, and such scattered along our path. They stop as we approach, quietly step aside and stand motionless with saddened expressions. They're at what civilians perceive to be attention. It's close; heels not locked together, but the intent is what's important. One woman wipes a tear away with the back of her hand. A few others are glassy-eyed. Have to be careful here and not let the emotion seep into my soul...although it's difficult to impede...like a neap tide running its course over a sand castle.

They wait for us to pass well beyond them. I can sense them holding their positions and staring in despair. It's a feeling, a sense, like just knowing someone is in a pitch-black room with you although you cannot see them. This occurs at several spots along the way, so even though we're not in or at the East Room yet, we're always, in Brit speak, "On parade."

We slide in next to our counterparts. They execute their prescribed movements in silence and depart. We side step into position, and start our thirty minutes.

Once settled and in this state of fatigue, my mind grabs snippets of my past barracks life. These flash before me like disconnected fragments of film. Whatever the form, it will help the time to pass and my thoughts drift to...

* * *

The summer of '63 sunset parades at the Iwo Monument on Tuesday evenings are fun. Yes, it's serious business, Showtime; however, it's great people watching. It's well attended by the public, although a more relaxed crowd and less formal in dress than the Friday nights at The Barracks. It's a pleasant, mild summer evening out for couples, families and the city's tourists...a picnic atmosphere. For us, game faces and cold, observant eyes.

We form slightly behind and to the side of the monument, waiting for the bugler to Sound Attention, and the D&B to strike up, Adjutants Call. Then we march on. Until that time, we stand at ceremonial at ease, and wait. Statues of living granite, a picture of military bearing in blue white dress. That picture alone, with the monument of black marble with the bronze figures of the Marines raising the flag atop Mount Surabachi on Iwo as a backdrop instills enough patriotism in one's heart to last a long time and make little ol' blue-haired ladies weep.

It also gives the shutterbugs a free pass to click and flash heaven. Close-up shots are premium...of Captain Kemp, or me, or my troops, because we're at the head of the formation. This evening a man in a red golf shirt, blue Bermuda shorts with a white belt asks, "Excuse me, sir, could you move your men just a little to the left so I can get a better shot."

Even though he's in patriotic attire, I stare through him impersonally, not speaking, stone-faced, until the expression on his face signals that the tiny light bulb in his brain-housing group has come on. Stunned, with eyebrows raised and silver dollar size eyes, he retreats, step-by-step mouthing, "Oh my God. I'm sorry. I'm sorry. I didn't mean..."

I don't change...a face of granite, and I would guess eyes as expressionless as those of a Hammerhead shark.

He turns to the woman with him and says, "Did you see that, honey? His look." She nods, stares and shakes her head. She's decked out in red, white and blue...white halter-top, nice. It's amusing to watch the reactions, and to know how the guards at Buckingham Palace must feel every day.

Yankee Doodle departs toward the seating area, talking to his lady friend and pointing back at me, surely relating the mannequin's mannerisms. Seconds later, a woman and her son approach me. She doesn't have him by the hand, rather allows him to willy-nilly his way along in front of her. In one hand, he holds a double-decker chocolate ice cream cone he is trying to manipulate and devour. His other hand shows all the milky dark, sticky signs of holding the two gigantic scoops on top of the graham cracker like funnel. His mouth is ringed in chocolate.

As he nears, I begin to feel the pangs of panic entering my brain's recognition and alarm cells. They start an impulse with cattle prod sharpness through my body, pricking all my nerve endings. I stand motionless, a living statue although my nerves are imitating Bojangles. I'm a prime target in my blue blouse and starched white trousers with a crease sharp enough to draw blood. My sword in front of me, firmly at its ceremonial at ease position. Add my shined brass buttons, glinting brass hilt on my sword, and the shined medals on my chest, and I'm a human magnet. The boy is fascinated by this picture and continues toward me like a paperclip slowly slipping into the magnetic field. The woman says, "No, no, Vinnie. Mustn't touch."

No shit, lady.

Then my mind instantly recaptures my own boyhood days and I realize that Vinnie has probably heard this caution several thousand times, and ignored them all. He keeps inching forward, like paperclips before they get within the full power of the magnet. His cone-carrying hand is reaching out toward me with the ice cream melting down over his chubby little fingers. I sense it's close to that moment when the clips will burst forward, captured by the magnets full force.

My granite like face and stare are not only not stopping this rug rat, but are enticing him. The mother moves up close but rather than grabbing this little twit, says, "Vinnie, don't touch that nice man."

Yeah, right. Nice man, my ass.

The little shit only hears his mother's statement as a challenge. A dare! He takes another faltering step, and with no facial expression other than my most ferocious Randy Recon look, and with lips not parting, I growl, "Get outta here."

Vinnie jumps back, frightened of the talking mannequin. He drops his cone in the grass, and raises his chocolate covered hands to his face adding to the ring of ice cream around his mouth. He adds nose, eyebrow and hair to his mask. I think, better his face than my white trousers. The woman jolts back a half step, and with the startled look still on her face says, "Well, I never...look what you've done. He dropped his cone. It's ruined."

Again, with lips imperceptibly cracked, and my face an expressionless mask, I snap, "Better than my white trousers, lady."

"Ohhh! Oh my G--"

The bugler sounds, Attention, breaking off her remark. She gets her mouth open to say something else when Captain Kemp calls us to attention. I do so smartly, my leather heels with the horseshoe cleats resoundingly smashing together at his command. She startles again. On Kemp's next command, I bring my sword to the Carry, its back edge thudding, "Thwack" against my shoulder seam. This time she jumps and Vinnie stumbles backward. I half smirk and say, "Move it, ma'am, you're about to get run over."

She jolts back another step and grasps Vinnie by the arm, jerks him up and to her side, then scurries back several more steps almost tripping. Then she looks around, side to side, I guess for some confirmation as to her wronging. Then looks at me again with astonishment, and leaves in a huff giving me one last "Oomph," and a well-I-never look.

We march on, past the lady and her precious Vinnie, leaving the melting and toppled double-dip for the ants. The woman will tell her husband and all of her friends about the nasty Marine. I'm sorry;

however, my "Trou" are still pure white, even if the Corps reputation isn't.

It reminds me of something I read that Eleanor Roosevelt purportedly said in 1945. "The Marines I have seen around the world have the cleanest bodies, the filthiest minds, the highest morale and the lowest morals of any group I have ever seen." I think she also said something like "Thank God for the United States Marines." Perhaps I enhanced some part of that reputation or legend this evening. If not, I kept my trousers clean.

The Magpies in my platoon have seen all this, are mumbling, and muttering, with some muffled snickers as well. The march-on music smothers these, so no one can hear them, and besides they, too, are accomplished ventriloquists. Besides, as soon as they get on the parade deck in front of the monument and are facing the crowd far across the field, they will be busy at their favorite parade pastime. Spotting and shooting beavers, and then giving muttered target descriptions to other Magpies. Ah, I love 'em, the Snuffies and Magpies in blue white dress... the McCloskeys, Pooles, Addisons, Greens, Timberlakes, Tallicks, Griffins, Slacks, DiLossis and Collins.

* * *

The White House
East Room
About 1710 hours
Sat, 23 Nov 1963

I snicker quietly to myself. It's time to change position. I do, and see an ever so slight grin on the two sentries at the foot of the casket...the wing wiper and Hooligan's Navy trooper. I sense a feeling of relief from the other two on either side of me at the head.

The priests seem louder this afternoon...probably my imagination. Should tell them to hold it down a little. I don't want to get emotionally involved if I can help it. However, my mind switches to its internal humor channel.

I wonder how many prayers they have offered. You'd think God would whisper, "Okay, I got the message. He's with me now." Barney, Barney...that's sacrilegious. Take your mind elsewhere before you are struck with a bolt of lightning.

I do for a flash, then backslide and wonder if any of the prayers were deflected towards me. I could use some help.

I turn off my audio system and let my mind drift off once more...

* * *

Ah, Dan Rader's namesake, the Dubious Achievement Award, or DAA pops up on my mental cue card. There's been some winners lately. Another lieutenant stuck his sword into the plush turf of the parade deck while passing in review during rehearsal. He recovered well, but did flick a chunk of sod onto the platoon marching in front of him. Since he had recently bragged about his proficiency with the sword, he was a unanimous nomination and selection.

Lieutenant Colonel Maloney, Ol' Melon Head, our Barracks XO, managed a colossal faux pas at the Iwo Parade. He gave an incorrect command for the march-off. Instead of Center, Face, he gave a Right, Face. The result was troops facing in two different directions since some executed the movement that was supposed to be next. It took some unceremonial corrections to right the situation. To be honest, the company grade officers sort of knew that Ol' Melon Head was a prime prospect for a blunder. He's from New York, and true to form, he talks fast, walks hurriedly, reacts or overreacts immediately and sometimes without much thought. Answers every question whether directed at him or not. Knows it all. You know, the center of the universe syndrome. Anyway, he was prime, and didn't let us down.

However large a mistake it is to us, the public either doesn't catch it, or maybe not care. It doesn't hinder the end, or the march-off. We pull it off anyway.

Two companies of Marines, clad in blue white dress, march up and around the Iwo Monument. The amber sky of sunset encases the bronze figures of the past on the monument, the marble and bronze representative of sacrifices made on the black sand and rocks of Iwo Jima. The sunset cloaks the blue white dress clad Marines of today as they march off and disappear on the other side. There isn't any more moving patriotic spectacle than this. If you've been to one, you know. If you haven't, you don't...and you should.

One end result is that a new parade field decree is issued. No matter what, execute the command the parade commander gives, and not the next movement in the sequence as we were supposed to do. If the command is wrong, the parade commander has to get the problem unscrewed.

Nonetheless, Lieutenant Colonel Maloney is a "hands-down" awardee of the DAA. The McKay, Milsap, Kruger trio, with the sanctifying grace of our Adjutant, their publicist and agent, Captain Jake Dennehy, administering it.

I love this place and these guys.

CHAPTER 26

White House
East Room
1710 hours
Sat, 23 Nov 1963

IT'S TIME TO CHANGE POSITION; go from attention to ceremonial at ease. It's all routine and practiced by this time. We move as one and settle into our new position allowing our weary bones to carry a different burden of weight. With the move, however slight, our fatigued muscles get some needed blood flow, or whatever physiologically occurs.

When the only thing I hear is the priests rattling their beads, I realize what quiet is, and what quiet will wreak.. My fragmentary newsreel clips once again start running across the screen of my mind. I have to focus on something other than the events of the day.

I need to call Gabby as soon as I get back tonight. She's probably wondering what the hell happened to me.

For some strange reason, I start having disconnected thoughts about her. Like how she is convinced that we are the handiwork of fate... or how quick her responsive quips are, and how she teases me about the nicknames Captain Milsap or the ones the troops have tagged me with. As I stand here at casket side and settle into position, my imagination allows me to feel the sunlight of that morning parade rehearsal when Captain J.G. fastened some more tags...

* * *

The day is cloudless with a hot morning sun. It feels humid this early summer Friday of '63. Probably the moisture being sucked out of the ground after the overnight watering of the parade deck. After parade rehearsal, and after the formal critique, Captain Milsap says to me, "Lieutenant Quinn, you are one smooth son-of-a-gun on the parade deck. I mean you're like a snake, a cobra, the way you slide and glide through the grass."

"Well, thank you, sir."

I wait for the other shoe to drop. After all our Drum Room and uptown antics, it's reasonable to expect.

He asks, "How the hell do you do it?"

"Seriously?"

"Yes."

He's sincere, I can tell by his expression.

I feel better, although I'm still sniffin' the breeze for a telltale sign of the shoe. Regardless, I say, "Well, you keep your toes feeling like they're pointed down. They're actually just level with the surface. Then slide your foot straight forward and down on the outer edge and just let it roll to the heel. Just one after the other. That way you can march, like a woman walks without the provocative ass shaking routine."

He laughs. "How come the jokers at the Old Guard do something like that, but their butts wiggle like a hooker?"

"First, they are...never mind. They take mincing steps, and quicker. Also, they step in toward the center, not straight forward. Like a model...walk the centerline. This is what makes them walk like a woman in a tight skirt. Ass wigglin' and a jigglin'. Cute, but not military. Almost makes you want to kiss 'em."

He asks me to demonstrate, and again I'm a bit leery, but I do. I think, damn, I am snakelike, a cobra...love the tags, along with the Great Stoneface, Crazy Horse, and Mustang Barney. The latter being one of the Drill Team's tags so I'm told.

* * *

A few weeks after the snake and cobra coronation moment, I'm called to Captain Kemp's office. He says, "Lieutenant Quinn, get in your blue white dress, with sword, and go up to Lieutenant General Haney's quarters at the post."

I tense up, my mind racing through my antics of the past several weeks. I try to determine what I could have possibly done to embarrass this General. I don't even know him. Never spoke to him. I say, "Captain, what the devil is this about?"

"Mrs. Haney is having a tea. She wants you to come up and walk for her and her guests. You know, do your cobra shtick, slick."

"What? You're kidding, right? Sir?"

"Nope. Just got off the phone with Colonel Weaver. You're to go now, they're waiting for you." Kemp lets a sly smile spread across his face before he laughs aloud.

Okay, he got me. It's a joke. Has to be.

So, I laugh with him.

He says, "Hey, I'm not kidding. Get moving, and quick. They're waiting."

"Oh, Jesus. You're not kidding. Captain,--"

"It's not a joke. Go, Lieutenant Snake."

* * *

I arrive at the Haney's quarters. The steward answers the door, leads me through the enclosed porch and directs me to the living room where a *baker's dozen* middle-aged and elderly ladies are sitting. They each have a cup of tea and a plate with little thingies on it...munchies and teensy sandwiches, precariously balanced on a napkin sitting on their knees. Mrs. Haney says, "Lieutenant Quinn, good afternoon. You're such a sweet dear for coming."

"Ma'am, I didn't have--"

"I've watched you on the parade field. You walk so beautifully. Just like a model, but of course, more militarily."

"Uhh? Ma'am?"

"Could you please walk back and forth in here so I can show my lady friends." She looks at the steward and says, "Corporal Fennell, move this coffee table out of the way, please." Fennell leaps into action.

"Ma'am, this is--"

"Please, Lieutenant Quinn. Barney, isn't it?"

"Yes, ma'am. It's Barney, but ma'am this is embarr--"

"Oh hush, Barney, it's not either. It's just amazing the way you walk, or march, or...you know what I mean."

"Yes, ma'am, I do, but--"

"Oh hush, Lieutenant. I won't tell your friends."

Corporal Fennell gingerly pulls the table so as not to disturb the several items on top. Off the carpet, he slides it into the vestibule and onto the hardwood flooring causing a stuttering, scraping sound.

Mrs. Haney frowns at the noisy disturbance, and then says to me, "Well, go ahead, darling."

Darling? Oh, Jesus, I hope no one finds out about this. Good God Almighty!

She continues, "Just back and forth a few times, maybe more."

I do as asked. I also glare at the steward, who is off to the side, hands folded in front, in his best ready-to-serve-somebody stance, but grinning like a circus clown. That sniggling jerk is going to tell the stewards at Center House, and that will get back to the Muv, or Milsap, or worse Kruger. I assume Dennehy already has wind of this, the damn know-it-all. Sometimes he has too much info. I do the parading, only the several steps the room allows. Back and forth, twice.

I look at the general's wife with my best pleading face. She waves back and forth indicating she wants a few more passes. I do it and I know I'm flushed to a scarlet color.

Mrs. Haney gushes, "Wonderful, wonderful, isn't it ladies. Oh, thank you, Barney." Then she waves her arm in a flowing motion around the room and says, "Wasn't that just delightful, ladies?" The word delightful sounds like a fingernail scraping along a slate blackboard. She adds, "You'll have to come to the parade, if you haven't already, and cheer Lieutenant Quinn on." The ladies complete my mortification by applauding. One even asks if I could do it just one more time. I do, because I have no choice since Mrs. Haney is flicking her hand, motioning me unto the carpet again. The steward smirks, nodding knowingly, with a smug look about him.

I choke out a, "Thank you, ladies. Mrs. Haney. By your leave, Ma'am." I salute, face about, and depart via the front porch door, to Generals' Walk. I hurry, not slide and glide, hoping not to be seen. It's a long walk. The Haney's quarters are the last in the row of five.

I return to Building #58, saying nothing to anyone. In fact, I'm ready to snap off heads should anyone poke fun at me. Gunny Elms and Gunny Blank have the good taste, and smarts, to say nothing. Sergeant Hapgood, more bullish says, "Hey, Lieutenant, I hear you were up--"

"Stow it, Sergeant. Just keep shining your shoes."

He laughs, and continues with his spit-shining routine. Elms and Blank are grinning, ear to ear.

I sulk the remainder of the afternoon, knowing what is in store for me this evening. I call Gabrielle from the office and tell her of the incident. She thinks it's delightful. The word causes me more pain than a bayonet stuck up my...in my gut. She says, "What was that sound?"

"Me, groaning with your choice of words."

"What word?"

"I can't even repeat it without pain. Do you realize what the guys in the House are going to do with this?"

"Oh, don't worry, BQ. Those guys won't say anything. They're gentlemen; at least they always are around me."

"Yeah, right. Call you later tonight."

"Okay, don't forget I have class. Do you love me?"

"I can't talk now, but, yes. Bye."

Elms and Blank are grinning again, and Hapgood is about to say something but I say, "And keep it stowed." He shrugs and grins.

Before dinner I have a drink at the bar. Chink and Jeff are here but say nothing. Captains Milsap and Kruger come in, order a drink from the Gunny, and say only hello.

Maybe that stinkin' steward didn't say anything.

Then Captain Jake Dennehy strolls in, says, "Hi," and orders a drink.

Oh oh. This is it. Dennehy is here for a reason. This is going to sting.

Captain McKay enters, orders a scotch and water, and when he has it, swirls the swizzle stick around clinking the ice cubes. This goes on for several seconds. No one speaks, but the looks on their faces are telltale. After his dramatic pause, the House Mother mumbles, and then it builds into a mutter slurping in his Carolinian syrup, and finally something discernible spills out. "Well, Mister Quinn. What did you do today to distinguish yourself? Cobra, isn't it? Or do you prefer, Snake? Did you have some tea and cute little finger sandwiches this afternoon, Looootenant?"

"Is that what they're called?"

"Hush now, Mister Quinn."

211

Milsap, Kruger, Dennehy and Chink feign falling off their bar stools in boisterous laughter as my face flushes to scarlet but not as deep nor as hot as this afternoon. Van Dell is no better. He's laughing also but he sounds less like a crazed chimp as the others do. Before I can reply again, the Muv adds, "Don't tell me. I've heard directly from an eyewitness, and his telling is much better than you can probably muster. My, my, my, Lady Bernadette, out for a 'delightful' afternoon with the little ol' ladies." He breaks into a loud, rumbling laugh. A chill, goose bumps, run down my back upon hearing the friggin word again. They are all squealing in laughter. All pleased with themselves. It sounds like the monkey house at the zoo.

No sense trying to recover. This is one story I can't deny and will only make my situation worse by trying. I just say, "Gunny, another bourbon and Seven, please. And none for these gents, they get giddy when they drink. Just give them some bananas."

I'm going to hear this tale for a long time. I can only hope it's not a DAA nominating type performance. My only recourse is to become involved in an antic that will push this to the background. I'll work on it.

The unmistakable sound of cleated footsteps on the hardwood floor snaps me back to the present.

* * *

The White House
East Room
1730-watch over
Sat, 23 Nov 1963

Ah, our relief is here. Off we go. Only one more to go today. I know if it weren't for my mind running off loose afield, I'd be about four times as tired as I am, and that is bone achin', bleary-eyed weary.

I go through the press and shine routine again, shave, then hold my head under the cold water faucet for several minutes until my brain feels frozen, but refreshed. I grab another sandwich, baloney this time, and a cup of black coffee.

Time to eat, rest, and be thoughtless...or let my mind roam at will.

CHAPTER 27

The White House
Galley area
After watch
Sat, 23 Nov 1963

I GO THROUGH THE SAME monotonous routine of press, shine, and wash up. I pass on the food table. I'll grab a sandwich and whatever after this watch, my next to last here. I check on my deathwatch unit and the other Marines from my Drill Team. All are tired, but will be fine. We're in the homestretch, at least for today.

I get a cup of coffee, sit and quickly melt into my newly acquired habitual daze. My fatigue sponsors outlandish thoughts. I think about some of the bizarre incidents at The Barracks. After some of the antics of the boys in blue white dress, Chesty is the next most ridiculous, and unfortunately, the nastiest subject to trek across my existing inane mind.

* * *

Tonight is what I call an off night for me. Gabby didn't come to the parade, so I hang out with the guys in Center House afterwards. I'll see her tomorrow after Bullwinkle, and will stay there the weekend. The break for an evening will be good. I didn't think it was possible but the woman is wearing me out with the lovemaking and the sightseeing trips. Also the domesticated errand and shopping ventures are eye-openers. However, I luv this gal and our time together is fun...and increasing.

Congregating in the Drum Room...the bar after a parade is good for the ego. Guests tend to ogle the parade officers, and want to gush how wonderful and beautiful the parade was and how magnificent you are. Occasionally, someone will comment on my walk...my gliding. It's all nice, but a tad embarrassing.

I shy away to a corner of the bar for a drink with the glib trio of McKay, Milsap and Kruger.

That sounds like a name of an Immigration Law Firm for Scots, Brits and Germans.

Anyway, Mush Mouth was the Parade Adjutant tonight so we got the Oxford, North Carolina version of parade commands, such as "Suh, thuh poo-rayd is foamed, suh." Beyond this is his rendition of the command, Fix, Bayonets, which is one of the two best and richest ever heard at The Barracks. It melodically rolls across the parade deck, Fix, BAYOUL-NETS. I always try to copycat him when I give this command to the Drill Team when out and about.

Captain J. G. Milsap, after a hard night of coordinating the show, orders his Kennedyesque scotch and water. He rests easy since the parade went well, what else? Julius Kruger had hosting duty tonight. He is a bit grumpy because some woman stepped on his spit-shined shoe as he helped her step up into the bleacher seating. If she'd been young, sexy and with a short skirt he wouldn't have cared, but she wasn't. He's a scotch drinker as well. I'm the only one that drinks bourbon and Seven, or as the Muv says, "Soda pop."

We laugh as Kruger retells the story about last Friday when some Staff NCO insisted that the dog handler bring Chesty down to their Club after the parade. He wanted to show Chesty to his guests. Why anyone would want to introduce his or her friends to that filthy beast is bewildering. Apparently, the handler tried to talk him out of it, but the Master Sergeant insisted, ordered it done. It was.

In came Chesty, on a leash, and from all reports, in a docile mood. He just swaggered in, looked around lazily, and seemed okay. He sat when the handler cued him with a tug on the leash and he slowly and gingerly scratched his ear several times, more of a rub. Then he turned and concentrated on licking his balls. Nice! Really cute. If there would have been a patio, he'd been out there...like in the well-known joke. But, there wasn't, so the handler tugged at Chesty to stop him as the Master

Sergeant waved him closer to his guests so they could pet Chesty. The guests had a small girl, around six or seven, dressed in girlish summer finery. Unfortunately, she was also dragging along a large stuffed rabbit, about the size of a smallish cocker spaniel.

As Chesty was being tugged unwillingly forward, he spied the rabbit. He came to life, charged forward, and jumped on the stuffed animal breaking it free of the adorable little girl's grasp. She squealed in horror as Chesty dragged it a few feet then proceeded to mount and hump the stuffed crazy wabbit. A melee of sort broke out among Chesty, the rabbit, the handler, the girl's father, and the hosting Master Sergeant.

The girl jumped toward her mother and grasped one of her mom's legs. The girl was saved, but the mother's skirt has now hiked up past mid thigh. The mom's face was beet red and the girl frightened pale and in tears as the woman tried to get herself respectful once again. Other folks present were either aghast at the scene or bellowing in laughter. The latter, mostly Marines from The Barracks. The handler was both embarrassed and pissed. The Master Sergeant apologetic. An unsympathetic Chesty was dragged out, hanging out as usual. The mascot was in disgrace yet again. The rabbit didn't care.

The three of us are in tears as Kruger finishes the telling. Each of us orders another drink. A new lieutenant at The Barracks is at the bar next to us. This is his first Friday night, so Captain McKay says to our barkeep, "Fix him up, Gunny," pointing to the new man.

The return nod and smile by the Gunny is one of understanding.

The lieutenant gushes out, "Thank you, sir."

The rest of us put on the best smiles our evil brain housing groups will allow.

"Fix him up, Gunny" has two meanings. One is, cut the freeloading bastard off by watering down his drinks until they reach zero alcohol content, at which time the person leaves. This is reserved for obnoxious guests. Lieutenant Paquette is not one of these. The second meaning is take this clown or new guy out with a specialty drink of the house, the Rattlesnake. This mixture of whiskeys and rums is deadly. Actually, Captain Milsap claims it should be called a Cobra since its toxins strike directly at the central nervous system in very little time.

He knows this not because of his scholarly wisdom, rather that he was a victim early on before his hollow leg became a subject of wonderment.

As soon as Gunny Richards serves us our drinks, we settle in to see how long it will be before the new guy seeks relief or crumbles. I should be more protective since my peer, First Lieutenant Walter Scott Paquette, has just replaced Jeff Van Dell in Guard Company.

Well, better him than me. Anyway, I need a supernumerary to put the "delightful" incident in storage.

Lieutenant Colonel Maloney approaches our huddled group and says, "Lieutenant Quinn, would you do me a favor?"

"Certainly, sir. How can I help?" He likes me although I seem to be a thorny rose that keeps pricking his finger.

"First, come over and meet my guests. Neighbors. He and his wife want to meet the Drill Platoon Commander. Are you being civilized tonight?" He laughs at his attempt of humor. The Muv chokes on his drink, and the other two snicker and snort. Paquette is still standing, although looking green.

"Of course, sir."

I move from my corner under the guidance of the XO who is pulling me along by the arm into the vestibule just outside the Drum Room. He introduces me. I'm civilized, and I politely answer several questions about the drill and my background...two of my favorite subjects. His guests are a retired Army colonel and his wife.

Maloney then says, "Barney, Mrs. Schmidt wants to see Chesty. Have the handler bring him in, on a leash."

"Sir, I don't believe that would be a good idea."

"Eileen wants to see him. She used to have English bulls."

"Sir, not like him."

"Just have him brought over here on a leash."

"Sir, the leash won't make any difference. Please, sir--"

"He'll be fine."

That remark is so absurd, I can't believe the XO said it.

"Please, sir, don't do this. Just make an excuse. Any excuse. The dog is at the Navy Yard, or on the way to Camp David for the weekend, anything, sir."

"Get the dog, Lieutenant Quinn."

I look at the Schmidts for help but they are talking to Mrs. Maloney so they don't hear any of this. "Sir, the Lieutenant really doesn't--"

He leans close to my ear, certain indication that this next statement is going to be ugly. He angrily whispers, "Stop your third person crap, and get the damn dog, now, Mister Quinn."

I lean back, shake my head, and mumble, "As you wish, sir."

I go topside, call the Guard Office and tell the Corporal of the Guard to have Chesty brought over to Center House, on a leash.

He says, "Beggin' the Lieutenant's pardon, sir, but that's not a good idea."

"Corporal, I know that. It isn't my idea, it's the XO's, and I fully realize it sucks. Bring the damn mutt over here, now."

The line goes silent but I can hear some muffled voices. The Sergeant of the Guard comes on the phone and says, "Sir, this is Sergeant Goodrich. Sir, I don't think we should do this, sir."

"Sergeant, nor do I, but the XO has ordered it, and I want that order executed right now."

"Sir, I--"

"Now."

"On the way, sir. Good luck, Lieutenant."

"Sergeant, luck is nothing more than when opportunity and preparation meet. There is no way to prepare for this. What I need is a miracle, not luck."

"Sorry, sir."

"So will be the colonel."

After hanging up, I pause in the second deck hallway.

In a way this is an opportunity. A barracks tale, a legend is in the making and I'm just an innocent pawn following orders. My name will be glorified in the retelling of this in the months, perhaps years, to come. Geez, I love my reasoning. However, most important, it will wipe away the tea party story...well, at least push it back in the far recesses of the mind.

I return to the vestibule. As usual by this time, word has leaked out among the younger officers of the forthcoming event. The clan is clandestinely gathering on the fringes. Except Mister Paquette. He is finished for the evening after one strike from the Cobra. He's on Muv's couch. I saw him stagger by in the upstairs hallway.

The XO must not be aware of the Staff NCO Club fiasco or his natural New Yorker character traits have obscured his judgment once again. The junior officers, of course, look forward to Chesty being... well...Chesty.

A slight commotion occurs on the porch as the handler enters with Chesty, under leash, but not key, and wearing his little scarlet and gold dog uniform coat. He's been reduced in rank to Lance Corporal since the incident at the beginning of the parade season. He strolls in the room, barrel-chested and bow-legged. Sticks his nose in the air to catch a scent. The XO, babbling about Chesty's background as he goes, leads his guests to the dog. As he waits, Chesty delivers a silent fart, noticeable first by the folks behind him scrunching up their noses, and then moving rapidly away. Then all notice, but are trapped in position. Fortunately no one shouted, "Fart," thereby causing a riotous rush for the exits.

Mrs. Schmidt reaches down to pet Lance Corporal Chesty, II. He leaps up and wraps both his front legs around the poor woman's forearm, and begins his humping routine.

There is a mad scramble to free Eileen, led by the retired Army colonel and our XO.

It's good to see senior officers still so spry.

Chesty and the woman have only a brief affair. She pales quickly in horror, and then brightens in embarrassment. Her husband is chalk white. The XO is a dazzling scarlet color darkening to purple rapidly. I'd say stroke intensity. Chesty is slobbering and panting heavily. He's in love. I look at Lieutenant Colonel Maloney and shrug my shoulder along with my best I-told-you-so look. Then I say, "Corporal, retire the dog." I got this command from the parade..."Retire the Colors."

As he drags him away, Chesty's backside to the crowd, I remember a Shakespearean quote, at least I think it was his. I mutter a paraphrased version, "Oh what manner of dog is this, that walks with balls twix parentheses."

The XO says to me, "What was that, Barney."

"I said, I need a drink. By your leave, sir."

"Oh, yes. Yes."

"I suggest we all have one, except Chesty, he gets nasty when he drinks." The colonel flushes and gives me an angry look.

The trio of captains is again in the corner waiting for me. We order drinks, turn our backs to the room, bend over the bar, and burst into muffled laughter. Muffled or not, the tears come. Chesty is not eligible for the DAA, and the XO already has one. However, we'll have to check with Jake Dennehy...the Colonel could receive a gold star in lieu of his second award.

The XO is probably going to start shying away from me. First, it was my remark to the WM. Then, just weeks ago in a meeting about what brand name liquors to carry at the bar, he said to me, "Lieutenant Quinn, you're a bourbon drinker. We need your honest opinion. What is a good bourbon?"

I replied, in the presence of the trio of captains and others, "I don't know or care, sir. I've never had a bad bourbon, just some better than others." He shook his head in bafflement and continued the meeting without any further input from me. And now this Chesty incident. He will most likely rationalize his involvement, point the finger of blame at me, decide to remain at a respectable distance from me in the future, and certainly not pluck this rose in blue white dress.

No matter. Both incidents remind me of something I read somewhere...don't remember where or when but it went something like this, "Some mistakes are too much fun to only make once."

CHAPTER 28

The White House
East Room
A gloomy 1930 hours
Sat, 23 Nov 1963

AFTER I DO THE READYING routine again, I make myself another roast beef sandwich and heap some more macaroni salad on my paper plate, grab a couple of deviled eggs, cup of black coffee and a tall glass of ice water. After I eat, I brush my Chiclets, and then hold my head under the cold water tap again. I'm really beginning to feel the fatigue all over, but especially in my legs. Apparently, my mind has been gone for hours.

The time has flashed by what with the chow and clean up. No time for daydreaming. My unit and I are up, dressed, and on our way into the East Room. The room continues to have its subdued overhead lighting and the candles at the casket cast eerie shadows and emit a slight, indistinguishable aroma. This, along with all the black mourning draping, and the somberness of the event, carries enough gloom to make the room look and feel like late dusk on a cloudy, winter evening. The priests are here, murmuring their prayers. Again, the clinking of the beads is audible. It's so quiet; you can hear the candle flames flicker.

This is this President's last night in the White House, and I get to spend a brief part of the evening with him. We're not alone, he and I, but I feel we have our privacy...and sadness. Camelot has passed.

My mind wanders the path of another moment with him, probably unobserved except for a few, however unforgettable for me... but only a fleeting moment for him.

* * *

It's another weekend after a parade in the summer of '63 when the President, First Lady, and family spent it at Camp David. The CD Presidential Retreat Site is located about seventy miles from the White House in the Catoctin Mountains of Maryland. Established in 1942, President Roosevelt called it "Shangri-La" after the mountain kingdom in James Hilton's book, *Lost Horizon*. It was renamed Camp David in 1953 by President Eisenhower in honor of his grandson.

Navy personnel operate the Camp, and Ceremonial Guard Company provides the guard of the day. One of our platoons is here all the time. When the President is in residence, the guard requires augmentation. Although it's normally one of the other platoons more familiar with the compound that goes, the Drill Platoon and I have caught the assignment this weekend.

It's an unbelievable compound. Double chained-link electric fences, jeep patrol around the inner perimeter road, and sentries back in the woods in what amounted to be hunting blinds. Jackie insisted on the latter to hide the men with rifles from the children's sight. It is truly an extraordinary place. Nothing...the water tank...sheds, nothing is what it appears to be. It's a command center. When the President is here, all sentries are armed with live ammo and all posts are challenging posts. More than one Secret Service agent out wandering around in the dark has been challenged, and if the truth be told, scared shitless. The Service is here, as always, when the first family is aboard. It is a no-nonsense environment for us, a vacation for guests.

There are beautiful cabins here, each named for a species of tree such as Dogwood, Maple, Holly and Birch to name a few. The Presidential cabin is Aspen. The camp has a small movie theater, bowling alley, skeet range, pool, hiking trails...it's secluded and striking. Each season holds it's own beauty here. To me, the fall is the most spectacular with nature's display of colors. However, since it's summer, I can live with this greenery and aromatic smelling mountain air.

Saturday morning, everyone in the immediate family is already here with the exception of the President. He has yet to arrive from the

White House. He will be coming by chopper, Marine One. It's about a half-hour ride. I'm sitting in the radio jeep at the helo pad, listening to the chatter on the radio and waiting for the arrival. Don't have to do anything really, just ensure all is ready, vehicle present, and all posts manned.

I glance down and there stands John-John, looking up at me with a toy metal plane in his hand. An always nearby Secret Service agent smiles. The agent and I have seen each other before. John-John's plane looks like a replica of Air Force One. He's harboring an inquisitive look on his face. I say, "Want up?"

His eyes grow large in excitement; he nods and starts to climb up. I give him an assist and let him sit on my lap. The radio's squawking draws his attention so I have the operator let John-John diddle with the handheld mike. I ask him, "Is that your Dad's plane?"

"Yes," with a nod for emphasis.

"Can I see it?"

He hands it to me. I fly it around with my hand and ask, "Is this how it goes?"

He grabs it back, anxious to show how it's supposed to be done. He diligently shows me how it should be flown, making great circles with his plane arm. He accompanies these patterns and loops imitating the noise of the jet engines.

Have to add the sound effects, I forgot that.

He lands it on the folded-down windshield of the jeep. A perfect wheels-down landing. He twists around in my lap, smiles and says, "See."

I nod, "Good job. Better than any pilot I know."

He beams.

The operator is talking, so I know Marine One is inbound, and close. Also, I hear the whump-whump-whump of chopper blades cutting into the thinner mountain air seeking lift for this big bird with its valuable cargo. It lands, settles easily, the blades shut down, and the front hatch opens and President Kennedy steps out and descends the fold-down steps. The Marine at the bottom snaps to attention, and salutes.

I lift John-John from my lap, ease him to the ground, and let go. He races toward his dad on his short and yet unstable legs. He stumbles a few times but stays on his feet.

Athletic little rascal...and excited.

When he arrives at his target of attraction, he takes a running leap into his dad's arms, gives him a hug and immediately starts chattering away. Like any boy when his dad comes home.

From my seat in the jeep, I see that John-John is talking, rapidly and excitedly. He's flying his plane with one arm, and pointing back at me with the other. He is also doing something that appears as if he's explaining how the radio works in the jeep. He animatedly rambles on, pointing and gesturing. The President looks over, leans down and forward slightly, half shades his eyes with his free hand, and squints. We lock on to one another's eyes. A look of recognition spreads across his face and it says, "It's you again, everywhere I turn...arrivals, Mona Lisa, cordons, and now here."

The President smiles, tips his free hand in a relaxed salute, and shrugs as he holds up his son. He points at me, mouths a "thank you," and puts John-John down. I nod and wave back. No salute, just casual, like pals. They walk away, hand in hand, for the stroll to Aspen...with agents trailing.

It probably happens to many people around the President, but these types of moments are no less personal, important and memorable to me. These brushes with fame occur with all of the lieutenants up here at Camp David. As strange as it sounds, it makes you feel like family.

* * *

The White House
East Room
2000 hours
Sat, 23 Nov 1963

I'm back, and fight off some emotion. I've had some personal moments with this man who lies here in front of me. I hear the heels of the next watch, clicking across the hard wood flooring of the East Room. The clack----clack----clack in funeral cadence brings me all the way back. My last watch of the day is about over.

I take in a deep breath through my nose...and let it out in a quick snuff.

Good night, Mr. President. Rest peacefully. I'll see you in the morning.

CHAPTER 29

Marine Barracks
Center House
0500 hours
Sun, 24 Nov 1963

I'M UP AT O-DARK-HUNDRED. DO my five "S's" then take the steps downstairs two at a time and into the dining room for breakfast. Orange juice and coffee are great booster shots but the bowl of steaming oatmeal with brown sugar is a rib-sticker, only surpassed by SOS.

Captain Milsap joins me at the table. The other residents join us within five minutes. The mood is somber. Captain JG and I talk about the details of yesterday and I thank him for his part in sending the Drill Team members for the twelve-man escort early Saturday morning.

After chow, I go to Building 58, and there I dress, re-shine my brass, and with my troops depart for the White House in our Marine Corps green, ugly bread truck. We stand as usual and hang on to the overhead straps. The driver is Atherton. He says, "Ready to go do it, Lieutenant?"

"Got you again, huh? Great, you do good work. Yep, I'm ready. How 'bout you?"

"Yes, sir. Clean sheets and hot chow make me good to go. No police escort this morning, sir. Won't need it. At least I hope."

"Shouldn't. It's Sunday."

"Yes, sir, but not a normal one."

"You can say that again."

"Yes, sir, but not a nor--"

"Okay, okay, Atherton. That's one for you. Let's move it."

"Yes, sir, but I was only--"

"I know...go."

Got near six hours sleep so I should feel rested, but the body aches, particularly the knees from the hours on that hardwood floor. It's goin' to be worse at the Rotunda. Atherton guns it as we roll through the 8th Street gate. This ol' van just groans and shakes, and picks up speed at its own pace. As we hit a pothole, a Magpie shouts, "Hey, Atherton, try not to hit every damn hole. You're jarrin' the hell out of my knees and back."

Before Atherton can respond another troop chimes in, "Yeah, but don't swerve at the last minute...the swayin' and the fumes in this piece of crap are makin' me sick already."

"I can't help the swayin'. This is nothin'. Wait til I make the turn on Pennsy."

I say, "Okay, guys. Knock it off. Atherton, pay attention to your driving. Just get us there, and open the window. The fumes are bad."

"Yes, sir." The others groan and mutter.

Nothin's changed. This green beauty is bouncin' and swayin' like always...and the Magpies bitch. The drive should be a snap this morning. Up to Pennsylvania Avenue and over to the White House. I glance out the windshield.

Good, not much traffic at all. Jesus, this is a piece of crap.

We easily arrive on time. Once inside we get with our own Death Watch groups. The Army officer will be on first this morning, the 0800 watch. I will go thirty minutes later. The President will be moved today to the Capitol rotunda, sometime late morning or early afternoon. The funeral cortege will go down Pennsylvania Avenue. I'm sure the street will be packed. Will be a huge procession; tons of troops.

With the oatmeal still stickin' to my ribs, it's time for me and my watch detail to stand our first of the day this saddened Sunday, the twenty-fourth day of November 1963. We enter the East Room at the funeral cadence and slide into position. Nothing has changed. Still quiet. Rosary beads and flickering flames are the only sounds. I settle in position.

Good morning, Mister President. It's me. Everywhere you turn, I'm there.

My mental conversation triggers my emotions once again. I need to clear my mind of this type of thought process and on to something lighter to occupy my time on watch. The silence and gravity of the moment prompt enough emotion without me adding to it with personal chats. I try but can't.

Big day today. Mr. President. All my buds, and others from The Barracks, will be involved somehow. The Body Bearers will have their work cut out...carrying you up the capitol steps. Tough, tough carry. Wish it weren't so!

Ah, I better change positions, been about ten minutes. And get on to something lighter, dummy.

We move to ceremonial at ease and settle into position. My mind finally shifts gears. We've got a helluva crew of folks at The Barracks. While we perform in the finest traditions of the Corps, we also amuse ourselves, and foolishly at times. The games in Center House. My mind starts to slip away as I think of the roguish nature of our antics. Ah, the thought of the asinine simplicity of these games takes me the rest of the way to...

* * *

These games mostly take place on the weekends when only its residents inhabit Center House.

Iroquois Leap...we and our dates suddenly leaping into one pile in the middle of the room. Loser buys a round, that being the last on the pile. Dead Bug...flopping over and playing dead, from any position to include bar stools. The winner is the best "dead" position. Midnight Lawn Romp...racing across the parade deck with a date; usually ended by the Corporal of the Guard turning on the sprinklers. The frolic ends and nothing is reported. Never a winner here.

Gabby's been involved...well, sort of. She watched each the first time and said, "BQ, Dead Bug is stupid."

I responded, "Of course it is, that's why it's fun."

"Well, not for me. You try for the Oscar; I'll just vote."

When Iroquois Leap was introduced, she said, "Barney, I'm not playing Algonquin--"

"Iroquois."

"Iroquois, Sioux, Comanche or whatever...I'm not jumping in a pile of drunken Marines."

"We're not drunk."

"Good, then let's go home and leap into bed. That I enjoy...and I'll let you call it anything you want."

"Yeah, that does sound better."

She did play Lawn Romp. Thought that was exciting. I asked her why that and not the others. She replied, "Because we get soaked and have to go home...and play Iroquois Leap."

Games in general are not unique to The Barracks. Roguish behavior portrayed in the form of contests are a part of Happy Hours and parties throughout the Corps, a rite of passage, such as Carrier Qual's at Air Wing clubs or wherever pilots gather.

My favorite, the Launching Pad race is conducted on two, two-person stools that have no back. They are slightly lower in seating height than a chair. A love seat. Stained wood with leather padding for the seat. All four legs have coasters making it doable for the race, and useless or damn difficult...maybe novel, as a "love seat." The participants lay on the stools on their chests, legs coiled with feet against a wall. After an appropriate countdown and on the command, "LAUNCH", they thrust themselves across the Drum Room floor by shoving off from the wall with their legs and feet. A blast off.

The race can be a sprint, just a half orbit across the bar room floor. The longer flight goes through the Drum Room and into the vestibule, living room, around the dining room table and retracing the path back to the bar. This requires the participants to push themselves along with their arms and hands much the same as some handicapped peddlers on city streets. Either race is great sport, with the latter requiring strength, agility, endurance, and some form of psychosis.

Tuesday evening, after the Iwo parade in late summer of '63, and after all the senior officers leave the bar, Captain Kruger challenges me to a Launching Pad race. I say, "Not tonight, Captain. Maybe Thursday after Happy Hour."

Kruger says, "You can't turn down a challenge, Stoneface."

"Yes, sir, I can, and do. I haven't had enough bourbon to get me motivated. No liquid fuel, no launch."

Captain McKay, who is sitting on his usual one stool away from the corner, chimes in, "Loooootenant Quinn. A request by a Captain is an order to you, Mistaah." He sounds like James Cagney talking to Henry Fonda or Jack Lemmon in the picture, *Mister Roberts*. "You will race. It will be the long orbit. May the better Captain win."

"Sir, there's only one Captain in the race."

"Exactly. You're very quick, Mistaah Quinn." He is pleased with his newly found accent. At least it's easier to understand than his normal Carolinian slurp and syrup mumble.

Captain Milsap is Launch Control when not involved in a contest. Chink is simply drinking, watching and laughing along with several other lieutenants. Paquette, the new guy is quiet, not yet having recovered from the Rattlesnake incident.

Julius has already aligned the two love seats, the rockets, against the front wall...the launching pad. We each get on one, and when ready, the Ivy Leaguer, Captain JG starts the countdown, "Five, four, three, two, one, LAUNCH."

We burst off the launching wall, collide at the door out of the bar, and while wrestling for position, a leg on my love seat snaps off and I tumble to the floor. The race is over. Vehicle malfunction. Uncle Julius declares himself the winner. I argue, "No way, my launching pad broke. I had to eject."

Kruger gets up and shouts, "Doesn't matter. The rules are the same as a car race. Mechanical failure; you're out of the race. The finisher wins."

The House Mother agrees and declares Kruger the winner. I don't give up, "Julius has not completed the race. He got up and off his pad. He didn't finish either."

Launch Control, Captain Milsap, rules that I'm right. JG is the authority; Captain McKay is just the Muv. The race will have to be rerun. Then JG adds, "First, we need to either fix the pad or report the damage."

After serious discussion, and two more drinks, we decide to fix the leg on the love seat. Captain Kruger has some wood putty in his room, God only knows why.

We refit the broken leg piece on the remaining stub and apply the putty. Captain Kruger cleverly covers the wood putty with KIWI brown shoe polish, and places the love seat in the corner of the bar, against the wall. He stands erect, hands on hips and declares, "That'll do it."

Our slim thread of hope is that no one will sit on it for a spell. We'll guide people away from it, and later come up with a reasonable explanation for its replacement.

Three days later on Friday night, after a parade, we are once again in the Drum Room, without dates, being nice to guests and having a few social cocktails...the boys in blue white dress in all their innocence, looking like mom's all-American boys, and not the scoundrels of a few nights before.

Our CO, Colonel Weaver, enters the room with his guests, makes introductions, and orders drinks for his group and himself. After handing out the drinks to his guests, he takes his own from the bar, and for whatever reason, decides to relax. The Colonel turns, looks at the love seat, and starts to sit. Kruger sees this move first. He chokes on his drink, coughing up his scotch back into his glass and bar top. Muv whines, "What the devil is wrong with you?"

Julius sputters softly, "Look." He points with his head and immediately slumps over his drink pretending to ignore what he's seen. We all turn our heads. We see what is happening. It looks as if it's happening in slow motion. Unfortunately, it's not. It's too late to warn him, he's on his way down, so we turn quickly, join Julius facing the bar, and pretend not to notice.

CRASH. The leg collapses. The Colonel is down. A groan escapes from the several senior officers and their ladies. He's in a heap on the floor having slowly slid off the now lopsided love seat. His starched white trousers stained with the soaking of his Bloody Mary. Several officers rush to pull the CO to his feet. The XO exclaims, "The leg broke. Gunny Richards, take this out of here. Get it fixed or replaced. Check the other one, it may also be defective."

"Yes, sir." His face is bright red but he stills manages a sly grin. The Gunny remains mute about the cause. He always does unless questioned, then of course, he can't and won't lie, and we wouldn't expect him to do so. Tonight, Lieutenant Colonel Maloney perceives it to be just an unfortunate accident, and for all to hear alluded to it being defective.

There is a God and he smiles on his roguish boys in blue white dress. There will be no cherry tree confessions.

The evening moves forward. Even though publicly exonerated, we culprits cower in the corner, order another drink, stifle a case of the giggles, and feel relieved that we have escaped the hangman. The incident passes quickly. Finally the Muv whispers, "No more races. All launches are cancelled."

* * *

The White House
Down below
Near the end
Sun, 24 Nov 1963

Our watch is over, and we slide and glide back to our subterranean hideaway to rest and prepare for one more watch before the President is moved to the Capitol.

The off-watch routine is the same, only more practiced. We are much more rested than the first thirty plus hours.

When time, we move into the East Room passing a few somber groups as we go. There is more activity now, a somber bustle if you will, now that we're close to the transfer.

I settle in position, suck in some of the musky air through my nose and release it quietly and slowly, relaxing.

Sure is a different environment than all those huge Camelot-like receptions and dinners...I think I can hear this ol' house sobbing, right along with the nation.

CHAPTER 30

The White House
East Room
My last watch
Sun, 24 Nov 1963

WE'RE IN PLACE ON WATCH and we can't hear the beads and the candle flames. The quiet is gone. People wander about, preparing for the transfer. In a way, I feel like they are trespassers, intruders on my time with the President but listening to them makes the time flicker by. I move my team to ceremonial at ease at the ten-minute mark, and back to attention again after another ten. The subtle and somber bustle of people scurrying about drowns out the murmured Hail Marys and Our Fathers from the priests.

I hear the next team coming across the flooring, clack----clack----clack. My watch is over.

Rest easy, Mister President. I'll see you at the Capitol in a little bit. It won't be as peaceful. Goin' to be crowded. Have to share you with the country. Gotta go now...By your leave, sir.

I feel the elbow of the next watch commander once again. I salute; step back, face about and my detail is on our way out. Our last time here...forever, I hope.

We freshen up, pack up and wait. When the time comes, and the last watch is finished, the body bearers will take over and move the President from the East Room to the horse-drawn caisson for his trip down Pennsylvania Avenue to the Capitol. Strange, or maybe not, but many of the troops that marched in his inaugural will be taking him to the Rotunda.

Each deathwatch detail leaves in its own vehicle, but in convoy. We head to the rotunda with a police escort, however, not near the problems of Friday night.

Once at the Capitol, we are escorted to a Senate Committee or Hearing Room. It will be our headquarters, our changing area. A chow spread is already on a table. As we wait for the cortege to arrive, we go over our route of march from this room to the rotunda. I see that as our path nears the rotunda it is cordoned off with stanchions and ropes. They are expecting people along here, probably a lot of them, and not the general public. We'll be "on parade" so to speak, all the way there and back. No problem, but no slack...a lot of eyeballs.

It's a longer trek than at the White House. It'll take several minutes longer, cutting into our preparation and rest time. In the Rotunda we discover what shouldn't be a surprise but is. The floor is a highly-polished marble. It is more slippery than an ice rink and harder than a whore's heart...and we're in leather-soled and heeled shoes with horseshoe metal cleats and metal toe taps.

This isn't goin' to be fun...is going to be a tight-cheeked walk.

I don't even want to envision a slip, but I do. I look around. Everything is already set up and in place...mourning draped catafalque, ropes and stanchions, and the TV folks with cameras and lights.

The Army officer will be the first one to go on here with his Death Watch detail. It'll be a long watch since there will be a ceremony accompanying the placing of the President in the rotunda to lie in state. Along with everything else will be the eulogies by Senate Majority Leader Mansfield, Chief Justice Warren, and Speaker McCormick.

We leave and go back to our room where we get the word that over 300,000 people were along the march route, and that the crowds to view the President as he lies in state will be gigantic...hundreds of thousands will be passing through the rotunda. I did this once before, in Philly, when I was a kid...for a Catholic Cardinal...but nothing this big. This is enormous. This is a world stage...no time for a screw-up.

The MDW Army Captain Graven informs me the ceremony is over, and it's time for me to effect the first relief. He's lookin' flustered again. Crimson-faced. This guy is a prime candidate to blow a gasket. I say, "Okay, sir. Ready to go."

"Good."

"Sir...take it easy. Everything is going fine."

"Yeah. Okay. Okay. Thanks." And the steam just keeps building. Not good.

The rotunda will be opened to the public at 1400 hours today, and will be open all day and night until sometime Monday morning. My detail and I head out to relieve the first watch and to see what awaits us on the ice rink.

Jesus, this hallway floor is slippery...glad we're at a funeral cadence and shorter steps. With these cleats and toe taps, it feels like I'm walking on ball bearings. I hope I don't look as worried as I am.

We approach the roped off area for dignitaries and the entourages that accompany them. It's packed.

Oh man, show time. There's that guy from Germany. What the hell is his name? Can't remember. The President was just there, well, in June... made that famous declaration, "Ich bin ein Berliner."

We slide and glide through this area and come into the rotunda.

Jesus! Cripes! Look at all the people. Two lines. Five...six abreast in each. TV cameras and lights. Suck it up, Barney ol' boy. Be careful; watch the floor, especially turning into position. This is not the time or place to go ass over teakettle.

We come into position to relieve the first watch. The procedure is exactly the same. I slide in next to the Army lieutenant at the head of the casket. I can feel or sense a sigh of relief. It's been a tough watch for him. I touch his elbow and we start. It goes well. He and his watch leave smartly, and carefully. I settle in, suck in some air though my nose careful not to give any sign of breathing. I survey the scene without my eyeballs clicking or blinking. Be a mannequin. Everyone is focused on the casket but I can feel hundreds and hundreds of eyes glancing at me, some staring...I'm sure they're waiting for me to blink or give some sign of life.

Oh-oh. The stanchions are too close. The crowd moving along both sides of the casket blurs in my peripheral vision. It's making me dizzy. The flashbulbs make spots in my eyes...can't focus properly...getting little green, purple, yellow men dancing around in my eyes, like when you get kicked in the…Anyway, the little jaspers are on my internal imaging screen.

I'm at the head of the flag-draped casket. The capitol doors to my front are open for the masses of people. The line goes to the door and beyond, until it drops off my vision, down the steps outside. The TV cameras and lights are directly behind me. Must be every network in the country, in the world, all with cameras turning. The cold air rushing through the doors is hitting me on my forehead; the heat from the TV lights is roasting the back of my head and neck.

Geez, I feel like I have an ice pack on my face and a heating pad on the back of my head. The contrast is nauseating. I'm in a cold, clammy sweat. This is the worst I've been. Damn, I might go out of here. Got to will this away, quick!

My mind is playing tricks. I envision myself fainting and falling forward on the casket. It topples over and the President rolls out onto the rotunda floor. Everyone is aghast. People in the crowd are pointing at me as I lay on the marble floor. I can't get up. My feet keep slipping on the slick surface. I can feel myself getting clammy. Cold sweat.

Good God, I'm hallucinating.

I pull myself together. Stare at a point over the heads of the people coming in, taking pictures at the center point, the foot of the casket. I start doing math problems.

Let's see. Long division…even number into odd. Tough. Okay, 48 into, ah…5,135……Oh crap. Too hard; too many decimal places. Try even into even, dummy.

I do. One-hundred and seven. It works. The perspiration is drying…my skin feels normal again. I'm back in control. I make the movements necessary to change position of the deathwatch. We go from attention to ceremonial at ease. It goes well, smooth. No one noticed a thing. The mannequin is back…with the mannequin's blood.

As soon as I get back to the room, I'm telling them to move those stanchions back several feet. I suppose the flashbulb situation can't be changed. Just have to deal with it.

Good, it's time to change the watch. This arrangement allows me to see the next watch coming into the rotunda and crossing over at the foot end. I bring the watch back to attention, silently and smartly once again.

Sorry Mr. President, I got a little screwed up here for a few moments. I'm back. Helluva of crowd. All here to say goodbye. Me too, but later.

I feel the elbow and sense the Navy officer on my left side. We effect the relief, I step back, face about.

That was damn tricky on this marble.

We move off, out of the rotunda, past the roped off area for the bigwigs and toward the Hearing Room. My first watch is over. The troops to either side of me had the same problem with the heat and the cold. The two at the foot of the casket had the opposite problem. Not an easy watch with all the emotions displayed by the people passing the casket, paying their last respects. No politics...just Americans.

In our rest area, I first do my shine routine. I pass on the food but take advantage of the head to splash cold water on my face. I sit down and let my mind wander.

I wonder if Gabrielle is watching this on TV. Hell it's Sunday. What else does she have to do but watch this, and look for me. Damn sure hope that's the case. I'll have to ask her if I looked as bad as I felt. Probably not, the ol' Stoneface never changes. I can't wait to see her when this is over. We're going to visit her parents over Thanksgiving. That'll be big. Talk about inspections. The IG will be nothin' compared to what's coming. What her dad might ask.

I hear something. A voice. How the hell did that get in my dream? "What? Huh?"

"Excuse me, I'm a reporter. Merriman. Freelancer. Do you have a few moments to speak to me, answer a few questions?"

"What?

"Lieutenant. Are you okay?"

"Who the dev---Oh, yeah. I was lost in my thoughts."

"About the President?"

"Yeah, yeah. That was it. What do you want to know? What do you need? I don't have much time...have to get dressed and go back out shortly."

"Let's start with your name, rank, and where you're from."

"My name is Lieutenant." I pause and watch the bespectacled Merriman react. He gets a puzzled look on his face. Then he frowns. He probably wished he had picked someone else. He starts to say something. I cut him off, "Hey, lighten up. It's a joke. It's a Marine

Corps thing. I'm First Lieutenant Barney Quinn. My given name is Bernarr Leslie Quinn...after my dad and I'm from--"...

Merriman smiles, relaxes and the interview goes on. Another reporter joins us, then another, and yet another. The questions are easy except for those asking about my feelings. The rest are basically bio stuff. Finally, I say, "Fellas, I've got to get ready and go on again. In addition, I need time to check my troops, collect my thoughts. See ya later."

I walk away, head toward my deathwatch troops. They're stirring, getting ready to go again. Good team...a Doggie, an Anchor-Clanker, Wing-Wiper and a Hooligan's Navy shallow water Dixie Cup... but lookin' sharp.

"Hey, guys. Let's go give the world another look at the deathwatch's finest team."

A chorus of "yes, sirs", accompanied with groans, then smiles follow.

I add, "Get ready, and no lipstick this time."

CHAPTER 31

The U.S. Capitol
Rotunda
1700 hours
Sun, 24 Nov 1963
LATE AFTERNOON AND STILL CROWDED. The numbers are
overwhelming. They keep streaming through the doors. I did talk to
Captain Graven about the stanchions and, by God, he got them moved
back. Can still see, or sense the movement, but it isn't as distracting.
The flashbulbs are still popping, but at least a few feet further away. The
emotions are somber with many people in quiet tears, and some openly
sobbing and muttering. The dignitaries come and go as well. They come
from off to my left front. Capitol police part the line; an MDW control
officer leads them to a spot off the foot of the casket for them to pay their
respects. They stand, heads bowed for the most part, and are there for a
politically correct amount of time.

*I wonder what their true thoughts are? Can't read the faces...only
can catch them in my peripheral vision.*

I settle in and fix my point of vision on the top of the front doors
of the Capitol, over the heads of the folks entering. Most people pop
their cameras at the foot of the casket, so by looking at the door, the flash
doesn't bother me as much. I just stare out into space and try not to hear
or see what is happening around me. Do my long division if necessary.
Be alone, in a crowd.

The emotions of the crowd are riveting. The rotunda hushed except for sobs, the quiet click of cameras and pop of flash bulbs, the shuffling of feet, the whispered voices. Sniffles and sobs seep through everything. Subdued or not, you'd think it would be noisy, but it's not. It's as if an invisible comforter is cast over the scene, muffling the sounds. The hum under this blanket allows me to drift off in a trance-like state. Good for daydreaming...and I do...

* * *

Sometimes this Post of the Corps is crazy. A dichotomy of actions. For example, the new guy, Paquette, fainted at a ceremony this summer at Leutze Park for some high-ranking naval dignitary. The park is adjacent to Building 58 in the Navy Yard. Tiny crowds. Just a bunch of naval officers and a few civilian bigwigs. Occasionally the SecNav. It was a typical joint Marine-Navy troop formation. Two platoons each. I with my Drill Team, Paquette with his platoon. It was hot and humid but no worse than many ceremonies in the summer months of '63 here in D.C. Not before thousands, not even two dozen. No big deal, but of course, it's a ceremony, and that's our business, let alone our pride. We don't want to embarrass ourselves in front of anyone, much less a bunch of Dixie cups.

So what does Paquette do? Blip, blop, flop. He faints. Goes to the ground in a heap of blue white dress. Lucky he didn't impale himself on his sword. The supernumeraries come out and ceremonially remove him. It's hard to look good under those circumstances...well, the super's do; he doesn't. Embarrassing. Can almost hear the anchor clankers snickering. Wish I could go over and pick him up by the scruff of his neck, stand him on his feet, and tell him to tough it out. Too late, he's counted out.

Afterwards, a big investigation. Always the inquiry follows whether it's something like this, or a ragged firing party volley at Arlington or a screw up on the parade deck. Questions about what he ate; did the night before, did this morning, and on and on and on. Maybe his cover was too tight...try it on and let's see. Or did he lock his knees and go tight, hence no circulation. The fact is, it doesn't matter...it happened. If you're feelin' poorly for whatever reason, you have to "Suck-it-Up!" "Tough it out." Every one of us here has had a bad moment at a ceremony or two. Just have to stand as straight as a steel door and make up your mind to stay on your feet. Then your mind and will power become as firm as the door.

By the time it is all over, Paquette probably wishes he had fallen on his sword. It didn't work out too well for him. The "To err and so forth" routine was in effect. He was transferred from Guard Company and from The Barracks shortly thereafter. Just another guy that vanished along with Light Horse, our former XO and of course Lieutenant Goen, the pre-med orator that Donnelly exiled. Paquette's replacement is First Lieutenant Jim Splittier. A few or more inches shorter than me, quiet, calm, an outdoorsman...a hunter. He's not a natural glider, but is serious about being ceremonial. Some are natural and some are workers. He's a worker type. He's married but with boomer tendencies. I like him instantly so I'll warn him about the Rattlesnake drink.

Therefore, in CGC we now have the West Pointer, Dan Rader; worker-bee Splittier; the quiet spoken ex-enlisted guy, Bob Reese, and me as Platoon Commanders. Good crew. Two pure homebodies, one half-and-half, and one boomer. All *Jack Armstrong types* for the stoic Captain Kemp to lead.

* * *

The contrast here is extraordinary. Just two nights after the Paquette passing, Captains McKay, Milsap, and Kruger, along with Chink and I go uptown for a few drinks, and maybe a White Tower burger on the way back. The House Muv is driving, and is speeding. Probably thinks he's in Palookaville, North Carolina or maybe even Oxford, his home. We're headed for Basins, our watering hole on 14th and Pennsylvania. Kruger, Chink and I are in the back. Milsap up front riding as the AIO...Airborne Intercept Operator. JG Milsap says, "Marsh, you better slow down. Goin' to get a ticket, or worse, kill us."

The Muv mumbles something indistinguishable.

Kruger turns, looks out the rear window, turns back and says, "JG, you screwed up. Missed a blip. There's a police car behind us with its lights flashing. He's got a target lock. We're toast."

Milsap says, "Might want to put it down, Muv. He's got ya."

Muv mumbles again, louder, more shrill, but still not understandable by humans. Maybe dogs can.

McKay slows, pulls over, bounces on and off a curb, and stops. Not a stellar demonstration of driving, more like a carrier landing in a heavy sea. The police officer arrives at the door. Muv has the window down already. The officer says, "Nice stop. Lemme' see your license."

While trying to get his license out, the House Mother fumbles around, drops his wallet. Cards spill out between his seat and the door. He finally locates his license which has fallen between his legs. He mumbles some explanation, which is mostly about why he is fumbling around in his crotch area. The police officer is either unimpressed or perplexed. The officer looks at the license after Muv hands it to him. He leans down, peers in at the rest of us, says to McKay, "Flyin' a little low, aren't ya?"

Muv mutters a refined and polite Yazza, sir which comes out as, "Yes, sir, officer."

"Hmmm, a Marine. Officer, huh? Wonderful! You all officers?"

We chorus a "Yes, sir." Always say sir when in doubt or in trouble...except to ladies, most of them would be insulted.

"Gonna give you guys a break. Slow it down. Don't make me call The Barracks."

The Muv gives his Carolinian version of "yes, sir" that comes out as, "Yazza, sir." He continues a muttering monologue with a bit of a shrill sound trying to explain something or other. The officer says, "Okay, okay. Why don't you stop while you're ahead." Muv stops, the cop turns and walks back to his car. We burst into laughter, and poke fun at Marsh.

Kruger says, "Muv, you need an interpreter up here in the North."

He growls or snarls something that sounds like, "I've got your interpreter."

The police car drives off. The Muv is angry, and while pulling away bumps and clangs over the curb. The car hits bottom, but we continue on our way. We're all still bustin' our gut as Muv delivers a monologue, which I think is on the subject of mocking and ridiculing friends. Can't really tell. The pitch is very high. Maybe we should get Chesty as the interpreter.

We arrive and the Muv decides to use the parking garage next to the National Theater. We get out and while doing so Captain JG says to the Muv, "Marsh, I think you probably did some damage to the underside of your car."

We're all out on the sidewalk. The theater must have just let out because there is a large crowd spilling onto the walk...Waiting for cabs; strolling toward the garage; standing and chatting. A fastidious bunch, almost all in evening attire. The House Mother opens his door, and with one hand on the steering wheel leans over to inspect for possible undercarriage damage to the car. His right hand slips from the wheel, and he tumbles out on the top of his head, then crumples the rest of the way to the pavement. In a way, he looks like a pile of dirty clothes. People stare, giggle, and shake their heads, reacting in different ways but all with some degree of repugnance.

We're laughing aloud. Can't stop. This is better than Bullwinkle or Wylie Coyote cartoons. The garage attendant is aghast; then a smirk appears, followed by a wide grin, and then laughter. The Muv recovers well, and that's worth style points. From his crumpled position on the pavement, with feet still in the car, he hands his keys to the attendant and says, "Park it, and be careful with it. No dings." He gets a "Yeah, right" response, then scrambles out and to his feet, brushes off his shirt and trousers, glares at us, walks past the four of us, and goes into Basins.

God, I luv him. He's one of the best Parade Adjutants on the deck, one of the best Course Writers at the Tute, and a disaster waiting to happen on liberty.

No one saw us, or at least no one who counted. The liberty uptown went on without further incident, even at the White Tower on the way back, and that's notable. The White Tower and its ketchup bottles induce "boomer" incidents. Our arrival back at Center House goes unnoticed. Life goes on without Paquette, who unlike Muv, did his flopping during a ceremony.

* * *

Capital Rotunda
Huge emotional crowds
1730 hours
Sun, 24 Nov 1963

I see the next crew coming into the rotunda. I stood the watch at attention again. Never changed positions. I do notice that the metal cleats and toe taps feel like farrier's nails driving up through my shoe leather into my hooves. This marble floor is hard. I mean there is hard, and then there is friggin' hard. This is friggin'.

241

We're off and back in our rest area. It is still packed with press people who are muscling in on our chow spread.

Got one more watch to go today...rather, tonight.

I have the last watch before the night crew comes on at 2000. Other than that first watch, it hasn't been too bad of a day as long as I can drift off quickly...the place is snug with emotions. And those damn TV lights...hot!

"What?" It's a reporter.

"I'm Marshall. I'm with..."

I straighten and smile. "What can I do for you?"

Need to think of something interesting or insightful. Maybe I'll create a character. Naw, I'm right for the part and I luv the spotlight.

CHAPTER 32

The Capitol
Between watches
1750 hours
Sun, 24 Nov 1963

AFTER GOING THROUGH MY SHINE routine, which includes all my brass and my shoes this time, I grab a sandwich from the spread. It's been picked over. The press people who are here hustling stories have helped themselves.

Gad, they're pushy folks, and messy based on the looks of the table. Not all, just the buck-a-day journalist types.

Them being here remind me of two fun experiences.

* * *

Just before the '63 parade season got underway, The Barracks arranged a publicity spot on one of the local TV stations. Captain Milsap was in charge and responsible for coordinating our participation. The day came and he had me, the D&B Drum Major, The Marine Corps Band Drum Major, my Drill Team rifle inspector, and Chesty all suited up in our ceremonial finery. He was present, working with the gal doing the interview, live. I thought we all did just fine. From the look on J.G.'s face, he seemed not to share that opinion. Milsap was fretting worse than a virgin's mother on a late night.

However, regardless, the ending was priceless. The handler brought in the uniformed Chesty and put him up on a table so the TV cameras could zoom in on him. He was facing the camera, as well as

JG, myself, and the woman doing the broadcast. The hostess, with her perfect TV smile, looks into the camera while introducing Chesty, and ends with, "And that folks is the face only a mother could love."

At that precise moment, Chesty turns around and gives the cameraman a bow-legged, short-tailed, wonderful rear-end shot... balls and all as they say. I started snickering aloud; John was beet red, started to stammer something then began laughing. The startled hostess blushed, then gasped, "And that's our show for today."

I don't know if the cameraman switched shots or did a fade out. Made no difference, Chesty had done it again, however, the woman had those two priceless lines.

The other experience was with NBC. They filmed a show this same parade season of '63; I think it was called Red, White and Blue for Project Twenty.. Big patriotic to-do for the Fourth of July period. They filmed us at the Iwo site, doing the parade. A lot of sequences in an all day filming. They dubbed my voice in for commands, plus did a lot of shots of the drill. It went well. Later, the Associate Producer, Robert Garthwaite, of NBC sent me a letter saying among other things, "NBC and Project Twenty now has recorded for all time the golden voice and the chiseled profile of the great Stoneface." I ate that up. Wore dark shades to the Center House bar that night. A star was born...if only in my mind. And of course the Barney Quinn Fan Club with T-shirts was added by the Center House group.

* * *

Capitol
Corner-Hearing Room
Hiding from the press
Sun, 24 Nov 1963

I sit in a far corner and eat. Seeking and getting some solitude. Only have one more watch to go today. I finish my sandwich and coffee, get up, stretch and settle back down, alone with my thoughts. Again, I think of my time, ceremonies with the President. My mind drifts back to...lets see, late August '63, I think...

* * *

I'm at another arrival ceremony. This one is for Halle Selassie, the Emperor of Ethiopia, and is being conducted at D.C.'s Union

244

Station. The only one we've done here. Probably because Selassie was in New York City first and maybe likes trains. Anyway, that was his mode of travel. There is a big crowd on hand. Many are here to see the arrival, like so many others. Some other folks are here to catch trains, and just hangout to catch a show while waiting. However, most are here because the press has played up the fact that Jackie is going to make an appearance. This will be her first since the premature birth of their son, Patrick, who was born on the seventh, and died just two days later. She's been recuperating and understandably grieving.

In my mind, the station is ideal for our type of ceremony. It's enclosed; the decks are all marble, cement, or asphalt so we can make what I call ceremonial music, the CLACK of heels and CRASH of rifle butts. Prior to this I've had some problems at MDW ceremonies with Army officers not in a "known to me" position of authority issuing orders to move here, move there, shift five paces to the right and so forth. Mickey Mouse type stuff...a nobody trying to be somebody. I complained to Milsap. He talked with folks at MDW. Later I was told to take orders from the commander of troops or the site control officer, and no one else.

Today we're in formation on a platform that runs perpendicular at the end of all the tracks. A large crowd is behind us on the other side of a tall, wrought iron fence that separates the concourse area from the tracks. We, the troops, are standing at ease, motionless, waiting. There is a delay. The commander calls us to attention, and then puts the formation at rest. Says, "Rest easy, relax, talk, and light the smoking lamp."

The other service platoon commanders do just that, and their troops begin chatting, shifting weight, turning, and many smoke. I face about, command, "Ceremonial, AT EASE." The command means that we will stand in that position, not move, not talk, and for damn sure not smoke. We're in the public eye here, and a large crowd at that. I face about, assume the same position as the troops, and remain motionless.

Soon, in minutes, I hear a rustling in the crowd and murmuring voices. I hear people in the crowd saying, "Look at the Marines. They're not moving." "Hey, look at those guys. The Marines." I hear several more comments that are similar. I know my troops in the Drill Team hear them and are not thinking about being pissed at me for not doing the same as others, but are getting prouder by the second. Standing taller, and probably with a glint in their eyes. I know I am.

After more than several minutes, an Army Captain comes to me. Stands in front of me and says, "Lieutenant, you are at rest. You and your troops can relax, talk, and smoke if you like."

In respect to his rank, I come to attention, leather heels cracking together and the sound reverberating as if in a deep cave. I snap my sword to the Carry, flashing it just past his head and popping it against the seam of my blue blouse at the shoulder. Thwack! "Sir, the lieutenant and his unit are at rest and we are not going to move, talk, or smoke. We are in the public eye. As far as I'm concerned, sir, the ceremony isn't over until I get on the bus to go back. So I ain't friggin movin', Captain. Get away from me. Thank you, sir."

He staggers slightly backward a step, a shocked look on his face. Stares at me for a second, apparently in disbelief. His face the color of a stop light. I return my sword to the order in true barracks style...letting gravity plummet the sword so it falls gracefully to the order position. When it drops to the bottom, I grip it hard so it rattles to a halt. Then I slam back to ceremonial at ease. The crowd stirs even more. All have seen, and some have heard the confrontation. The troops, who have heard the conversation, stand even taller, and I'm sure with slight smirks on their faces.

The Captain hustles off to my right front with his dress boat cloak flowing out behind him. He stops, within earshot of me, in front of an Army Major, a site control person I suppose. He tells him what happened, pointing to me. I hear the Major say, "Oh, the Marine. Oh, yeah, I forgot to tell you. He's supposed to do that. Leave him alone, he doesn't make mistakes, and he bites." The Captain departs hurriedly, face aglow and his boat cloak again streaming behind him. Why he would wear that thing in August is beyond me.

Anyway, I've seen scolded dogs leave with more pride. The troops grew another inch. The legend grew immeasurably. Slowly, each of the other platoons sense what is happening. They put out their cigarettes; become quiet; and get into a more ceremonial posture. The crowd sees all this.

Tell me. For the young men watching, what outfit do they want to join?

246

We all are called to attention. The ceremony is about to start. The train is in and Halle Selassie arrives. The Presidential entourage is here, and the crowd lets you know that Jackie is present. She enters to applause. I'm astounded. She lights this ol' railroad station up like it has its own huge halo. She is beaming, tanned, vivacious, and gracious. She is wearing a bright, sunshine yellow summery light jacket and skirt with a white blouse beneath the jacket. In addition, she is wearing what I believe is a trademark and trend-setting matching pillbox hat. The dark, dreary platform area of the station is aglow with her radiance.

The arrival ceremony starts; honors are rendered to Halle Selassie; and he and President Kennedy troop the line as normal. Once again, the President recognizes me. This time with only a smile of recognition and a wink, no double take.

He's probably thinking, this guy won't go away. He's right. I'm not, at least for a while.

The ceremony ends and we stand at attention, motionless, waiting. The dignitary, his party, the President, First Lady, and their party all leave. We stand and wait for the station to clear before marching off to our buses parked outside. The crowd, which has grown steadily since our arrival, also waits.

When the President and dignitaries are well clear, the troops commander orders, "Platoon Commanders take charge. Return to your transportation. Dismissed." The crowd is still waiting and watching. For them this is all part of the show.

These folks want to see what we, the Marines, will do. I feel it my bones...just know it. It's all based on the earlier incident. This is goin' to be a killer of a day.

We normally leave in reverse order, junior service first. So, as customary, I allow the Coast Guard...Hooligans Navy to depart first. The wing wipers, then the Dixie cups follow them. I wait, feign speaking to my troops until the Army lieutenant grows impatient, and he departs going around me and giving me a disgusted look. I smile. I have what I want...the stage to myself.

The other services left looking okay, perhaps good. They receive mild applause.

The crowd is waiting...wanting us to do something different. Expecting it. Maybe they just know a ham when they see one. Okay folks, we're gonna knock your socks off.

I move a few paces closer to the platoon. I less-than-whisper, "We're goin' off in style. Listen up. When we get moving, we're goin' to start with a long pendulum manual, then we'll do a marching manual, then a caustic manual. Next, I'll order a delayed cadence count, and then we'll finish out with another marching manual. Don't forget, we'll board in a column from the right, at Carry Arms. If you've got it, click your eyeballs."

"Click," followed with a proud smirk. They sense the same thing I do.

I call them to attention, face 'em to the right, give them Forward, MARCH, and from this they go immediately into the long pendulum manual. The remainder I command as we go. We're off; rifle butts crashing on the hard station deck; hands cracking the rifles as they move from one position to the next; rifles thwacking into the shoulder when moved there; and chrome bayonets flashing in the overhead lights as the rifles move and spin. I must admit, this is orgasmic. I see the Army lieutenant looking back in shock. Underlying all of this, our metal-cleated heels click out our marching cadence.

We are gliding and sliding, ten feet tall. The crowd gobbles it up.

I'm right. They love it...MDW won't, but these folks are drinkin' it in.

Some people cheer; all applaud. And somewhere from the back of the crowd come several "Oouh-Rahs." Better yet, some young boy, no more than nine or ten, is running after us with his mother chasing and screaming, "Randy. Randy. You come back here." He did, thank God. However, I bet he joins the Corps when he's seventeen. The applause is overwhelming, and ripples along with us as we pass through and out of the building.

We get to our bus, and as normal for us, we load at the Carry Arms position, and marching. Like the fat lady at the opera, the ceremony ain't over until we're on board and the door closed, or she sings.

One helluva day. I am guessing that Captain Milsap will get a call from the site control officer about my conduct. I put it all down on my after ceremony-reporting chit. I tell our new company commander, Major Hank Cronin, and our company XO, Cap'n Kemp about the incident, and my departure. They shake their heads, smile with that will-he-ever-change look.

I'll be told by the new barracks Ops officer, our former CO, Major Bill Kendell to tame it down, with a tongue in cheek tone. He still jerks my chain about the Drill Team guys tipping over all those cannons in Leutze Park. Maybe it was Tallick, Griffin and McCloskey, or more likely, Van Weel and Powers.

Captain Milsap and I laugh over a drink that night. The fact is it had more value than all the recruiting brochures ever published, including *I Want You.*

Geez, I love this place and I love the Corps...and the Drill Team Snuffies...and Magpies.

And straight men with boat cloaks.

CHAPTER 33

The Capitol Building
Hearing Room
1915 hours
Sun, 24 Nov 1963
"Ready to go, Lieutenant? What are you smiling about?" It's Captain Graven, the site control officer.

"Yes, sir. Just getting' on my feet. Twenty-hundred watch. Last one of the night for the day crew."

"Yes. Nevertheless, what were you smiling about? A pleasant daydream again?"

"That it was, sir. However, it's up and at 'em time now and I'm at the top of my game, Captain."

I get up, slip on my unnie and accoutrements. Check my detail, and we move out of the room to form up in the passageway. I remind my watch team of the marble deck and tell them we are going to remain at attention for the entire watch. I smile at the groans, "Toughen up guys. We're the best out here and we're goin' to prove it again."

That gets smiles. I call them to attention and we're off.

Hmmm, a crowd in the roped-off area but I don't recognize anyone as a dignitary. Probably too late in the day for them.

We continue along and enter the rotunda.

Damn sure not too late for the general public. Jesus, must be thousands and thousands of people outside. They'll be here all night.

The rotunda is jammed with its two lines, five or so abreast, somberly shuffling past the flag-draped casket. We move gingerly but lookin' tuff, clack----clack----clack across the marble floor and into position. The TV lights snap on as we approach. It doesn't take but seconds for the place to heat up, as I would imagine a Broadway stage does.

We settle in position. The crowd's attitude hasn't changed in its solemn procession past the President. Sobs, sniffles, crying, murmuring, whispering, and the click-pop-flash of cameras. The contrast between the TV lights and the cold air is even greater now that it's nighttime...ice cubes and heating pads.

Tonight I don't fix my stare over the entrance doors but instead stare straight ahead at the people as they enter and struggle with their emotions at the foot of the casket, then somberly pass. All manner of dress; all manner of people. I allow my sense of hearing to work its magic with the sobs, murmurs and the shuffling of the feet. My sense of smell takes in the rich autumn air swishing through the doors, mixed with the musky scent of people, the flower wreath at the foot of the casket and heat of the TV lamps searing the other two. I fight off and will away my poignant feelings by mentally flicking away these fireflies of emotion.

The time is up so fast that I feel as if I've only been here seconds. I see the next watch coming on duty. The night team, headed by Staff NCO's with non-rated sentries. I see one of my Lance Corporals in the unit, looking tall and tuff.

Well, it's just about over for tonight, Mr. President. I'm going to leave you in able hands. See you in the morning. Good night, sir.

* * *

Center House
Marine Barracks
2200 hours
Sun, 24 Nov 1963

I'm back in Center House and have eaten some much-needed hot chow. Before I left Building 58, I got my uniform, brass and shoes ready for tomorrow, Monday, which has been declared a National Day of Mourning.

I call Gabrielle. Her girlish squeal tells me she is excited to hear my voice. She quickly lets me know she has seen me on TV, her parents and all her friends have seen me at her insistence. She adds, "They're eager to meet you. What time do you think we can be there on Thanksgiving?" Her parents live a little north of Philly.

"Let's leave early, say, six in the mornin'. We can stop and get breakfast on the way, and still be there easily by late morning. How's that?"

"Wonderful. Are you coming over the night before?"

"Yep."

"Better than wonderful. You might not be able to leave at six." She says this with a seductive giggle.

"That sounds ominous, or challenging...and fun. If I can't, you can drive."

"Are we taking the Vette?"

"Sure. Goin' to take your Dad for a ride and scare the B-Jesus out of him."

She laughs then rambles on about how great I looked on TV ending with, "The real Stoneface, even more so than the parades. Kind of sexy in a way."

"Really. How so?"

"Well, just think, I've been in the sack with a TV star."

"Geez, you're somethum' else."

Nonetheless, my not-so-humble shoulders gladly accept the praise. We chat seriously for a while about the tragedy of this whole event. She asks, "How can this happen in our country, Barney?"

"I don't know, honey. It might be something more than some nut runnin' loose. Time will tell, and shortly I hope."

"Do you mean someone or whatever planned this?"

"I don't know, we'll see. Listen, I've gotta go, luv. Have missed you. See ya Wednesday evening."

"Okay. Bye. Love you...and, Barney--"

"What?"

"Think of me while on watch instead of doing math problems. Guaranteed to be more fun."

"Sure it would be, but the thoughts might put me in a non-ceremonial posture."

"You're terrible. Is that all you can think about?"

"When I think of you, yeah."

"Good...me too."

* * *

All of the house residents are in the bar. Like me, all are having a nightcap before heading topside for some Zs. Monday will be a long day for all of us...as it will be for the country, but nothing like it will be for Jackie, the kids, and the family.

* * *

The Barracks
Washington, D.C
Early again
Mon, 25 Nov 1963.

My routine this clear, crisp autumn morning is the same as yesterday. Up early, grab some rib stickin' chow, go to Building 58 and dress. My deathwatch detail and I leave for the Capitol, again in the van. The driver is Atherton. "Atherton, are you just our driver or are you a spy for Captain Milsap?"

"Yes, sir. I mean, no, sir. Captain Milsap just told Motor T he wanted the same drivers assigned to the same details as much as possible."

"Okay. Just checking. You look like a spy."

"How's that, sir?"

"Must be those slits you have for eyes this morning."

"I'm tired, sir."

"That must be it. Okay, get us there on time...alive."

"Will do, sir."

"Which one, Atherton?"

"Both, sir."

Damn, can't seem to get in the last word anymore. Was gettin' to be good at that. Shoot, Gabby got the last word also. Hell, she always does.

Today we need a police escort to get there and around all the crowd control barricades along the streets and at the Capitol.

My first, and as it turns out only, watch will be the 0830 one. The President will be taken out of the rotunda around 1100, put on the caisson and taken to St. Matthew's Cathedral for services. The Army lieutenant will bear the brunt of the longer than normal watch again this time since he will be on watch when they begin to move the President.

The first watch hasn't gone on yet so I have plenty of time. I get a cup of coffee, sit, relax and think about what the after-effects of all this will be. Not the country, just as it relates to us here...

With President Kennedy and Jackie there was a lot of activity. More like a reign than a term. They went to Camp David often. Then, all those arrival, wreath laying, and departure ceremonies for visiting heads of state...and all those State Department functions and the White House dinners, and of course, the parade at The Barracks for him.

Then there was the night of the White House parade when we took the show on the road, to the South Lawn. What a day and night that was. I was draggin' by the time it was over. It was...

* * *

Another busy, busy week. End of August '63, hot as usual. Today, the Drill Team and I have the arrival ceremony for yet another foreign dignitary at the White House. I'm doing so many of these I lose track of who's in town. Later, in early afternoon we stand the Wreath Laying Ceremony at the Tomb as part of the visit. The day is long from over. I still have the White House cordon to do and the biggie. We're going to do our Friday night parade, or some version of it, on the South Lawn for the President and his guests sitting up in the balcony. Like Buckingham Palace, or Camelot, I suppose. The adrenaline levels throughout The Barracks are high. The Barrack's err and forgive policy is prevalent.

After the Wreath Laying, the Drill Team and I rehearse all the versions of the silent drill routine. By the time we finish, it's chow time. After we eat, we get dressed in our blue white uniforms and leave to do the cordon at the White House for the formal dinner given for this foreign head of state. No slack today. Beside the ceremonies and the practices, we max out shine time. My index finger is actually sore from all the spit shining today and I probably smell like Kiwi shoe polish and Brasso.

After we do the cordon, I take the drill team across the street and rehearse the drill one more time, in the pitch darkness of the Ellipse area. We get to the South Lawn and join the rest of The Barracks parade formation. We have several minutes to relax, if you can call it such. My company commander, Major Hank Cronin, comes up to me and says, "Well, how are you and the drill team doing?" Captain Kemp is with him and although he looks worried, it is less so than the telltale frown the good Major is wearing. Kemp also was at the cordon as usual.

"Tired, but ready. What version of the drill are we doing?"

"Don't know yet."

"Well, for Pete's sake, sir, it would be nice to know more than a few seconds before we start. We need a little think time."

"I know. I know. Not only tired, but testy, huh?"

"Sorry, Major. Long day and it ain't over." *I need to take it easy. He's a good guy, easy goin'. Besides, we're golf buddies.*

As I finish, Colonel Weaver, The Barracks CO, my resident mentor, strides briskly up to us.

If looks mean anything, I'm guessing he is about to meddle some more and not with my career. At least not directly.

"Good evening, Hank. Lieutenant Quinn. Are you and the drill team all set, Mister Quinn?"

Mister Quinn, huh. All business tonight.

"Yes, sir. Do we know which version yet, sir?"

"Yes. The middle one. Any problems?"

"No, sir. Middle one it will be, sir."

"Will it be perfect, Mister Quinn? No mistakes?"

"We'll try, as always, sir. That's always our goal."

The colonel squints his eyes, leans forward just a tad and says, "I want a perfect drill. No mistakes. None. I want a guarantee that it will be flawless. Your word."

"Guarantee, sir?"

"Yes, your personal assurance that it will be just that. Otherwise, I will delete it from the parade tonight."

"Yes, sir. It will be perfect. The colonel has my word, sir."

"All right. I'll hold you to that."

He leaves without another word other than, "Hank," and Major Cronin scampers along after the CO. Captain Kemp shakes his head, shrugs, and says. "Remember Lieutenant, to err is unforgivable; to forgive is unthinkable; to guarantee is stupid. Think about it, Barney. Have a nice evening." He winks, smiles, and walks back to his position in front of Guard Company.

I look at my troops who have heard this conversation. They're wide-eyed and waiting. I shrug my shoulders and say, "You heard the man. Flawless. So let's make it so. No sweat. Middle version." I get a nod of heads and eyeball clicks. The kind that tell me, right on. Perfect it will be.

I love these guys. Tough, hard working and reliable... even if they're a little touch and go on liberty.

The parade goes well. The D&B sounds and looks as good as ever. No change here. Our drill is sharp and flawless. At the end, to everyone's surprise there is a huge fireworks display put on by Zambelli. They do all the biggies in this area. It must be a surprise because shortly after it starts, the air is filled with wailing police and fire sirens racing toward the White House. Probably more excitement at 1600 Pennsylvania Avenue than they've had in years. Someone is going to have some explaining to do. I suspect not the President.

When I get back to Center House, I'm exhausted. Have been on the go the entire day. Four ceremonies and several rehearsals...and a retired Marine officer's funeral detail at Arlington tomorrow sandwiched in between the Iwo rehearsal and parade in the evening.

Whoever said that we used to have wooden ships and iron men, but today we have iron ships and wooden men, doesn't know a base plate from a paper plate. These guys at The Barracks are just as tough as anyone that sailed on the two-and three-masters.

* * *

U.S.Capitol
Hearing Room
0750 hours
Sun, 25 Nov 1963

"Lieutenant Quinn. LIEUTENANT."

"Sir. SIR." It's Captain Graven hovering over me.

"You look like you were gone again? My God, you just got here. Just want to let you know that you'll have just one detail this morning. They're going to move the President just before 1100. The first watch is going on in several minutes."

"Aye aye, sir. We'll be ready. Thanks, Cap'n."

He's lookin' worse today...this guy needs a break.

The cortege will go from here to St. Matthews, then all the way to Arlington. Long haul for the massive troop formation in the cortege, particularly at the dirge step. All the services and the academies will be

256

represented. Also two foreign military units; pipers from the Scottish Black Watch; and twenty-four Irish Cadets at gravesite. Then there will be the cordons of military and police all along the route of march. Helluva procession.

Up front with the caisson will be Jackie and the family, followed by two hundred and twenty foreign dignitaries, nineteen heads of state, and royal families from ninety-two countries. Even the Russians sent some Deputy Premier.

Nikita didn't make it; I suppose he's still uptight about the missile showdown.

* * *

I'm dressed and ready. It's already 0810. Just before I'm about to leave the committee room, a civilian in a not-so-spiffy business suit approaches me.

He's not press. Wonder what this clown wants. Who the hell is he anyway? He's not supposed to be in here.

He fronts me and says, "Will you please put this rose on the casket for me when you go up there?" He's pushing a single long stem red rose toward me.

"What?" I push the rose aside.

"Please, put the rose on the casket for me."

"Who the hell are you anyway?"

"Doesn't matter, just please do this for me?"

"The hell it doesn't matter, pal. Not just no I won't, but hell no. I don't have time to fool with this, or you. Go see that guy over there," as I point to Captain Graven, then shout, "Hey, Captain Graven, this guy needs to see you, and you better check him out...I think he's nuts."

I give the man a shove in that direction, then another as I push past him, and get my troops set. It's time to go on. As we leave I see Graven leading the man away toward a Secret Service agent and a Capitol policeman.

That jerk's day is goin' to get complicated real quick.

We pass the roped off area and it is packed with people again. We slide and glide into the rotunda to find it jammed again with viewers. They're going to cut this off around 0900. Graven had said that there were 10,000 or more people outside waiting to get in and see the President...I believe him.

We slide into position and affect the changeover flawlessly. It's all robot-like now. I settle in at the position of attention. I've told my guys we're going to do our last thirty minutes standin' like steel doors. Mannequin time.

Everything is the same. People shuffling by both sides of the flag draped casket. Flashbulbs popping every second. Cold air on the forehead; TV lights searing the back. The murmurs, mutterings, sobs, and tears of the folks shuffling by...the nation saying good-bye. Says something about the people of this country. They care.

Of all the ceremonies I've stood with the Drill Team, this could be my last. I'm on the Captain's promotion list and should be picking up my railroad tracks in a week or so. Chink and I at the same time. For me no more traveling with the Drill Team to half-time shows, state fairs, Fort Henry, Canada, and all those neat places and ceremonies.

I see the next detail entering the rotunda.

Man, the time flew by.

About another minute and they will be here and alongside.

Mr. President. I'm leavin' in a few seconds. Not prepared for this. All I can think of to say is, have a safer journey than you had. I'm sorry... or ashamed...or something. I'm goin' to miss the excitement of you being around. God Bless.

The Navy officer slides in next to me. He and I, and our details execute a smooth exchange. My detail and I face about and start our trek away from the casket and out of the rotunda. Clack...clack...clack.

I want to look back, but of course I can't. All I can do is my mannequin murmur...

By your leave, sir.

CHAPTER 34

Navy Yard
Building 58
At work
Wed, 26 Nov 1963

WEDNESDAY, 26 NOVEMBER, 1963 AND I'm at work at Building 58 in the Navy Yard. Not much happening. The funeral is over, however, the nation certainly hasn't settled. It will be stirred by speculation, investigations, inquiries and conspiratorial theories I'm sure. The country will go on, the pace will pick up each day and one day it will be business as usual. That seems to be the way of life, at least in our country.

I got plenty of sleep Monday and Tuesday nights. Feel completely rested now. I'll take a short leave over the Thanksgiving holiday that's on top of us. Need a break; so does the country. I'll be seeing Gabrielle tonight and we'll leave Thursday morning for her parent's home. They live north of Philadelphia, in Wyncote. A pretty suburb, parts wealthier than others but not wallowing in money. It's nestled between Glenside, Jenkintown and Elkins Park. Gracious homes of wood and stone, also some red brick, and mostly two story surrounded by sprawling yards spotted with huge elms, oaks, and firs.

Asphalt two-lane roads wind around the comfortable neighborhood, leading to schools and the small, local grocery markets, drugstores, shops, and the railroad station. Nothing but commuter trains these days. Hilly area, and all seem to slope or run toward the station. Once upon a time, the Reading Railroad's Crusader rumbled along these tracks headed to New York. It all smacks of mom and apple pie. Since Gabrielle's an only daughter, only child, I assume her dad will be asking some penetrating questions.

* * *

When I arrive at Gabrielle's late Wednesday afternoon, she throws her arms around me, smothering me with kisses as I step inside her apartment. I stagger a few steps forward as she pulls me along, reach behind me, pull the door shut with one arm, and drop my clothing bag with the other. I return her hankerings, trying to catch up with her lips and tongue as they search my mouth, neck, and ears. Finally, our lips meet and linger. She tastes like sweetened strawberries and her hair smells like pastures of fresh wildflowers in the morning sun. She takes my breath away like the summer heat in California's low desert.

She says, "I'm so happy to see you, I can't help myself; so anxious to hold you again. It seems like ages."

"Hell gal, it's only been a few days over a week."

"Seems longer."

She's wearing a long, flowing, sheer gown again. It clings to her seemingly swelling breasts and hardened nipples. It's so transparent it doesn't alter or hide her freckles, the color of her fair skin, or her thick amber hair.

I step back, caressingly holding her by the shoulders and say, "Jesus, you're beautiful."

She takes off my jacket. I mutter, "Seductive too." Her fingers dance down along the buttons on my flannel shirt and leave it in a heap with my coat. I kiss her and say, "Long-legged, sexy wench." And as she unbuckles my belt, unzips my trousers and lets them fall to the floor joining the heap around my ankles, I add, "And I might add, pectorally superior."

I help by shucking my loafers and then snatch her up, cradle her in my arms and our lips meet yet again, linger, tasting, enjoying each other as if a fine, mellow wine. I stroll and rock with her still draped in my arms, hers clasped around my neck, toward her bed.

She murmurs, "I love you, Barney. I love you...adore you."

"I love you, Gabby...love everything about you."

She lifts my chin away from her neck and says, "Pectorally superior...where do you come up with these...these phrases?"

"I had too much time to think lately. Sounded better, more sophisticated than huge tits." The bed is invitingly turned down.

"Breasts."

"That's what I said, and let me linger for a--"

"Here...take it, and me. And hurry, I'm so wet I'm--"

"Damn sure are, woman. Whoa, nice and easy."

* * *

I lay here, worn out like an old shoe.

This lady is out to set world records, or kill me. She's combustible... hotter and wetter than a Houston summer.

"Barney, you look pensive. What are you thinking about?"

"I'm wondering if I'm goin' to be alive in the morning."

"Come on, Barney, let's do a quad."

"Good God, you're horny."

"No, just sexually focused."

"You talk about me. Where do you come up with these one liners...Quad, sexually focused?"

"I use to skate and just like you, BQ, I had too much time to think."

I pull my arm from under her, manage to sit up and say, "How about we get cleaned up, dressed, and go to that little Italian place 'couple blocks over?"

"Only if you promise."

"Promise what?"

"You know damn well what. I want you some more."

"Now I fully understand what Admiral Nimitz meant."

"What?"

"He said, 'Uncommon valor was a common virtue.'"

A slow seductive smile spreads across her face. She mockingly bats her eyes, licks her lips and says, "Well, good for him." and runs her hand down my chest, walking her fingers along the way. Then leisurely to my abdomen, pausing here for a moment, then finishes her journey traveling only a tad further. "Barney, let's prove him right, at least about you."

"Good God, give me a break, woman. Let's get showered, dressed and have some pasta...I need it."

"So do I."

"Need what? Never mind. That's not what I mean."

"Okay then, let's do it." A sly smile creeps across her face as she slides off the bed.

Damn fine ass, too. Damn fine.

* * *

The shower feels wonderful, but I manage no rest. Her smile was indicative of her intentions for a quad. Once we start soaping each other with that strawberry smellin' gel we're off and goin' again. She's in what I think of as her NASA gravitational straddle position. The marble floor of the Capitol was nothing compared to this soapy tile and her gyrations. I hope LBJ makes it a full term because I don't think I can last through another deathwatch, unless it's my own.

We step from the shower. I hand her a towel, grab one for myself and shake my head.

"What's goin' through that mind of yours now, Bernarr Leslie?"

"I was just thinking. You have great legs, triple threat type."

"Is that a compliment...or a dare?"

"Yes it is. Both. They're made to order for sitting astride, straddling, and strapping on."

"Good, and my...what was it you said, pectorally superior---"

"They're All-American. Double threat. And I vote for me first, then motherhood. Let's go eat before...before...keep your hands off me, Monjeau. I need pasta...carbs...raw oysters. Maybe even a transfusion."

"Okay, but I'm goin' want a transfusion when we get home."

"I love threats and especially when you talk dirty."

She giggles and says, "Do oysters really work?"

"I don't know. Last time I had a half dozen, and only four worked."

"You're sick. You need to see somebody."

"You make me that way."

She smiles and says, "Who, me?"

"Yes, you. Who else?"

"Better not be anyone else."

Doggonnit, I can't get the last word with this woman...and I can't get enough of her.

* * *

We enjoy the food and ourselves at Rizzo's Ristorante Italiano... and I have oysters on the half-shell. Six. I eat four and give her two, and say, "Try these."

She says, "Maybe you should have all six, BQ."

"This is an experiment."

"No, the experiment will be at home."

She tries one loaded with sauce and squiggles up her nose and shakes her head, "Yuk. That's nasty." She pushes the plate back to me still making a face.

I eat the last one 'cause I'll need it.

We pass on dessert. It appears it's to come so we head to her apartment for the serving. It's a crisp and cool walk in the November air. Short, and all down hill, thank God. I need both the fresh air, and time.

As soon as we're inside, we shed our clothes, I open and pour a nice mellow merlot, and enjoy it and ourselves in front of her fireplace. I push the ottoman out of the way, she pulls some sofa pillows under her and we're off and runnin'. Gad, she tastes like that body wash, fresh strawberries and maybe some cream.

Breakfast at Wimbledon can't be this good.

* * *

Morning comes, and none too soon.

Damn, I'm alive. There was a time last night I didn't think I was goin' to make it.

We get up and take separate showers, thank God. Throw our stuff together and head for the Vette. She says, "I hurt a little this morning again."

"Hell, I'm havin' trouble just standing."

She giggles. We load up and ease out onto Columbia Pike. We'll get some breakfast on the way, certainly be at her home by noon at the latest.

We motor along, chatting about everything and nothing.

Where is all this is leading?

CHAPTER 35

Pennsylvania
On the road
In the Vette
Thanksgiving Day, 1963

ON OLD YORK ROAD, ABOUT five or so minutes out of Jenkintown where we'll turn and head down the hill to Wyncote, Gabrielle says, "What are you going to tell my dad?"

"That he raised a nymphomaniac."

"I'm serious."

"So am I. Easy...just kidding. Tell him what?"

"About us. He's going to want to know what your intentions are."

"Oh, oh, one of those type of fathers."

"Barney!"

"Okay, okay. I don't know what I'll say if he asks. I don't know myself. Don't know where my head is. Damn, honey, I've never had feelings for only one gal at a time. At least not for very long. Maybe a day or two, tops. That probably makes me some sort of bastard, and I guess I am, or was. You have me off my feed. You're the first one I've really cared about."

"Do you love me?"

"Yes, you know that. I've told you that I do, haven't I?"

"Yes, sort of."

"Well, not sort of. I do, and I'm not just saying that."

"Good, then just tell him that. You and I can continue this conversation later this weekend. You're sounding like a relationship-challenged person."

"There you go again."

"What?"

"One of your screwy phrases, like, sexually focused."

"Well."

"Well, what the hell does that mean?

"It means, afraid of commitment."

"Ahh...lets see. This is your street, isn't it? Greenwood."

"Yes. Some are saved by the bell, you by a street sign, huh?"

"I suspect only momentarily."

* * *

I pull up where she directs. The mailbox says Mosher. I point and say, "What's this about...Mosher?"

"My father changed the family name. Mosher is anglicized. I like my name much better."

"Okay. So do I. For the same reason I love Gabrielle."

"Love Gabrielle? Me or the name."

"Both."

The greeting at the door is all warmth, smiles and hugs for Gabrielle. I get a polite hug from her mom, also a fair-skinned redhead, and a friendly, firm handshake from her dad. The handshake is accompanied by a slight smile, more a squint, and a penetrating stare.

She's right. He's going to ask, and more than that one question.

As we enter, he looks back and takes in the Vette, frowns, then gives me a harder look. I respond and let him see the Stoneface stare first hand.

Good, we're even and maybe done playing hardass.

We all sit in the living room and chat. Her dad serves sherry. Not my taste, but I can survive with grace. After about ten minutes, Gabrielle and her mom get up and go somewhere, arm in arm, whispering. The kitchen I assume. Her dad, Henri, tells me he saw me on TV at the Capitol. He says that Gabby sent him some pictures of me in various other ceremonies. He asks about them, in particular about the Tomb.

I explain what happens at each, especially my favorite, the all-Marine wreath laying. The first ever.

Then he says, "The one I have the most interest in is the one at Fort Henry, Kingston, Ontario. I lived in Canada for a time, am French-Canadian as you know or guessed. I've visited the fort, but never saw any ceremony. Only saw a soldier guarding the entrance."

Since he lived in Canada, and has seen the fort, I don't bore him with the details of Fort Henry sitting on Lake Ontario, and guarding the entrance to the St. Lawrence River. Or that it sits on an island between Kingston, Ontario and the small town of Cape Vincent in upstate New York.

"You do know that all of the troops there are college students?" I pause for his answer, which will tell me where to start.

"No, I wasn't aware of that. Just that they wore old-fashioned uniforms."

"Yes. They work there, the largest number during the summer months. They're paid a monthly salary and a bonus if they grow a beard common to the time. The uniforms are British, 1867 vintage. They stand post at the entrance, a drawbridge over a now dry moat, and they perform changing of the guard ceremonies daily. Also, the entire unit performs their battle reenactment drill weekly."

Henri nods an understanding, so I continue. "I took the Silent Drill Team, Color Guard, and the Drum and Bugle Corps up there for a four-and-a-half hour ceremony. Tattoo it's called, fashioned after the same at Edinburgh Castle in Scotland. Hell, it was great. Makes anyone stand two feet taller."

"Tell me about it. We have a little time before dinner. Keep it as short as you can without leaving too much out. I want to take a ride in your Corvette before dinner."

"Okay, Henri. You've got a deal. They call the ceremony a Tattoo. I know you've seen the fort but I'm goin' to paint the picture again...so you feel it. The fort sits on a hill overlooking Lake Ontario and the St. Lawrence. It's a stone fort, granite I think, about two, three stories high...maybe sixty, seventy feet high including the ramparts. On the top, mostly facing the lake and river entrance they have Armstrong Cannons, sixteen-pounders...several cannonades, and a few huge, old mortars. All operable. Gettin' the picture?"

"Yep, I remember."

"Yeah, but can you see it?"

"Yes."

"Good, then you remember the floor of the fort, the parade field, is asphalt…was grass at one time. They have bleachers, maybe ten rows high around this entire inner rectangle. More seating around the archways or arcades on the second deck, and portions of the ramparts have bleachers as well. The place seats about fourteen thousand or so. A large, old, wooden drawbridge, made of huge oak timbers is at the entrance. It spans the dry moat.

"A single road winds its way to the fort from the bridge into Kingston. The Tattoo ceremony was done at night, under the lights, our last night there."

"Sounds beautiful, magnificent. How long were you and your men there?"

I gather my thoughts.

I've got to get this right so he can see the fort vividly, feel the awesome electricity in the air that night. I can feel it still.

"We were there for three days before the actual Tattoo. During that time, we participated in sharing the guard of the fort with their student soldiers. They had a sentry booth at the entrance, at the drawbridge, very much like the British at Buckingham Palace. Stoic position, the mannequin bit we emulated on the deathwatch…well, in fact at all ceremonies. The night show was stunning."

"Okay, get to that."

"Started at dark. The bleachers and other seating were packed. In fact, it was SRO…over fifteen thousand inside. The overflow was standing in the upper arcades and in between bleachers on the ramparts and below on the square. Five miles of cars stopped along the road coming up the hill. No more room. People just got out and stayed put. Another five or six thousand standing outside the fort, just watching troops form up, and listening to the music coming from inside. And the best part was, the bigger percentage of the crowd were Americans. Tourists I suppose, although probably a good number were from nearby upstate New York.

"The excitement of expectation alone was like standing in a field of static electricity. You could feel it...hairs on your arms standing up. Goose bumps. Chills. Emotions were runnin' on high octane."

"And Gabrielle got to see all this?"

"Yes, sir, sure did. She and a couple of her girlfriends flew up. Hence some of the photos. Others were taken by professionals and given to me, as well as the LP album the Guard sent to me later."

"Go on."

"First, we were formed up outside the fort, at the drawbridge. Myself and my guidon bearer in blue white dress. Then the Drum and Bugle Corps in their red white dress. My Silent Drill Platoon and the Marine Corps Color Guard followed them. These troops in blue white dress as well.

"As we approached, the Fort Henry guard atop the wall over the drawbridge shouted, 'Halt, who goes there, friend or foe?' I responded in kind, 'Friend, a detachment of Marines from the Marine Barracks, Washington, D.C.' He then responded, 'Enter.' With that, the drawbridge was lowered. Creaking, groaning, chains clanking until it dropped the last foot with a resounding thump that shook the ground.

"I commanded, 'Sound Adjutants Call.' The D&B responded, followed by a Sousa number. We marched in, over the drawbridge and under the entry arch. The fort was dark inside. The guidon bearer and I first. BAM! We were hit with a spotlight just as we emerged from the tunnel under the archway and the fort exploded into thunderous applause. Then the D&B came through the tunnel. The bugles and larger horns blaring, cymbals crashing, base drums booming and the rat-a-tat-tatting of the snares...all reverberating off those old granite walls pumping blood into the crowd. Then once fully out of the chute, they burst into the Marine Hymn. POP, the spotlights hit 'em and the crowd went bonkers.

"Then came the Drill Team, bayonets fixed, doing a marching manual and other spin manuals on the way. Now we have bedlam inside, and a roar from the outside. Suddenly the lights go out, we keep marching, in the darkened inside square. Our Color Guard comes into the fort, Stars and Stripes fluttering, alongside our own Marine Corps Battle Colors, battle streamers flowing behind the flag. The spotlight hits the color guard just as they enter the parade deck and holds for several seconds. The crowd is on its feet; shouting; applauding; cheering; whistling...you name a sound a proud American can make, and it was being made.

"Then all the lights come on and we move into formation, in line and facing the long axis of the parade square. We halt. The Drill Team comes to order arms; twenty-four rifle butts crashing on the asphalt as one. The D&B Drum Major raises his mace, lets it drop, and the music stops. A second of silence, then the crowd bursts into applause again. It must have taken five or more minutes for the crowd to settle."

Henri starts to say something, pauses, slowly shakes his head and says, "It's hard to imagine the emotion of the moment, but I'm getting the picture. Hard to know what it compares to in my life. Probably nothing."

"Henri, I don't mind saying, my eyes were glassy, and not from the lights."

"I bet...I understand."

"Then the Fort Henry Guard entered, at their cadence, a British one. The foot soldiers in their red coats and black trousers and hobnail boots. The artillery in black short coats and black trousers both with red piping. The dusty white coats and black trousers of the Drum and Fife Corps. The crowd erupted again. The unit formed directly opposite and facing us.

"From this point, we did a formal changing of the guard ceremony. The contrast was stimulating. The slow, methodical, drawn out high pitched, British style commands and cadence versus our more abrupt, crisp, upbeat and baritone tone at one-hundred and twenty beats per."

"One-hundred and twenty per, what--"

"Means a cadence of one-hundred and twenty steps per minute. Our marching cadence, except for the drill itself."

"Oh, and theirs?"

"About a hundred. I was asked to better show the contrast by marching our entire unit, twenty paces forward to assume the guard of the day. The new guard. And was to do this at a slow march cadence. The D&B routinely does it on Friday nights. First, I give out our type commands, then immediately go to a British style, just to show the contrast. Hell, I loved it...and maybe, just maybe, hammed it up some. For example, it went, 'Marine Detachment, By the Cennterrrr,

Sloooowwwww, Hut.' Drawing out the command, letting my voice fall off at the end, then a sharp, shrill HUT to finish. Hell, it was orgasmic."

"It was what?"

"Just a turn of phrase, Henri. Your daughter understands...it's her word."

Henri's mouth drops open; eyes widen.

Better get on with the story before he has time to think and respond.

I hear something behind me, look around and see that Gabby and Colleen are in the room. They've heard. Gabrielle smiles and motions me on. Colleen flushes and glances at her.

I continue. "Next, they leave the fort. We reform along the long axis to do our Battle Color ceremony. First the D&B does their twenty minute drill and concert routine. Man oh man, they're better than any D&B in the world, and that includes the great American Legion ones. The music is stirring and the formations are precise, brisk and unique. No funky or rinky-dink college stuff. All military. The crowd is stunned into silence...waiting and wanting to applaud but perhaps doesn't know when. Then it begins, between numbers along with cheers and vocal whoops. When they finish, they return to our formation to a deafening applause and booming yells and more whoops."

Henri says, "What was--"

Gabby interrupts, "Daddy, just listen and take it all in...let Barney tell it...you just feel it."

I smile and nod. "Now, Henri, picture this. The lights go out again. The square is pitch black. The crowd falls into silence. The contrast after the music of the D&B is dramatic. I could almost hear people in the crowd breathing. I pause for several more seconds. The crowd stirs, restless, waiting, even wanting. The anticipation and excitement builds. I step off and sixteen paces later, CRASH, the drill team starts with the rifle butts smashing onto the asphalt. The spotlight comes on and hits the platoon coming off the line and into their drill routine starting with our long pendulum manual.

"We do the long version of the drill...all four hundred and thirty-four counts. Rifles spinning, butts crashing on the asphalt, leather heels popping, chrome bayonets flashing. But not a command. Believe me, eerie. Not a sound other than the rifle butts crashing and the hands swacking the leather of the rifle slings. The crowd is at first shocked into silence by the contrast. Then a murmur begins, and builds. Then applause and hoots after each segment. After each progression, the reaction increases. You have to know that the Americans in the crowd were proud, and the more than a few former Marines roared, 'Oouh-rah.'

"We finished the drill and came into our long line, rippling rifle movements up and down the line. Then we did our double rifle inspection, at fixed bayonets. We never were allowed to do it with bayonets fixed at The Barracks, but on the road, we did. The rifle inspector finishing off both inspections with the patented behind-the-back and over-the-shoulder return of the weapon to the man being inspected. When he faced and marched-off, the roar was deafening. Incidentally, he is a Pennsylvania lad."

"Really?"

"Yep. Sergeant Collins. Norristown."

"How long will he be there?"

"He'll be getting out at the end of this year. We have his replacement all ready to go. He's the Corporal on the second inspection, the mirror."

"Hmmmph."

"After that, we returned to formation, presented our colors along with the Marine Corps Battle Color narration. The folks were silent while listening; they applauded and roared approval when it finished.

"Then we marched off to the D&B playing the Hymn again. Out the gate, through the tunnel and over the drawbridge. The place went absolutely nuts...bonkers, crazy. All of our eyes were glassy now, and I bet so were the good folks in the bleachers. If you were there, and not proud of being an American, not shedding a tear or two, then you were dead or dying.

"Once outside, the several thousand out there burst into cheers and applause. They hadn't seen a thing; just heard the music, crashing rifle butts, applause, hoots and roars from the crowd. It was the proudest time of my life, and I loved my troops and the Corps more than any moment before. This was why I came to The Barracks. Damn, I love the Corps. I realized once again, it's not a branch, it's a breed."

Henri is a little flushed, and I detect a hint, just a hint of fluid in his eyes and it tain't Murine. He says, "You're making a believer out of me. Was there more?"

"You bet. Do we have time?" I look at him, and then turn to Colleen and Gabrielle. They nod. Gabrielle has tears in her eyes...but then, she was there, so she probably can still see and hear it...feel it.

"Okay, but I'll hurry though it, and not because it wasn't a knock-out performance...just because I can smell that turkey and fixins', beside Henri wants his ride in the Vette."

Colleen says, "Don't worry, you have time, and don't leave out too much. We're enjoying it, aren't we, Henri?"

"Yep."

"Okay, I won't. Next in the parade square was the Fort Henry guard. They do a battle scene reenactment using the old formations and commands. The British red line, you know the thin red line...firing muskets, blanks of course. Firing by volley by ranks, then falling back to regroup toward the cannons. When they arrive at the two smaller Armstrong Cannons, they form two ranks. One kneeling and one standing. The cannons fire in support to repel the enemy...two lines of infantry between the cannons are firing volleys by rank. Then at the end, they kneel with musket butts in the deck, bayonets angled upward, ready to repel a cavalry charge. Ahhh, it was great! The flash and boom of the cannons. Rippling volleys of musket fire. Smoke billowing up from the parade field mixed with the smell of powder. It was Orga...fantastic."

"Orgasmic," Henri chuckles.

"Right on, Henri. Then a Canadian Pipe and Drum Corps came on, marched the entire length of the square, and then countermarched playing famous pieces like *British Grenadier* and some Scottish pipe numbers. They were dressed in plaid kilts, knee-length woolen stockings with white leggings at the boot level, and bright blue coats. They were every bit as good as the famous Black Watch.

"After this, all the units reformed on the parade field for the finale. This was the lowering of the colors, then a firing of all of the Armstrongs, cannonades, and mortars off the ramparts reenacting the repelling of an attack by the enemy frigates on the lake. The big ol' mortars belched flame; the Armstrongs did the same showering fire and sparks over the lake. The commands by the gunners were chilling...'Number one gun, ready, SIRRR.' 'Mortarrr, ready, SIRRRR.' 'Armstrongs, readddyyyy, SIRRR.'

"Then, 'Mortarrrr, FIRE.' Boom. Then, 'Armstrong Number oneeee, FIRE.' Boom, and so on. Some twenty or more mortar and cannon being fired."

"Wow!" Henri is alive, eyes expressive...no longer just slits. He's in the moment.

"Yeah, wow. When the smoke cleared, all grew silent. Then came the sounding of taps by a lone, spotlighted bugler on the ramparts. Then the echo from another, outside the fort. No light on him. The haunting sounds grip your heart and slowly tear it out.

"Then a hush draped over the entire fort. An unbelievable, God-like silence. As if the world was empty, void of all life. Then, POP, all the lights came on and the crowd was up on their feet, cheering and applauding...hooting, hollering, yelling and a smattering of 'Oouh-rahs.' It must have lasted ten minutes, maybe longer.

"When the applause died down, we started the march-off by units. The clapping started again for each unit. Once outside, we needed a police escort to get to our buses."

I look at Henri. He's glassy eyed again. I got to him all right. Colleen and Gabrielle have turned and are headed for the kitchen. Both are dabbing their eyes.

Henri says, "Barney, I'm stunned. Wish I could have been there, but this was the next best thing."

"Not necessarily so, Henri." His head snaps back. "However, I appreciate your comment. The next best thing is a copy of my LP with the entire ceremony on it. I brought it for you. It's in the car. I'll get it for you after dinner. Play it some night when you're low, or you think the country is goin' to hell in a hand-basket. Play it when the blue-flamin' liberals in the country are shrieking how bad it is. It'll get your blood pumping and make you believe again."

"Thank you, I don't know wh—"

Gabrielle pops in the room and says, "Dinner's served, guys."

I look at Henri and say, "Henri, give me a Oouh-rah."

Henri chirps something that sounds like, "Boo-ah."

"Come on, Henri, let's eat. We'll work on that after dinner, in the Vette."

CHAPTER 36

Wyncote, Pa
Gabby's home
Morning
The day after

I WAKE TO SUNSHINE STREAMING through the upstairs bedroom window, and I sense someone standing, staring at my lifeless form. This is the guest bedroom, next to Gabby's old room. Her back is to the window. She's silhouetted in the sunlight, smiling and looking down at me. I look up. She's already dressed. I whisper, "There's nothin'. Absolutely nothing, more beautiful than your hair in the morning sun."

She sits on the edge, leans over and whispers, "Thank you, again. I love you too." Then a signature kiss on the tip of my nose, "Get up. Breakfast is ready. And get set for my dad."

"Why? What's up?"

"Not you." She giggles then bursts into laughter.

"Hey, be nice."

Then another giggle. "They heard us last night. You know, doin'... making love."

"Oh, great."

She giggles some more, then kisses me again. She's flushed just a bit.

I say, "You mean they heard you. I told you. I warned you when you snuck in here. But, oh no, you wanted to...what was it you said?"

"I was just—"

"Wanted to christen the guest room. It'd been a virgin too long. Great line. Be sure to tell your dad that."

"I know, I know. I couldn't help myself. When you get me started, I...I, ah--"

"You're a moaner and groaner. A screamer. Jesus, this is going to be embarrassing."

"Well, you can't hide up here. Come on down and face the music." She swishes her hair about with a flick of her head, giggles again, and leaves the room but not before she picks up my skivvie shorts and tosses them back over her shoulder. "You'll need these at the least."

I thought last night was painful with all his questions about my intentions. This is going to be excruciating.

I think about last night as I get to a sitting position and fumble for my shorts on the bedpost where they landed...

* * *

Last evening after dinner, I took Henri for a ride. We drove over to 611, Old York Road, between Jenkintown and Elkins Park where I could show off the Vette's stuff. Let him drive. Not much there between the towns.

When we got to Church Road, we stopped at the old Flat Iron Building. Went in to the taproom for a drink, and to give him the opportunity to get the inquisition off his chest. He starts subtly with, "What are your intentions regarding Gabrielle?"

"Don't know. I haven't thought about marriage if that's what you're referring to."

"It is."

I try joking at that point and say, "Someone once told me, marriage changes passion. Suddenly you're in bed with a relative."

That went over like a fart in church. No laugh, no smile, not a word.

I didn't learn well enough that silence is golden. I tried another line I had heard. "Henri, I want to be happy, arrogant, unburdened...not forever, just for awhile." That too struck an odorous note. Sometimes it takes a few moments for my humor to grasp the funny bone. I waited. It didn't.

We chatted some more and I looked him in the eye and told him I thought I loved his daughter and was serious. Further, she and I would probably be talking about this very subject over the weekend. That seemed to satisfy him, although I still didn't get even a chuckle over my attempts at humor.

We drained our drafts and headed for home. I drove and he sat silent. No matter, the ride was short. I made it to the safe haven of Gabrielle and her mom.

* * *

I lollygag down the stairs and saunter into the kitchen. Gabrielle is frying bacon and her mom is busy poaching a mess of eggs. Hash is on the stove.

It's not SOS; that's going to come from Henri.

I say, "Good mornin' folks."

Henri is glaring at me, lips shut white tight. He takes in a deep breath and says, "I have something I want to say to you. This is my house, my home--"

Colleen says, "Henri, not now. Just hush up."

"No, I want him to understand that--"

"Sir, if you are going to give me a lecture about last night, you need to include your daughter. In fact, you might want to address her directly. I tried to tell--"

"He's right, Daddy. I instigated it. And, it was me you heard. So hush up, please."

Good, finally, someone got to finish a sentence. She's shifted the focus. I'm going to stay out of this if possible. Silence is often misinterpreted but never misquoted. Heard that somewhere; goin' to see if it's true.

Colleen jumps on the pile. "Dear, Gabby's right. Hush up. Let's eat and enjoy these two lovebirds while we have them at home. At least we got them at the table. How much trouble can they get into here?"

"The way they behave, plenty."

"Hush. Sit."

I laugh at her humor, well, at both of them. Gabrielle flushes a bit, and then starts laughing as well. Colleen turns red. Henri frowns, shakes his head, and then succumbs to the moment and the laughter. He sits down and says, "Oh well, let's eat."

The breakfast goes along without another word of last night. I have trouble on occasion as I glance at Gabrielle. She flashes a sly grin, seductively licks her lips, and starts giggling softly.

Cripes, if he sees her he's goin' to blow a gasket.

I finish eating; thank Colleen for breakfast...and especially for the homemade orange marmalade on wheat toast. I spread it two-ply thick over the peanut butter.

Colleen responds, Henri mutters something but agrees aloud about the food. I smile thinking of last night...and we've got another night to go.

Gabby and I spend the remainder of the day visiting old haunts, see a few friends from long ago and have a late lunch at Rizzo's Pizzeria in nearby Glenside. Nothing fancy, just some great pizza and a Coke. Same name as the place in Arlington but not the same family. We went to school with Ann, the daughter of the owner of this place.

We invite Colleen and Henri out to dinner tonight. He wants to go to a place close by in Abington. Since I'm paying, I talk him into driving to a small French restaurant in Doylestown. It's cozy, with brick interior walls, and candlelight. It's a new restaurant but it looks old. It's what I imagine Paris to be. Colleen loves it. Henri does too after he stops grumbling about the drive. The rack of lamb is superb. The wine that Gabrielle selects is mellow, soft, with a hint of wildflowers. I decide to have some fun with her so while holding my glass of wine and talking to her father I drop my other hand to her leg and slowly crawl my fingers up her thigh.

Bad mistake. Very bad mistake. I should have known better. She leans over, and whispers into my ear, "If you don't stop, I'm going to start something right here, on the table." She nips me on the lobe. Her mother hears her, flushes. Her dad sees and hears nothing, thank God.

Hard not to love her. She's a hoot.

It's a pleasant evening and the conversation stays the narrow trail...work, golf, neighbors, old friends and Gabrielle's youth. Parents love to tell stories about their kids, some can be embarrassing but none of those tonight. We took care of that last night. Everyone's walking on eggshells and not the ones from breakfast. All except Gabby. She's got her hand on my leg...playing.

After dinner, we sit, enjoy the ambiance and have some brandy. I'm happy because the restaurant has apricot brandy...pancake syrup. After more small talk, we leave and Henri takes it slow and easy goin' home so by the time we arrive its well after eleven.

All of us go upstairs and head for bed. Some secret pact must have been made because we start the night in Gabrielle's room. Under a warm comforter, the snuggling leads to foreplay and then we're off again. I whisper, "No damn screamin'."

"Gag me then 'cause I can't stop."

The hell with it. I'll take the heat in the morning, 'cause I'm not goin' to turn it down tonight. Ol' Henri is either going to have to wear earplugs, or get Colleen moanin' and groanin'...it's gotta be genetic.

* * *

I'm last down again this morning. The breakfast table is set for four again. I was hoping Henri had eaten early and was out raking leaves. Not so. Colleen is pinkish in color. Henri is stern; and Gabrielle is giggling.

I hope nothing is said. I believe faith is the ability to not panic. Heard that somewhere...hope this is true also. My life seems to hinge on one-liners; those I utter and those I've heard.

Nothing is said, at least not about last night. The talk is mostly about our plans for today and Sunday. We linger at the table, Colleen trying to draw out the visit.

We leave shortly before noon amidst hugs and tears by Gabrielle and her mom. I hear her whisper, "Mom, I think he's the one. I love him." Her mom nods and smiles, glances at me. Then a hug and a stern look from her dad. Then he caves in, smiles, and kisses her on the cheek. Me, I get a peck on the cheek from Colleen and another long look and smile.

That's a mother-in-law glance and smile. A sizing up-gaze. The figuring what- the-kids-will- look-like grin.

From Henri, a who's-got-the-best-grip handshake again, along with hard eyes. He really doesn't have either. It's just his best dad's stare and relates to his daughter and the jerk she's brought home.

* * *

We leisurely drive back, drop our stuff at the apartment, shower, dress and go out for dinner nearby. Nice place, Chinese. Good, we both like the same restaurants, the same type of food. After dinner we have an additional glass of Plum Wine, then leave for the apartment shortly after eight.

We shed our clothes for something comfortable. I just go barefoot and throw on my faded Swift, Silent and Deadly shirt that barely covers my jockey shorts. Gabrielle puts on one of her sheer nighties. If it wasn't for the lace and a few strings, it wouldn't be anything. If we're goin' to talk, it won't be for long. I pour us each our usual cordials and sit cross-legged on the floor. She joins me, leans forward, puts her hand behind my neck, kisses me warmly and slowly, then a peck on my nose and says, "Need that before we talk."

"So much for impressing anyone."

"What?"

"Nothing. Talk? You're distracting me in that thingy."

"Good, I mean to...now then. What did you tell my father when he asked you what your intentions were?"

"You mean my serious remarks?"

"Don't tell me you joked about this. You didn't throw out any of your one-liners, did you?"

"Noooo."

"Barney?"

"Okay, just two one-liners...but they were good."

"Bernarr Leslie, you didn't? What did you say? No, I don't want to know...just tell me what you said in seriousness, if anything."

"I did respond seriously. I told him that I didn't know for sure. That I thought I was in love with you, and that I was serious about the two of us. And, that it was something you and I were going to discuss this weekend or one day soon."

"You're not sure? You told him you 'thought' you were in love with me?"

"Well, I'm not sure. I think I'm in love with you. This is all new to me. I told you that."

"Okay, so let's talk about it."

"How about one day soon?"

279

"No, now is a good time to start. What do you want to do? Keep going on the way we are, or something else? Something more... more permanent?"

"You mean getting engaged or something?"

"Yes, and something is marriage."

"Marriage? As in..."

"Yes, and stop acting like this is all a big surprise. We've been together for over a year now. I love you, more than I thought possible. I do not have a doubting heart about you. I'm so in love with you, Barney, I think of you everyday, and every night you're not with me. How do you feel, really? Be straight with me."

"I think I love you. I know I love makin' love to you."

"Barn--"

"Now don't go phoofin' up your feathers, let me finish. I just figured I had some time. Goin' to make Captain next month. Want to see what they're going to do with me. I mean, I know I'll lose the Drill Team. And I need to check my finances. Hell, I don't hardly have peanuts saved. Been spending my money on uniforms, upkeep, my car and liberty...havin' fun."

"Barney, your feelings...in your heart?"

"Gabby, I think of you all the time, but I just haven't thought about where it's leading."

"I know you're going to be promoted. You told me. You're acting as though you're treading water. Barney, I love you. I adore you. I want a life with you. I want to extend my love, our love, into something long term. Permanent. Marriage."

"Are you askin' me to--"

"No. No, you're going to ask me. And knowing him, probably my dad. I'm just telling you I want you. In bed, in my life, in my world, all of the time. But you have to want that too." She leans over and kisses me softly, long, passionately, hands cradling my face. I respond, gladly. I need think time, if even only seconds.

She leans back and says, "You know, your buddies are leaving you behind. Muv is gone, transferred. Julius leaves in a month. JG is getting married very soon. And those beautiful gals that walked into Center House together, and met your buddies. Well, your buddies are all married, just that quick. Gerry Dugan didn't even last four months.

Chink married and gone shortly after that. Even the new guys are half hooked. And here we are, over a year and--"

"This is not a damn race. I know I need to think about this more seriously than I have."

"Your two new running mates, Mike McDuffy and Bill Howard are serious. They're as good as gone."

"Yeah, I think the married officers' wives have formed some cult...with a secret pledge to marry off every bachelor that reports to The Barracks. The objective is to break up our antics and forays uptown."

Gabrielle shakes her head. "Oh, Barney, that's hogwash and you know it."

"No, I'm serious. Ever since Mush Mouth conjured up that plan about having a married officer and his spouse to dinner at Center House on Wednesday evenings, something has changed. After the CO and his wife, and a few other senior officers and their ladies, everything seemed to take on a different flavor. The younger ones, the Captains' wives in particular, had that...that look on their faces."

"What look?"

"That look women get when they're plotting, designing. It's an unmistakable, devious look...you can see the wheels turning anytime they see a happy bachelor. It's in their genes or hormones or something."

"That's crazy. Be serious. Marsh was just trying to improve the reputation of the bachelors. Show that they had some class, and not prone to languish around playing those silly games like Bug, and Iroquois, and those damn launching pad races."

"Well, yeah, that was part of it, but the wives got together like some witches and put spells on us, or wanted to introduce us to...to--"

"They did not. Besides, Barney, all that has nothing to do with us. We've known each other for years. We were apart, but this is fate. We rekindled our past, fell in love and are made for each other. The wives have nothing to do with it...we have everything to do with it."

"You're right. Hell, you're always right. Let me regroup and think about this. Let me get through my promotion, see what's going to happen with me here, or somewhere. Maybe--"

"You're staying here, aren't you? They wouldn't transfer you just because you make Captain, would they?"

"No, I think I know what's going to happen but I'm not sure. Let it run its course."

"Promise to think about this seriously. I love you. I need to know. Barney, we're not kids anymore."

I knew that clock was tickin'. Just knew it. Damn, this is a full court press, but she is something special...real special.

I lean over and put my hand gently on her face. "I know. I promise. I do love you, Gabby. I do."

"That's great, luv bug. Now put down your wine glass. I'm about to show you what you've got to look forward to."

I don't wait for her to move. I take her in my arms and kiss her as hungrily as I can, because I am. And, I can see that body beneath the nightie and I want it...maybe forever. She responds as athletically as ever as we push the ottoman out of the way and clear off the coffee table.

CHAPTER 37

The Marine Barracks
1600 hours
Officers' Walk
31 January 1964

IT'S A CRISP AND CLEAR late afternoon this winter of discontent. Darkness is slowly draping itself over The Barracks. I'm standing on Officers' Walk, along with the other Barracks Officers and Staff Non-Commissioned Officers. We're waiting for Colonel Weaver to lead Captain Jack Kruger, Julius the Only, to Center Walk for the next step in his play-off.

Criminy, time slips away so fast.

Days, even seasons, blend into a mere moment. It seems like just yesterday that Mush Mouth left, but it was last September, before the JFK assassination. He is aboard a carrier, I think the *Kearsarge*. She had been involved as a recovery ship for the space program splashdowns in the Pacific. Now she has returned to the 7th Fleet in Southeast Asia, keeping an eye on unsettling problems.

Gabrielle and I had two wonderful weekends together since Thanksgiving weekend. Out to dinner on Saturdays. One at Hogates on M Street and the other at Rive Gauche in Georgetown. Both times we followed dinner with drinks at one of our favorite spots, The Fireplace... listening to Blues. Then home, her apartment, to talk and make love...in either order. Jellybeans, jellybeans, jellybeans!

Gonna' need another jar soon.

Both Chink and I have been promoted. He's still at the Tute and I am now XO of Guard Company and the parade company commander for at least this year. Great! A dream job here.

Now, here we are. Julius is leaving. Today. The second of the trio. J.G. is still here at the show but not for too much longer. He's married now and his uptown time has been blunted, however his tongue and wit are still sharp and prickly.

Okay, here we go. Julius and the colonel are out of the office where they had their private session, and headed down Generals' Walk.

The Barracks XO, ol' Melon Head, calls us to attention. Next to him is the relatively new Director of the Tute, Lieutenant Colonel Ernie Reid. Tall, quiet, squared away Texan...nicknamed Curly for his blond curly hair. Is grey now, cut short like our so no curls. Doesn't matter. We don'[t call him curly, just his first name, Colonel. He's goin' to look "tuff" in the show on the parade deck.

As the CO and Julius approach Center Walk, and just before they execute a column left, Kruger flashes his infamous smile...a cross between a ferocious sneer and an evil grin with squinty eyes that blink like neon lights in a window of a waterfront bar. Colonel Weaver and Julius turn and spot themselves on Center Walk, facing the Drum and Bugle Corps.

As the D&B strikes up their first number, my mind wanders...as usual. At any given ceremony, I am prone to drift away. It all started at the Death Watch. I must have a short attention span, or it's just a habit now.

The music is great. Love the D&B. For some reason the music is saying something to me. What? What is it? I got it. Yep, I just said it. It's a show.

It's clear to me. This, The Barracks is Broadway. Yeah, think about it. Finally, after two parade seasons and everything else, it occurs to me. We're a show. The parades, both of them, are shows. Every ceremony is a show but particularly the parades. We have seasons. We're the same as the Great White Way or whatever it's called. We have all the ingredients.

We have a producer and an assistant producer...the CO and XO of The Barracks. They prepare a budget and go to Headquarters for funding. The show's Director is the S-3, the Operations Officer...

this season it will be Major Bill Kendell. His Assistant Director is still Captain J.G. Milsap. Cripes, the J.G. even sounds Hollywoodish. The rest of us in the parade are the cast. The supernumeraries are understudies, waiting in the wings...the arcade. The Escort Detail each week are the ushers in our theater. We have it all.

Now is off-season. We have a new cast. We'll rehearse. Do some street parades or something as our off-Broadway bit. Then, in the late spring, we open the season. New cast. Same show and it will be SRO every week. During the season, the Drill Team and the D&B go on mini tours, bring the little show to some off-Broadway towns or events, but always return for "the show."

Then, when the season is over, some of the cast leaves, moves on. We say our goodbyes, like now, then new cast members come aboard, and we start the off-season all over again. Some of us get to be long-running stars. Headliners, I believe is the show-biz term. We're all starch, polish, glint, gleam and lights. Lookin' pretty, dazzling our audiences and advertising the Corps. An irreverent Lieutenant once stationed here, by the name of Miles something or other, purportedly said, "The Barracks is a large pile of manure with a large white sheet over it." I don't think that's true...but its funny.

The real Marine Corps is in the field...at LeJeune, Pendleton, and Okinawa or on a deployment afloat somewhere, waiting to strike if need be. The only time we here at The Barracks get close is when we're firing for qualification on the rifle range or when we get to do some training in Hog Company, which isn't often.

Jack is going to the real Corps again, like Mush Mouth before him. Where we all came from and want to return. These thoughts bring Gabby flashing across my mental silver screen.

She really doesn't know the Corps. Just the play, the show. I need to clue her in.

In the meantime, we are at the Post of the Corps and it's Showtime...The Play-off...A cast party.

The music has stopped. Jack is speaking to the D&B. When he finishes we'll adjourn to Center House for the remainder of the proceedings...the CO's remarks, Julius' attempt at the four-second club, and then his monologue. He's been rehearsing both...the chugging and his spiel.

Then, who knows, several of us will probably venture uptown, Basins or who knows where. Stir up the natives, and finish the night at the White Tower for a rock-hard hamburger...and maybe a karate chop to a plastic mustard container. If not, a parking meter. Both are Boomer's specialties. First Lieutenant Bob "Boomer" O'Malley seems destined for immortality here...will become a legend of sorts; most likely a Dubious Achievement Award candidate; and if not, his "Oouh-Rahs" will continue to reverberate through the rafters of Center House...and downtown.

* * *

The Barracks
The Drum Room
1630 hours
31 January 1964

All is finished outside. We get comfortable at the bar in Center House. The officers order a drink. When all is settled, the CO begins his remarks. As he talks, I think about where Jack is going. Like most, folks are ultimately headed for the Divisions at Pendleton or in Okinawa. Away from the show and toward the real world. As is usually the case, my mind drifts away during the colonel's remarks. I think about Gabby again, the boys in blue white dress, and this past Christmas...

* * *

Christmas Eve of '63, it snows. Two in a row. Script made to order. Center House is quiet. Kruger and the new guy, First Lieutenant Will Howard are headed uptown. The bar here is closed so they want to get some holiday cheer.

Julius says, "Stoneface, come along with us. We'll treat the indigenous personnel to a few Ho-Ho-Ho's."

"Can't...goin' to Gabrielle's. Her parents are in town. They're staying over so I'll be back tonight. And by the way, Julius, they're called citizens here."

"Oh yeah, citizens...civilians. Anyway, not stayin' over? You having a decency spasm?"

"Ah come on, be nice, Julius. It's Christmas."

"I'd rather be a pri...be a Scrooge. It's lonely around here this time of year. It's hard on my mind."

"Not good for your health either. Get happy and stay loose. I'll be back later. Just going over for dinner and a visit. Spending tomorrow there also."

"Okay. Go."

"Save some holiday cheer for me. I may need it when I get back."

Lieutenant Howard pipes up, "Sir, you mean my leader is not--"

"No, I'm not, Lieutenant."

"Sir, you mean you don't want to--"

"Loooootenant. I don't need one of my platoon commanders haranguing me, particularly one who is so careless to get caught in a well-known, obvious speeding trap in Virginia."

"Sir, I--"

"I'm not finished Lieutenant. Then since you had insufficient funds to pay the fine...you had to phone Center House and beg for money. Beg for gratuity to alleviate you from your sins."

"Sir, can I speak, sir?"

"Mister Howard. I know you can speak. If you're asking, may you speak, the answer is yes, and be brief. Lieutenants generally have very little of value to say."

"Sir, I was just going to remind you, sir, that the Captains present at the time waited so long before responding that it appeared that I might be spending time in the hoosegow. You let me sit there and worry, forcing me to call several times."

"Lieutenant Howard. Slick Willie, isn't it? That's what your running mates call you...right?"

"Yazza, sir."

"Yazza. Who the hell started that?"

Kruger says, "You did...with Mush Mouth."

"Oh, well then. It must be okay. Anyway, Slick, you are most fortunate that we responded at all. As hard as it is to believe, Captain Kruger actually came to your aid. Go with him this evening, you owe him. Care for him and spare me your advice. That means bring him home safely...and sober if possible."

"Sober! Sir, I'm just a lieutenant. Not capable of this immense challenge."

"Then just bring him back safe and sound. And, bring me a bottle of Apricot Brandy as well. I'll need some when I return. Well, I'm off for a challenge of my own."

"Yazza, sir. Yazza."

"Do you need some coins for the brandy?"

"No, Massa, no."

"Mister Howard!"

"Sir?"

"Enough."

"Yazza, sir. Yazza."

Good God! There's always a lieutenant getting the last word. Where did it all start?

Slick's part of the new cast for the show. Has the third platoon, the third herd, in my company and is pretty smooth on the parade deck... slick actually. Bob Reese replaced me in the Drill Team. In fact, the entire cast of platoon commanders is new to the show.

I nod at Julius, and leave...headed out in the snow in my Vette to Gabrielle's for dinner and a chat with her dad.

* * *

Marine Barracks
Center House
The Drum Room
31 January 1964

The colonel finishes his remarks. The beer is poured in Julius' pewter mug and he has his customary I'm-ready-for-anything sneer on his face. With a final squint of his always bloodshot, watering eyes, he chugs and gulps. It's gone. He's the newest member of the four-second club.

He wipes his mouth, takes his congratulations mildly, accepts his souvenir mug humbly, and begins his farewell monologue that assuredly won't be humble but mumbled, nor mild but melancholy. The second of the trio, the triumvirate, about to be gone.

I listen...sort of, it seems like old hat. I've heard so many of these, and in particular almost all of Julius' ravings.

Oh well, off-Broadway is about to begin. The winter of discontent will end, and the show season will soon be here along with the fresh aromas of spring...and more, perhaps different, boys in blue white dress.

CHAPTER 38

Arlington, Va.
Snowing
Christmas Eve
December 1963

I ARRIVE AT GABBY'S IN good spirits and attired to impress Colleen, and maybe, Henri. I'm in a white turtleneck, gray slacks and blue blazer. The trip isn't as beautiful as Christmas morning a year ago. Everything was so pristine looking then...no tire tracks in the snow, no one on the streets, only birds perched on the telephone wires along the way. Tonight there is some traffic resulting in the slushy streets. However, the evening still holds the magic of the season with all the bright, colored lights in the shops. On the side streets, and especially on my left up the hill, I can see homes trimmed in lights as well as many lighted Santas, sleds and such on the lawns.. Most important is that my mind is bright and my heart is pounding. I feel good. It's Christmas and I love this woman.

Even though it seems pointless, I buzz Gabby from downstairs pretending I don't have a key. Don't want to bristle Henri's neck hair; he had enough of that over Thanksgiving.

This little act jingles a thought...maybe I'm meant for show business. I love pretending. I should have been a thespian except I don't like the sound of it.

Whatever, Gabby buzzes me up, going along with my pretense, and is waiting for me at the door. She's dressed in a sweater and slacks in holiday colors. She gives me a sensual hug, rubbing against me. I whisper, "Better stop, or you'll cause--"

"Shhh...Kiss me; I love you, and Merry Christmas...Eve."

"Love you. Merry Eve."

We enjoy a long kiss, which is interrupted by subdued coughing sounds from inside. She follows with her signature peck on the nose. I go in, get a squeeze and a peck on the cheek from Colleen; a handshake from Henri...firm but not a strength contest this evening.

Her parents circle the coffee table returning to their seats on the couch. Gabby says, "We're having a glass of wine. Want one?"

"Sure. I'll get it."

"No. Sit down. Relax. Chat. I'll do the honors."

"Great. Thanks." I sit, look across at Colleen and Henri and ask, "How was the trip down? When did you get here? What'cha been doin'?"

They take turns telling me. Henri grumbles about the traffic while Colleen tells of the sights and holiday decorations along the way. Both continue chatting about their three-day visit. Henri always returns to the tour of the Smithsonian. Gabby and I have been there, more than once. It is fascinating.

Henri adds, "Gabby didn't come with us. Said she'd been there, done that...tons of times with you."

"Yes, it's one of our favorite spots."

Gabrielle hands me my wine and says, "One of yours. Mine's the shower."

I almost drop the glass and feel myself flush. Henri misses it... Colleen doesn't.

I take a sip and say, "A good Burgundy...spirited, like you. Appropriate for Christmas." She giggles. I add, "Thanks, Love Bug."

She gives me a sinister grin, wets her lips seductively and sits on the ottoman in front of my chair after she pulls it off to the side just a bit. Then pats the seat next to her. Colleen has seen all this foreplay. No grin, just a smile in her eyes. Henri has the look of a person that has obviously missed something as he glances from his wife to Gabby and back.

I move to the ottoman. We're facing her parents. All of a sudden, I feel like I'm in an interrogation room. Henri's wine glass looks like a rubber hose.

There is a lull in the conversation. Henri takes the moment to say, "Nice wine. Cozy evening, huh?"

I take in a deep breath. Kiss Gabby on the cheek and say, "Henri, this may not be the best time, but I'm going to seize the moment with the wine and the cozy atmosphere to ask you a pretty straight-forward question."

"Huh?"

"Henri, Colleen, I ask you for your daughter's hand in marriage. Gabby is not awa--"

Gabrielle's gasp interrupts me. She almost drops her glass. Henri takes a quick sip and puts down his glass on the coffee table. Colleen tears up. I continue, "aware of this, so if I have your permission, I will turn to her and ask her to marry me, with her parents as witnesses."

Gabby gushes, "Oh, Barney. I have--"

"Shhh. I need an answer from your dad first. Henri?"

"Yes. Certainly. I'm honored." He says nothing more.

I ask, Colleen?"

Colleen manages a nod, and a mumbled and tearful, "Yes."

They stand. I motion them to sit, holding my hand up as if a policeman stopping traffic. Then I turn to Gabby, get down on one knee, and say, "Gabrielle, I love you. Very much. Perhaps I always have and didn't know it. Will you marry me?"

She gathers herself after tearing up and says, "Yes. Oh yes, Barney. I love you. I believe I always have, and I know I always will." She throws her arms around me, kisses me, and holds me tight as her tears flow.

Her parents make another move to close. I give another hand and arm signal to halt. Gently push Gabby away and say, "Folks, I'm not finished yet." I reach into my coat pocket, bring out the ring box, open it, and say, "Love Bug, I want you to have this engagement ring as a symbol of my commitment and my love."

Gabby helps me put it on her finger. It's difficult...she is trembling and I'm a tad nervous. We fumble through it somehow, smiling at each other. Once on, she pulls her hand from mine, raises it to eye level, and stares at the ring. She wipes the tears from her eyes with the other hand, then breaks out into a beaming smile and says, "Oh, Barney, it's beautiful." Before I can say a word she wraps her arms around my neck once again and we kiss. Then she gets up from the ottoman, and steps toward her mom.

I say, "Okay, folks. My act is done. Let's have a drink. I need one. I was nervous...was shakin' worse than a cat sh--"

"Barney!"

"Peach kernels on a marble floor. What?"

Never mind. You're irreverent and irreformable...Thank God."

Henri comes across the room, shakes my hand, and then gives me a hug. I say, "Careful, Henri, I don't know if I should trust a Frenchman. They're a little quirky."

Gabby mutters, "Truly incorrigible."

Finally Henri catches a drift and laughs.

Colleen closes on me as smooth as a parade deck glider. She hugs me, tightly, and whispers in my ear, "She loves you; she adores you; and so do I."

Wow. This has gone well. Is getting to me. I need some air.

Henri says, "Let's toast. To the two of you, and a lifetime together."

That'll be better than air.

The four of us raise our glasses and murmur, "Hear. Hear."

Gabrielle sits back on the ottoman, then leaps to her feet and says, "I've got to serve dinner. I'll never get through it. I'm so excited."

Colleen snaps to her feet as if drawn by a magnet. The two of them sashay toward the kitchen, arm in arm, whispering and giggling.

Life is good. I don't even hear my mistress, the Corps, gagging although I think I hear her muttering, "If I wanted you to have a wife, I would have issued you one."

* * *

After the meal and another glass of wine, I return to The Barracks. Any celebrating of the occasion with Gabby will have to wait until her parents leave tomorrow, after an early Christmas dinner at the apartment. That way they'll get home before dark and I can work on my theory...understanding of course that tonight represents one of those irreplaceable jellybean events.

Tonight I get to have my Apricot Brandy with Slick Willie and Julius the Only. They have mellowed-out after their trip uptown.

I wonder why we call it uptown when to the rest of the world, its downtown. Must be that from this neighborhood, it's an upgrade.

The only damage from the foray, as I understand from Slick Willie, is to Julius' pride since he slipped on the icy pavement in front of some watering hole and fell into the slushy gutter. Apparently, Julius mumbled something to which Slick said, "What?"

According to Lieutenant Howard, Julius replied, "I did that on purpose. Wanted to see how many times I could chin myself on the curb."

Slick laughed so hard he got sick to this stomach and threw up.

So, one doesn't look so good...and the other doesn't smell so good.

I have told them of the events of my evening. Julius seems depressed and is muttering one of his monologues of despair. Lieutenant Howard dutifully listens, a true disciple.

For me, the brandy tastes sweet as it slides and slithers down my throat, warming my innards...matching my feelings.

Life is truly good...it can't get any better.

CHAPTER 39

Center House
The Drum Room
Happy Hour
7 May 1964

THURSDAY NIGHT HAPPY HOUR...LOVE IT. This will be busier than most because the first Friday night parade of the year, show-time, is tomorrow. Rehearsals done, off-Broadway finished to include a trip to the Worlds' Fair in New York by Lieutenant Reese, the Drill Team and D&B. His first official off-Broadway show. The cast is set. Tonight will be fun.

Won't see Gabby tonight. Tomorrow she will come in and meet me for dinner and the parade. I told her, "No big deal. My third season in the show."

She replied, "It's a big deal to me. You get to speak, or holler, or--"

"Give commands. A command voice, not hollering."

"Okay, command voice. Should I applaud every time?"

"No. Geezit, no."

"All right, I'll just tell everyone that I've slept with you and you're good there also."

"How about just sit quietly and applaud and do the oohs and aahs along with everyone else."

I laugh to myself at my thoughts of her. Oh well, tonight will be mild. I will, of course, be irreverent, but well behaved. Won't make the mistake as I did on my birthday in early January when I proclaimed,

"There isn't enough bourbon in this bar to get me drunk." Jesus, what a night that was...

* * *

Julius leaped from his barstool, swished an imaginary cape at the bull, me, and shouted "Ole." Then he ordered me a drink...a double. Sometimes the bull wins, but not this time. There was enough bourbon. Unfortunately, I fully realized this the following morning. Julius the Only and Milsap the Yalie took my car keys that night to save me from myself. They did this just before I wandered out to the parade deck near the cannons on the south end and hit a beautiful, high, soft draw with my six iron. I was goaded into this by Major Hank Cronin, my company commander and golfin' buddy. He claimed I could only hit fades. For a dollar I'll do most anything.

Then, as the reconstructed story goes, partially from a cabbie, after the shot I left and walked, rather staggered down 8th Street to M, then the several city blocks to Hogates Restaurant before falling, to chin myself, just as the dinner crowd was leaving. They ignored me in obvious disgust, so the cabbie said. Since I was in uniform, the hack brought me back to the gate where the sentry assisted me in the debarkation process which was only slightly less awkward than climbing down a cargo net in choppy seas.

Actually, after having hit such a superb golf shot, and worrying about the possible immediate repercussions, I merely went for a walk to clear my head. Having done that, I hailed a cab and returned home to the camaraderie of my mates. The driver doesn't know squat. The difficulty getting out of the cab was due to darkness and the icy gutter. At least that's my story and I'm stickin' to it...and as always, it seemed like a good idea at the time.

Nonetheless, the golf ball bounced off the Commandant's House, onto his patio, then one more high bounce onto the parade deck. Colonel Weaver found it there the next morning. He asked the Adjutant, Captain Jake Dennehy, to investigate as usual. Jake didn't have to since he was in attendance, but pretended to, and of course came up with a shielding but believable story that cast no shadows on Center House or me.

That's all in the past and although I think about that event and others, I sit here at the corner of the bar, watching and listening to the lieutenant's rev-up a notch. First Lieutenant Burl Likens is warming up, which means he is beginning to stir the pot of uptown notions. A silky-smooth ceremonial officer, albeit short in stature for here, is probably destined for a Dubious Achievement Award in the near future. It's only a matter of time.

He's always smiling, or it seems that way. Even when he's not, his natural look is a sly grin. He brings great joy and relief to the Majors when he departs Center House for home.

I like him and his sense of humor, but he's going to wrinkle early in life with that ever-present smile.

He first distinguished himself while the XO of Headquarters and Service Company. When serving his first tour as the OD at this, the oldest and most prestigious Post of the Corps, he made the obligatory trip to Guard Company to inspect the mess hall and sample the evening meal. All the troops were eyeballing him, a stranger from up the street at The Barracks. Burl thought it was because he was looking sharp in his Dress Blues. It wasn't. He had his Sam Browne belt on backwards, meaning the shoulder strap was over the wrong shoulder. The troop's smiles were not of admiration but rather of amusement at, in their words, "The Little Elf from Heat and Steam", the latter referring to the H&S, or Headquarters and Service.

That was in December of '63, and it not being enough, he further distinguished himself within a month. Before General Brown moved in as the new Commandant in January of '64 replacing General Shelton, the Corps was renovating the CMC quarters at the north end of the parade deck. First Lieutenant Likens, as XO of Heat and Steam, was given responsibility for the security of the quarters while it was being gutted and redone.

This meant regular visits and the enforcement of a no-smoking ban in and around the quarters. He would make the tours during daylight hours, however, the OD would be responsible for the inspections after hours.

On this occasion, while "The Elf" had the OD watch and was about to make the mandatory after midnight inspection of the quarters, he arose to find The Barracks parade deck and surrounding area filled with smoke. It obscured many features, including the Commandant's home. Burl, assuming the worst and not asking the Corporal of the Guard, alerted the entire guard section, and the CO, then raced to the quarters, sure it was afire. He bravely and boldly battled the smoke, no more than a mist, only to discover that the fire was simply elsewhere in SE Washington and had blanketed The Barracks. The guard of the day knew this but let "The Elf" do his thing.

Geez, I wish he had called the fire department...Sirens, trucks, flashing lights. All the generals along Generals' Walk outside watching. And there would be Burl, trying to explain the non-event...would have been legendary. However, as it is, doesn't qualify for a Dubious Achievement Award nomination...not even a drink. Well, maybe one.

I'm back to the present and catch his eye as he continues to stir the pot. I mouth the word, "Fire" and he flushes immediately, then grins...and stirs some more.

Another thought about Burl strikes me. He is married, attends Happy Hour religiously, and is constantly in the forefront of uptown forays. After each, he tells his wife, Sharon, that he was ordered to stay and go uptown by one of the notorious Captains...Kruger, Word, Milsap or me. Now that the natural fall guy, Julius, is gone, the honor usually falls on my head. I don't care. I consider it a badge of honor.

One time Sharon good-naturedly confronted me. She was seeking some form of the truth, a confirmation of what she already knew. I went along, as all before me did, with Burl's story. She never believed it for a second, but it was fun.

The ironic part is that the current Drill Team commander, Bob Reese, is Burl's neighbor. The two of them are tight as ticks, as are their wives. Bob is always home early, never stays for the patrols uptown. Burl never misses and doesn't have a chance when he arrives home. You have to hand it to him, he keeps goin' and blamin'..

Anyway, one by one we change into civilian attire thereby masking our identity and saving our Corps' reputation. Good thinking! Yeah, right. Our white sidewall haircuts, Boomer's "Oouh-Rahs" and karate chops, along with our general demeanor is enough to reveal ourselves... particularly since we always return to the same haunts...and have been cited before.

As we prepare to leave, it boggles my mind that we are still welcome at these watering holes. Oh well, off we go, with our over-used battle cry and excuse well engrained.

"It seemed like a good idea at the time......Sir."

CHAPTER 40

The Barracks
8ᵗʰ & "I"
Parade night
First Friday, May 1964

THE FOLLOWING EVENING, THIS FIRST Friday in May '64, the "Show" opens to SRO again, rather as usual. Almost a completely new cast. The Parade Commander is the tall, soft-spoken Texan, Lieutenant Colonel Ernie Reid. He's popular with the lieutenants and captains in particular. He seems to love 'em and their antics. Maybe because he spent most of his time when a lieutenant as a POW in Korea. I think he enjoys us because he's making up for the time he missed. Maybe not, but it sounds good and I want to believe it.

Anyway, his staff is new. The Platoon Commanders are new with the exception of First Lieutenant Reese. Captain Word and I are holdovers, and as Parade Company Commanders, we are not just walk-ons but now have speaking parts, headliners. We worked our butts off during rehearsals making changes to various sequences in the parade. We changed Officers Call to make a more exacting half column movement going into the arcade. Improved Officers Center making it more precise and eliminated most of the commands so it flows more smoothly as one continuous sequence. Other changes as well were made, particularly in the march-on.

I even get the Band to change some music and play *"Men of Harlech"*, a stirring Welsh piece for Officers Center. If the Band Director had known it was my idea, it would have never happened. He and I have crossed swords, or rather my sword and his poisoned-tip baton, on occasion.

Once the parade, the performance, is over, the cast adjourns to Center House for refreshments and to reap the rewards of a stellar show. Joining the cast are special guests to include the guest Reviewing Officer, barracks wives, other guests, and some dates of the few remaining bachelor officers. Most of these bachelors have already been scheduled to leave that blissful state...others are targeted by the secret society of barracks wives. I'm no longer a target, however, the society may be a little stressed since they did not choose my soul mate.

Nonetheless, all are excited about the new season, me included. After all, this was a new part for me, and I am pleased that the changes went well and were at least noticed by the insiders. The general audience isn't aware. They're just caught up in the patriotic pageantry. They applaud and cheer everything we do. Gotta love it...I sure do.

I have Gabrielle here tonight. We started the evening with dinner in Center House. Then I turned her over to the last of the triumvirate, JG and his wife, to escort her to the parade.

After a few drinks, I go upstairs, change, and Gabby and I leave for her place and the weekend. We zip down M Street and over the 14th Street Bridge wasting no time in traffic with the Vette.

We go up, enter, flick on a few lights and head into her room to change into something more comfortable. After over four months of being engaged, nothing has changed. Well, not exactly true. She has purchased a huge jar and is putting jellybeans in it. Tonight, I see that she has three laid out on the dresser next to the jar...one red, one white, and one blue or a dark colored one anyway. The message is clear to me so I find no reason to delay, although I do miss seeing her in the thingy. The scent of strawberries in the room and the lingering taste of them still in my mind trigger my feeding frenzy.

Later we spend what is left of the night, or rather early morn, snuggled up on the couch...she with a snifter of Bailey's and me with my Apricot Brandy, or as the Strawberry Princess says, "pancake syrup." We talk of tomorrow, our trip to Mount Vernon, and decide on a restaurant for Saturday evening. As I listen to her other comments about the two of us I begin to think she is right, that fate is weaving our lives into a fabric of its choosing. I like the job it's doing.

* * *

The City
Assembly Area
Early afternoon
4 July 1964

What a great day, and it's a Saturday. Makes for a short weekend but doesn't detract from the holiday spirit. It's all red, white and blue. We, meaning Guard Company, are formed in the assembly area just off Pennsylvania Avenue readying for a huge parade. All the service units in MDW are present since this is a joint-service venture. There are a large number of other non-military units here also, but the joint service unit will be the headliner for this event.

The streets are lined with people from the city, from surrounding areas, plus a ton of tourists. The age-old saying is correct, "Everyone loves a parade." This is one of those off-Broadway stints we do, and is fun. The day will end with a huge patriotic show for the general public at the Washington Monument tonight, and of course fireworks, probably Zambelli's.

We stand at Ceremonial at Ease on a side street, waiting to start and move down Pennsylvania Avenue. People are watching us, even here in the assembly area, milling around the units, taking pictures and getting "up close." We, Ceremonial Guard Company, remain motionless. As with the Drill Team, so it is with my company. I believe once out here, it's Showtime. Have to give the folks a show. They want to see the highly disciplined Marines, even here in the "get ready to get set to go" area. Don't really want to see a bunch of military guys taking a smoke break, talking, and shifting from one foot to the other. That's what's happening around us with the other services. What the hell kind of picture does that present?

We are in company mass formation, directly behind the Army unit, The Old Guard from Fort Myer, and ahead of the Dixie Cups, Wing Wipers, and Hooligan's Navy.

The Old Guard is as usual in the Army's dress blue uniform which dates back to our Civil War, but is far less embedded in the American consciousness than our own Dress Blues, or even our Blue White Dress.

301

I see a boy and his dad strolling near-by, stopping on occasion to take pictures. They walk towards me and as they get close, I remember the youngster at Iwo with his Mom. However, this boy has no chocolate cone. He is waving a small American Flag clutched in his right hand. His other clasps his pop's, and he's wearing a white T-shirt with I Love America stenciled in red and blue on the front.

I've never seen any shirts with I Love My Government on them. There's a difference. Politicians seem to forget that. They're supposed to serve, protect and enrich our country and its heritage...not screw it up.

They stop in front of me. The father takes a picture of us. Then they move up to within a few feet of me and he snaps another...I mean a breath-smellin' close up. I'm wearing my Stoneface, no glare, just the face. After all, there are no chocolate cones. The father smiles, the boy stares wide-eyed. Then the man snaps another shot and murmurs, "Thanks."

He takes a few steps backward and says to his son, "Son, see these guys?" pointing first at me, then my troops behind me. "Those are the Marines. I don't know who those guys are in the funny uniforms standing in front of them," as he hikes his thumb over his shoulder pointing to The Old Guard.

Sometimes it's difficult being a mannequin. This is one of those times for sure. I suck in some air through my nose but probably cannot hide the sparkle in my eyes. I would rather just laugh, and say something to the "Old Guard" in front of me. I know they heard it. My guys behind me did. I can hear the Magpies murmuring. For me, this is just one more small victory in our competition with these jokers. So, today, Marines One, Old Guard zero, and we haven't even started to move yet. Then it will be a runaway.

Damn, I love the Corps and these troops. I love a parade. Hell, I love the Fourth of July. And for doggone sure I love America...

* * *

The Barracks
Officers' Walk
Late in the Month
July 1964

It's another play-off. This one for the last of the trio, Captain J. G. Milsap, the Yalie. I'm sure there were trios before Mush Mouth, Julius, and JG, and if so, good. I don't think however, there was, or will be, one just like them, these boys in blue white dress. I suppose however that Slick, Spike, The Elf, Boomer, and lately Mike McDuffy, a new lieutenant, might be considering a challenge. They may even give them a run for the money, but if I were to advise them I would suggest they settle for place or show money. The triumvirate was one of a kind, as is their publicist, Jake, the diminutive Irishman who is still here and he's not taking on any new clients.

Once again, as I wait here on Generals' Walk for the CO and Milsap to appear, I realize that all time is fleeting. The very thought of JG leaving, and of this new cast, causes my mind to wander and reflect on the "Once Upon a Time" world of mine.

* * *

It's spring, '64. We're still in the off-season, but working our way out of the winter of discontent. One of the events that make it somewhat difficult goes unnoticed by the world, the country, and this city. However, not by The Old Guard at Fort Myer, nor by Captain Milsap and me. Sad news. Captain Robert Graven, the Army Officer who worked with us on the JFK Death Watch died from a sudden heart attack just months after the funeral was over. He was a young fella, and I enjoyed working with him and had fun jerking his chain from time to time. He was a good man and had a sense of humor.

This evening however, starts as a typical Happy Hour Thursday. No parade tomorrow, but with the normal rehearsal starting immediately after morning colors. I'll be there early; want to see colors; love seeing the flag go up here at The Barracks...anywhere really.

Here at the bar in Center House there is the normal din of Happy Hour. It seems the decibel level increases by rank. Lieutenant colonels and majors converse in a raspy, bass whisper; captains speak in a slightly louder tone and with new-found authority; the lieutenants are still louder, more shrill, care-free and certainly laugh more. In time, as expected, the field grade officers bail out early, sliding down the ropes leaving the ship in the hands of those junior to them. Smart move actually.

However, one major always seems to remain, and tonight it's none other than Major Roberts. Ol' "No White House Clearance" Dave. He is at the bar, being baited. However, in his mind I'm sure, he is baiting two lieutenants, Slick Willie and Spike Splittier. Both mine from Guard Company. No one is drunk, just rowdiness happy and roguishly reckless.

I butt-hop a few stools to get closer. I hear Lieutenant Howard, Slick, say, "Is that right, sir? Is that right? That's pure bullshit, sir."

The Major replies, "Yes, that's right, Mister Howard. Lieutenants nowadays don't have the color, the flair we did when I was a junior officer."

Spike chimes in with, "No flair? No color? Is that right, sir?" It's obvious this has been going on, festering, for more than several minutes.

"You've got it, Mister. Both of you. When I was young, me and my buddies really raised hell. Nothing or nobody was safe. Yep, you guys today just have no, ahhhh...no dash, no pizzazz."

"Really? How's this for friggin' pizzazz?" as Spike sends his half-filled mug of beer hurtling down the bar like an out of control downhill skier. The mug rides up and over the raised curved edge of the bar like it was a mogul on a ski run, and through the window overlooking 8th Street. The windowpane explodes and shatters.

The room cascades into silence that ends with the Major sputtering and stammering, "What the--"

His words hang in the air, interrupted by Slick Willie leaping on top of the bar with two revolutionary-era cutlasses in his hands. He has torn these souvenirs from the Drum Room wall. He tosses one to Spike and bellows, "On Guard, Matey."

Spike catches the cutlass, retorts, "Arrrg, defend yourself," as he climbs up and over a bar stool to the bar top and assumes a dueling position opposite Slick. They feign a sword fight kicking over glasses and mugs. The only thing missing is the leap from the bar over a damsel and onto a table full of food. Nonetheless, everyone scatters to avoid the splash, splatter and spray. Hell, it's just like the movies...a swash-buckling scene in the castle. Oh, if we only had some damsels in distress here this evening to vie for these buccaneers. But, alas, none are present, only a stunned group of junior officers, plus a lone major.

Major Roberts yells, "Stop. Someone's going to get hurt. Dammit, you guys are out of control."

I look at him and say, "Out of control, sir? No color, wasn't it? Or was it no flair, no pizzazz. You haven't answered Spike's question, sir."

"What question? I was just kidding around, and this is--"

"This is what, sir? I know one thing for sure, Major."

"What's that, Captain Quinn?"

"You're the senior officer present, sir. And the instigator. You'll have to explain the property damage come morning, and report whom or what prompted this outburst. Let me see, sir. Just who was that, sir?"

"Captain--"

"Or, sir, if the Major chooses, he can make up some story that'll fly."

As he looks around he mutters, "Have all the--"

"Yes, sir. They left. Long time ago. You're it, sir. Again......Sir." and I give him my best leprechaun smile.

I look up to my two swashbucklers and say, "Get down, guys. Put up the cutlasses before you hurt yourselves or accidentally run the Major through. And start cleaning up this mess."

Slick and Spike get down, smile at each other, then me. Spike says, "Nice flair, Slick."

Slick laughs and retorts, "Great pizzazz, Matey."

The Major leaves but not before getting the story straight with Gunny Richards about the window. The glasses will not need explaining... normal breakage and probably not missed until inventory. Besides, the current House Mother, the rosy-cheeked Irishman, McPeters, is the Assistant Supply Officer so it's a no-brainer. However, the window must be reported to Maintenance to be repaired and Colonel Weaver might get wind of it somehow. If this happens, he'll ask about it and who the senior officer present was. Major Roberts hopes it won't get to that point. He's been there before, and rumor has it, it wasn't pleasant.

Nevertheless, I believe he secretly needs to be a part of the shenanigans, maybe because he didn't get to go out and play as a kid. Whatever his role or reason, we're most willing to allow him to be the fall guy. He's such a natural.

* * *

The Barracks
Still on Officers' Walk
1600 hours
Still late July

I'm back...in this world. Milsap is going to miss these antics. The duel was certainly unique and more exciting than Iroquois, Bug, or Launching Pad races. Moreover, thinking of this and Milsap, here he and the Colonel come...across Commandant's Walk.

As they head down Generals' Walk toward us, I can see Milsap wearing his impish grin. It's his ever so faint cat-that-swallowed-the-canary smile. He was always stirring the pot, making imaginary potions in the form of soothing words, and then giving tastes to Mush Mouth and Julius that prompted them into monologues, action, or the games. Then he would sit back and sprinkle just enough of his magic vocal dust to keep it going. Through all this, he uttered more one-liners than Henny Youngman.

The two of them hit their spots on Center Walk. The D&B play a number they selected for Milsap, then one he requested. When the D&B finishes its short concert, JG advances toward them, and when close, halts. They know him well. As he approaches, most of them grin. He addresses them in a tone only they can hear. Besides being the Assistant S-3, he is also the Public Affairs Officer...Advance Man as it were for their performances throughout the country.

As JG starts to speak, I drift back and recall a performance he set up at Annapolis...The Naval Academy. I suspect it might even have been his idea to get us to a place where we would make a lasting impression...on the middies and for the Corps. Man oh man, what a day it was...

* * *

August '63. I have the Drill Team, and take them, the D&B, and the Color Guard to the U. S. Naval Academy. We're there to put on a show that will let the Plebes, the mid-coolies, REALLY know how to march...to "troop and stomp." This time of year is the end of Plebe Summer that starts right after the Fourth of July. The Academy grounds are spectacular and absolutely reek with years of lore and tradition, let alone the saltwater aroma from the Chesapeake that makes you think Navy. We're going to put on our Battle Color Ceremony in Halsey Field House.

It is packed inside with Plebes, midshipmen, instructors to include the Marine Staff, Marine enlisted, and the Command Staff of the Academy. Shoot, I bet even the grounds keepers and maintenance crews are in here. A Navy Captain from the staff has been selected to be the Reviewing Officer.

Everyone is in place inside. From our position outside I can hear the stirring and the pre-ceremony murmuring. Have to wait for just the right moment...on time, but the right moment. Anticipation is everything.

I hear the stirring grow inside and sense the senior naval staff looking at one another, questioning, wondering. My internal clock dings. It's time. I call the unit to Attention, and then give Right Shoulder, Arms. Pause slightly, then command, Sound Adjutants Call. D&B sounds the call, and BOOM we come blasting through the open end and inside Halsey Field House. The music is reverberating all throughout the building. The acoustics are not good, but it is loud and we are looking sharp...ceremonial tuff.

The middies at first are stunned or shocked into silence. A momentary hush drapes over the crowd. Then some Marine, high up in the bleachers bellows out, "Oouh-Rah" and the crowd bursts out with a roar and whistles. They're goin' nuts.

We march in, do a couple of column lefts at the far end and bring ourselves back and on line, come to the order, and face center. I cross the hard-packed dirt grinder to the reviewing stand, face about and command, Fix Bayonets, letting the word bayonets roll off my tongue as Mush Mouth did with his Carolinian accent. D&B strikes up the music and the DT fixes bayonets to the distinct beat of the music. The middies go bonkers again. Then the DT Platoon Sergeant moves them into a long, single line, serving as a backdrop for the D&B.

The Drum and Bugle Corps starts its twenty minute drill and concert routine. Dressed in their Red White Dress, it doesn't get any better...anywhere in the world, nor by any Drum and Bugle Corps. None are as good. None.

The middies, instructors, everyone applaud and cheer at almost every maneuver and piece of music. The drum line rattles the rafters in this ol' field house named in honor of the famous Admiral Bull Halsey. In their concert formation they play Anchors Aweigh...it brings everyone to their feet, of course. They follow with other sea chanteys.

When finished, the D&B returns to their original position on the parade deck, halt and the music stops. As they do so, the Drill Team Platoon Sergeant quietly reforms the DT into three ranks of eight. The building shakes as the applause bursts out and the cheering erupts for the D&B as they finish. Everyone is on their feet.

If we did encores, this would be a time. However, not the case, at least not yet. The D&B snaps to parade rest. The applause dies out, and a reign of silence creeps across the crowd. Again, timing is important.

There is some stirring, murmuring in the stands.

Timing, Gunny. Remember, timing, timing, timing.

Gunnery Sergeant Elms steps off toward me where I stand between the reviewing flags on the far side. Sixteen counts later, CRASH, the rifle butts hit the deck and the silent drill commences, without a command.

Great!

The Drill Team in their contrasting Blue White Dress moves forward and centers itself in the field house. They continue the twenty minute drill routine without commands. Rifles popping, snapping, and spinning as they move from one formation to another. They do the multiple rifle exchange movements, tossing it back and forth, chrome bayonets flashing, between one another in their squares formation. With each move, each exchange, each toss comes applause, the oohs and ahhs, and some scattered "Oouh-Rahs" from the Marines in the peanut gallery...and most important from the "Marines to be" among the Plebes.

The DT finishes in its long line doing the manual of arms movements in rippling effects up and down the line. This is topped off by the two rifle inspection routines, done by Sergeant Gary Collins, at fixed bayonets. Each spin, toss and throw movement at each of the two inspections draw the oohs, ahhs, wows and overall roar of approval from the middies. Collins is perfect again.

There's going to be one hell of a lot of dropped rifles and splintered rifle stocks around here tomorrow.

At the end, as the DT marches back to position, it is pandemonium in the bleachers. Knocked them dead!

Again, waiting for the quiet, and when it comes I present the colors. We have the Battle Color narration read as the Marine Corps Colors is dipped with all of its battle streamers fluttering ever so slightly in the salty breeze that's creeping off the Chesapeake and through the open end of the Field House. The Color Guard and the narration receive a standing ovation.

Then we pass in review, countermarch at the far end, and march out of the field house playing the Marines Hymn. Bonkers again... standing ovation...hoots, hollers, cheers and "Oouh-Rahs" bounce off every wall and rafter in this place. Once outside we hear the crowd still applauding, cheering and stirring. I look at the D&B Drum Major, Gunnery Sergeant Eugene Belchner; give him a sign and mouth, "Encore", he nods. I call the unit back to attention, back to right shoulder arms, and Belchner sounds Adjutants Call once again. The hell with it...break protocol; break procedure or whatever. These folks want more, and after all, this is show business. We'll give 'em more. We come bursting back into the Field House playing Anchors Aweigh. The DT is doing marching manuals and caustic spins. It stops everyone in their tracks. Those starting to leave, the Navy brass, turn and watch. The applause and cheering commence again. We march to the far end, countermarch, and head toward the open end, playing first Men of Harlech, and go off to the Marines Hymn once again.

One helluva day. Days like this make you love America; love the Corps; just flat out love life...and even love the Dixie Cups.

   * * *

I'm back. Captain Milsap has finished his talk with the D&B and is passing down the line of SNCO's, shaking hands. Next, he will come down our line of barracks officers, do the same, and he and the CO will go into Center House and the play-off will continue, and end, as will JG's tour here at The Barracks.

I will miss him...as I do the other two. I surely will.

CHAPTER 41

The Barracks
Center House
Friday
28 August 1964

ANOTHER PARADE, OR RATHER, ANOTHER show under our belts.
It went well as usual, maybe more response from the crowd tonight than
normal. Don't know why, sometimes they just have the juices flowing
early; it catches on and builds and builds, then a standing ovation at the
end. However, when the lights are dimmed and echo Taps is sounded,
it always brings a sobering hush over the crowd. No matter how many
I do, it always grabs at my heart and makes my blood rush and pour
through my body like a cascading river.

Gabby didn't come tonight. I will be going there shortly. She's
leaving next Thursday for her parent's home. A planning trip. Good
timing since we have already finished the Iwo parades for the year. Last
one was on the 25th...and just four more Friday nighters. The wedding
will be in Wyncote. She and her Mom are busy, busy, busy. It's scheduled
in October, after the parade season is over. We're going to tie the knot on
Saturday, the 31st...Halloween! Only Gabrielle would do this. She says
it is because it's spooky the way we met and I already have my costume...
my Dress Blues. Gad, I love everything about her.

Tonight's show was somewhat special to me. Earlier in the
day, I met with our new barracks CO, Colonel Richard Marney. He
is an upbeat, partially balding, grey haired gentleman with generations

of military service running through his family. Guard Company's CO, Major Cronin is leaving. Colonel Marney informed me that he wants me to stay another season and has given me actual command of the company, a major's billet. He wants me to stay on the parade deck as the company commander as well. He humbled me somewhat by heaping praise about my performance and my contributions to the parade. Well, maybe not humbled me. I really don't have a humble bone in my body.

This is great news. It's the premier job at The Barracks for a captain. The colonel is the first CO I've had here that didn't know me from the past. However, based on our discussion it was apparent that Colonel Weaver filled him in on every detail to include all my mentors and probably some of my incidents here as well... I think he likes colorful characters. Good, because there are enough of those parcels here to fill a couple of mail bags.

Maybe because of the news and the praise I was standin' a little taller tonight. Whatever, the show is over and I have a drink in hand at the Center House bar, and answer questions by some of the guests... and watch my lieutenants bask, deservingly so, in their pride of another job well done. In a few minutes when the guest of honor leaves and the crowd thins a bit, I will change and head to Gabby's.

* * *

I arrive at the apartment, buzz Gabby, let myself in, and go upstairs. She's waiting for me inside the apartment door wearing a thingy again. This one is new and so transparent it is almost colorless...I can't believe they can make anything so sheer and manage to sew it together.

Good Lord, she's beautiful...stunning. Oouh-Rah!

She has her hands behind her and is seductively swaying from side to side as I enter. I close the door and she gives me a sensuous, draping hug. Then crawls up my body and kisses me...long, warm, and wet. She steps back, holds up her hand with a jellybean between her thumb and forefinger, and places it in her mouth, curls her tongue, and it's gone. So am I.

I really love' the smell and taste of strawberries, but jellybeans... they're the best.

* * *

311

Later as we sit on the patio, her with a Bailey's which is now becoming her favorite, and me with my pancake syrup, she leans over and says, "Barney, I want you to know that as far as I'm concerned, nothing is going to change after we're married. Nothing."

"Yeah, I know or at least I hope so."

"No, I mean it. Nothing. I know from others that the lovemaking drops off. Well, I want you to know that it's not going to happen to us. I won't let it, and I hope you won't either."

"Sounds great to me. My kind of woman." .

"I'm not kidding, so stay in shape BQ because just like the saying, 'shop till ya drop', we're goin' to 'make love till we drop'...like minks."

"Based on our record to date, you've convinced me."

"Barney, really, I'm not ki—"

"I believe you. Really! But, let me ask you a question."

"Shoot. How's that for Corps lingo?"

"Great, however...let's see. What's the average life-expectancy of the American male these days...age 65 or something?"

"Don't worry, if you don't make it, you'll be the happiest man in Arlington."

"Listen, Luv Bug, speaking of Arlington. I met with Colonel Marney today and he told me that I will be commanding Guard Company, both for real and on the parade deck...so I'll be staying another parade season."

Gabby squeals, jumps to her feet, wiggles onto my lap and wraps her arms around my neck murmuring, "Oh, Barney, that's wonderful. I'm so happy. Aren't you? We get to stay here a while longer."

"Yep, at least until next Fall."

We kiss, and then again. She gets up and says, "Let's have one more toddy before the playpen. I'll get 'em so you can get a few more minutes of rest. Okay?"

"Sure. And bring me some raw oysters."

She laughs and leaves. My mind drifts back to the news reports earlier in the month. The Tonkin Gulf incident. Not good. We're goin' to get more involved, and if we do, I'm gonna want to go. Will need to. However, now's not the time to talk about this, or at all until we see how things play out.

Gabrielle returns. Hands me my brandy; slips onto my lap again; wiggles just enough, clinks my glass with hers and says, "You look pensive. A sip for your thoughts."

"Just happy. Happier than I've ever been, sweetheart. Life is good and getting better. I love you."

"I'll sip to that."

* * *

Building 58
My Office
Saturday
5 September 1964

I'm in at work today and have finished conducting an inspection of our training section troops. I hold it in Blue White Dress, just like the real show. New Snuffies in the company undergo two weeks training and preparation before being turned over to one of the ceremonial platoons. I started this to make it easier on them and the platoons when they are assigned. The old troops, the "Salts" that have been here all of a year or two, expect "Tracks" to be tough, and want the new guys to sweat bullets. My actions at these inspections have gotten to be a source of wild sea stories. The Magpies hang out the barrack's windows to capture some morsel they can start spreading. I always try not to disappoint them. These type rumors are good for morale, and by the time they reach Tuns Tavern, bear no resemblance to the event. Nevertheless, that's what makes sea stories and legends...a little fabrication and some exaggeration is the spice for spin.

I've changed back into utilities and will eat noon chow down below in the mess hall with the troops today. No need to hurry. Have some administrative chores to do. Besides, Gabby left Friday for the Labor Day holiday at her parent's home, so my weekend is free; lonely, but free. She and her Mom are having one of their wedding planning sessions, and I guess a girl-to-girl giggle-fest.

I finish up the pogey-bait paper work and look at the stack on the Major's desk. I shrug and mutter aloud, "Better him than me," although ironically every item there passed through me for his signature. Then look at my empty "In Box" and say, louder, "Chow time," and I stand and head for some good Corps chow.

In the passageway, as I head toward the quarter deck, the Duty NCO, Corporal Belinsky, stops me and says, "Call for you, sir. On line one."

"Okay. Who is it."

"A Mister Mosley or Mosher, sir, I think. He was hard to understand, sir."

"All right, Corporal. I'll take it at my desk."

"Yes, sir."

I wonder what ol' Henri wants?

CHAPTER 42

Building 58
Back in my office
Noon time
Labor Day weekend

I REENTER MY OFFICE AND hustle around my desk, sit in my swivel chair, spin around facing the phone and window. I glance down at the blinking light for line one and sigh.

Jesus, ol' Henri has been calling me every other week since I asked Gabby to marry me. We'll need an unlisted number or somethin'.

I pick up the phone and say, "Hello, Henri. What's up?"

"Barney, are you alone? Are you sitting down?"

Corporal Belinsky was right. The connection is bad, a rushing noise, plus Henri's voice is husky.

"Yes, to both, Henri. What's wrong? You don't sound so good."

"I'm not." He's sobbing and having difficulty speaking. He sighs deeply, then blurts out, "Gabby's dead. She was killed in an accident in Delaware, near Dover, sometime late last night. Colleen and I are leaving for there now."

I feel like someone punched me in the solar plexus. I manage to stammer, "Gabby? Auto accident?"

"Yes, Barney."

I'm stunned into a year-long silence but it's crammed into a moment. I can hardly breathe. I suck in a deep breathe of air through my nose. My mind is ricocheting around in my skull like a squash ball.

Labor Day weekend. My dad was killed in a car accident on this weekend...thirteen years ago. This can't happen to me again.

My eyes moisten.. I stammer, "How did it happen? Are you sure it's Gabby?"

"I don't know much yet. Don't have many details. The description of Gabby and the car fits. And the title of course is in her--"

He pauses. I can hear him trying to control his sobs... trying to collect himself. He continues, "...her name. Barney, let Colleen and I get moving and I'll call you as soon as we get there and know more. I'll tell you exactly what happened, and where you can meet us, if you want."

"Ah...Late last night. What time?"

"Near midnight."

"That doesn't make sense. She was supposed to be at your place before that."

"I know." He's sobbing again.

"Ahh, okay. " I pause gathering my thoughts. "Absolutely. I'll be there." I'm still having difficulty. My mind is playing leap frog and my heart is pounding so hard and loud, it's about to come out of my chest.

Henri says, "Will you be okay? Where can I reach you quickly? It was difficult for me to get through to you this time."

"No, I'm not okay, Henri. I'm...I'm..."

Will I be okay? Hell, no. Jesus. My dad when I was seventeen; my mom when I was eight; my grandfather only a few months after my mom; and now this. All the people I love gone before I can really share a life with them.

I continue, "I will be at Center House, here at The Barracks. Do you have a pen handy?"

"Yes."

I give him the number.

"Call me, Henri, please, as soon as you get there and know something, anything."

"I will, Barney. Promise." He's choking up again.

I tell him I will come up immediately. I need to be there, with Gabby, and them. I barely get through this conversation.

He adds, "Colleen says to tell you we love you."

He hangs up. It sounds more like a water-tight door slamming and sealing than a phone being put down. Maybe because it's just that to my life. I slump back in my chair and take as many deep breaths as I can without hyperventilating.

There's a knock on my office door. I choke out, "Enter."

It opens. Corporal Belinsky says, "Sir, excuse me. The Mess Hall is going to close shortly. Is the Captain coming down, sir?"

"No, Corporal. I can't make it today."

"The troops will be disa..Sir, is the...is the Captain all right, sir?"

"No, not really......Yeah. Yes, I'll be okay. I'm going to make a few calls then leave for Center House. Have to see the Colonel."

"Aye aye, sir. Good day, sir."

"Carry on, Corporal."

Good day?

Carry on?

Yeah, right!

CHAPTER 43

Marine Barracks
Generals' Walk
Friday
20 November 1964

TIME DOESN'T FLIT BY, BUT, it's gone. However, emotions remain hidden in the deepest corners of my heart with thoughts of Gabby frequently interrupting my brain housing group. I am the Great Stoneface, but not a granite heart. My past has installed mechanisms that allow me to push the pain deep inside, and the Corps has taught me to move forward, always. So I do.

Once again, it's play-off time. This one is for my diminutive Irish friend, Captain Jake Dennehy, The Barracks Adjutant. He's also been the publicist and agent for the blue white dress triumvirate of Mush Mouth, the Yaliee and Kruger and a friend of all, particularly the company grade officers. He is the single most valuable information source at The Barracks. As many of our roosters have crowed, "If ol' Jake don't know it, it ain't worth knowin.'" Lieutenant Burl Likens, the Elf, is a Jake disciple. He may be challenged or at a loss for words without Jake's fodder of information that Burl twisted to suit his liking in his fun poking, pot stirring ways.

We're all standing on Generals' Walk, waiting for Jake and the CO, Colonel Marney, to come out and get this portion started. It's a chilly, gray November day and it matches my outlook although it's been over two months since Gabrielle's death. I think about her everyday and worse, at night. I think of the accident that took her so quickly and of the funeral, unlike JFK's, simple, and no death watch...just Henri, Colleen and me. I stand and wait for the playoff to continue as these thoughts of her push others aside.

Jake was great, as was the colonel, in helping me get to Delaware that Sunday, and then again the following week to Gabby's home and the funeral. I didn't miss any Friday night parades, just one funeral at Arlington.

The police didn't close the case entirely but classified it as an accident with suspicious surrounding circumstances. Apparently, in trying to avoid a four-car pile-up, she swerved off to the side and hit a concrete abutment head on. The police could find no skid marks and at first thought she just plowed into it. However subsequent investigation found that her brake line had been partially cut thereby slowly draining fluid. They don't believe it was accidental or caused by the accident itself. Neither the police, Gabby's parents, nor I have a clue who or why, or even if. I wish I did, but I don't. Nothing makes sense to me. I drove the car just the week before and it was fine. In fact, I had taken it in that previous weekend for an oil change, lube and had them check over everything. She never did that stuff...just drove the hell out of it. What I do know is she's gone, and her parents are devastated. I'm not much better, but my past, my make-up and my job keep me slidin' and glidin' forward...Stonefaced..

I hope this and getting ready for the next parade season...and time, will suture and heal the wounds. If I can just get through the Christmas period, I believe the healing will get on with itself. Henri and Colleen want me to come up, but I declined. Am just going to take some leave, go south, visit my pal and mentor, Stoop. He's stationed at Parris Island, South Carolina. He's been up to visit me here on two occasions. We went to a One-Five reunion and he and I went to a Edson's Raider Battalion reunion. I was a guest of General Barto. I don't want to forget Gabrielle, just let her reside in some secret recess of my mind for a spell, maybe forever. I read something a long time ago. It went something like this, "Some people come into our lives and quietly go. Others stay for awhile and leave footprints on our hearts, and we are never the same." Gabby left all of that, and more, on my heart and my soul.

319

I'm back. Here comes Jake and the Colonel down the walk. Jake's face is slightly flushed...must be his Irish blood flowing freely. They stop on the Center Walk spot as normal, and the D&B strikes up their first of two numbers selected for the little guy. I've been with the D&B so many times I've heard everything they play. This is no different so my mind drifts along with the beat of the music and it collects thoughts and images of Jake...

* * *

He's covered up so many of our incidents it's hard to remember them all. He must have a pocket full of IOU's. I would bet someday he'll get me off a hook again. He never did anything dishonest to help but he always kept a lid on what he could, and always looked as if he had whatever it was under control, thereby allowing it to fade into the aura surrounding The Barracks, or maybe under Miles' mythical white sheet. Also, he always had the straight scoop, about everything. He had his own incidents as well, of course. We all do. He was no different...like the weed in the Commandant's garden, and at another time making things right for the neighborhood paperboy. Then there was Pop Sterling.

Pop was a fixture at The Barracks, and part of the lore here. He was officially identified as Master Sergeant L. E. Sterling. He entered the Corps in 1932, served in the Banana Wars for a few years, and elsewhere, and then was assigned to The Barracks where he stayed for about twenty-six years. He never did go overseas in WWII. For years he commuted by trolley from his residence in NE Washington. Later when the trolleys faded into history, he rode the bus and walked. He never owned a car, and probably couldn't drive.

Simply put, he was a master cabinetmaker, small appliance repairman, and picture framer of broad and well-deserved reputation. He had a wood shop under the mess hall. He was adored by the generals and their ladies living at The Barracks.

In appearance, Pop was the antithesis of every characteristic of a ceremonial Marine. He was much too short. His hair was grey and much too long. He wore Coke bottle-bottom glasses, had a droopy mustache, and was authorized by some long ago, unknown Commandant or Barracks Commander to wear dress shoes instead of boots with his utility uniform. However, the generals' wives loved him and that had everything to do with his longevity. Lieutenant Colonel Donnelly, our former dictatorial XO, never looked at the man. Pop knew he had to steer clear of Donnelly, stay away from the "flagpole" so to speak, which he did better than many a young lieutenant. He was almost never seen outdoors. The only time he was in uniform was for his retirement, and the only three in attendance were one of the generals' wives formerly at The Barracks, the Assistant Supply Officer, Captain McPeters, to whom he reported, and Captain Jake Dennehy, his friend.

Why Captain Jake? He was the Adjutant; always had his finger on the pulse beat of The Barracks, and was a warm-hearted soul. Not soft, warm-hearted...there is a difference. Pop took a liking to Dennehy and would stop by his office two or three times a week to chat for a few moments, and then return to his wood shop where he created distinguished looking pieces for the generals' wives of The Barracks. His extraordinary skills were only part of the story. Somewhere along the line, Pop had married a black woman. As sad a commentary as it may be, The Barracks in Washington apparently was about the only place he could serve at the time with relative anonymity regarding his personal life.

As Captain Jake tells it, one day during one of Pop's visits, he learned that Sterling had missed coming to work only one day in all these years...just one day! Dennehy said, "I didn't ask why. Didn't think it was my place to do so."

However, Pop offered, "That was the day we buried my wife."

I only saw Pop a few times, walking toward his shop in the shadows of the arcade...just shuffling along, quietly. After Donnelly left, Pop didn't have to scurry anymore. I'd say, "Hi, Pop, how ya' doin'?" He'd smile, nod, mumble something and continue to scrape along. In fact, it was after one of these chance encounters I stopped at Jake's office and asked, "Jake, what's the whole story about Pop?" He told me the tale.

Pop certainly wasn't one of the boys in Blue White Dress, but I always thought of him as much a part of the tradition and lore of The Barracks as any yarn, event or ceremonial Marine.

* * *

D&B is finished and Jake is headed toward them, as all others before him, to pay his respects and thank them for the concert and his selected number in particular. Bob Reese, my Drill Team Commander has been promoted to Captain and will be replacing Jake. Lieutenant

Slick Willie Howard will be taking the DT and remain in Guard Company with me. There also will be a new alignment of lieutenants in the platoons of both Guard Company and MCI Company, and Burl Likens has replaced Milsap in the Three Shop.

After the holidays, and beginning with the New Year, we all will get back to preparing for the "shows", Iwo and Friday nighters, and of course the several special parades on Thursday night...command performance type. That will keep me busy, plus the MDW ceremonies, White House Cordons and funerals at Arlington.

Jake's done talking to the D&B and we all head into Center House for the remainder of the festivities. I doubt that Jake will make the four-second club. Unlike most Irishman, he always has been a sipper of fine whiskey...never a suds guzzler. I assure all around me who care, that his departing monologue will be discreet but laced with humor and elegance. None of us will need counsel.

After all the speeches, the serious drinking starts and the conversations commence with the field grade speaking just above a whisper, the company grade a tad louder, and the lieutenants, boisterous as always. This is good for me. It's really my first time out mixing with folks other than brief appearances after each of the last four parades in September. I didn't stay long after those. It was lonely without Gabby.

The Elf, newly promoted Captain Burl Likens, sidles up to me, buys me a bourbon and Seven and says, "Hey, Barn-Barn, comin' uptown with us tonight?"

"Since you made Captain, you little twit, you've been waitin' to call me by name, haven't you?"

"Yeah."

"Yeah? So where did you come up with this, Barn-Barn, crap?"

"I thought it sounded friendly and all of your other nicknames seem so hard-nosed. Thought this might help give you a better image... a softer one."

"Yeah, well I don't like soft, and further, an aunt of mine had a scraggly, old, grey cat named Barn-Barn that wasn't worth a hoot. Nasty damn cat, and he was an 'it'. I'm not an it, and I like my hard-ass image so just call me Captain, or Sir, or Stoneface, Snake, Cobra, Tracks, Iron Horse. If you feel it absolutely necessary to be friendly, call me Barney. Never Barn-Barn or BQ."

"Huh?"

"And yeah, thanks. I think I will go uptown with you tonight. Who's goin' on this patrol?"

The Elf smiles. "Great. Boomer, Mike, Spike, Slick, the Word, and Major Bruce Black said he might tag along."

"What? Is he nuts? Oh, I get it. You need someone senior to come along so you have your he-made-me-do-it alibi for Sharon. No more Captains to blame. Have to find a Major now that you've been promoted? Well, you ought to be ashamed; you work for him."

"I know. I am ashamed, but, what the hell. You do what you have to do. I really think he'll drop out when he finds out it's not just him and me. No matter, I have you to blame again."

"When he finds out the cast of characters going, his heels will pile up dirt like a front-end loader. He'll be like ashes in the wind."

"Yeah, probably."

"Burl, let me buy you a drink, you little shit. I know what you're doin' and I appreciate it."

"Anytime, Barney. Listen, I have a beautiful cousin who is..."

"Burl."

"What?"

"Knock it off. Let's just go uptown."

"Okay. Seemed like a good idea at th--"

"Elf."

"Huh?"

"That's the punch line for after."

"Right, let's go attack some mustard and catsup bottles, and a few parking meters."

CHAPTER 44

Marine Barracks
Navy Yard
Building 58
19 November 1965

THIS YEAR HAS SLIPPED QUICKLY by except for the weekends and holidays. As usual, time and activity are natural healers. It's my last day, and appropriately, it's a Friday. My Play-Off will be later this afternoon, near sunset, which is also fitting. I'm in my office, sitting on the ugliest and probably oldest leather couch in the Corps, maybe the world. It's a stagnant pond-green hand-me-down probably from the stable hand's lounge when this building was a barn. If not, from the fire of 1812. It has more wrinkles, creases, and scars than my grandfather's craggy face... nevertheless, it's comfortable, like his lap was to a young boy. It also reminds me of a Marine story, or perhaps a joke. It goes like this...

The Air Force when building a new base, builds the Officers Club and Enlisted Club first, then The Barracks. Runs out of money, therefore they ask Congress for more funds to build the runway. Get it. Build hangars and run out of money again. Ask for more, and build the runway.

The Army builds The Barracks, then the "O" Club, "SNCO" Club and the "E" Club. Runs out of money. They ask for more money to build the training facilities. They get it.

The Marine Corps builds the rifle ranges, firing ranges, tank courses, obstacle and confidence courses and runs out of money. They ask for more money to finish the base. Congress sends them tents.

It might not be true but its close, and if not, we in the Corps believe it to be.

My Winter Service "A" unnie is pressed, rigged, and hanging up ready to go for this afternoon. I've spent a lot of time in this office on Fridays after parade rehearsals, unfortunately with Chesty. After he had gotten loose several times on Fridays at The Barracks, it's decided by the powers to be to keep Chesty here until shortly before parade time. Then the Handler would come down from The Barracks and pick him up. At least someone from Guard Company was spared the job of walking that mongrel up 8th Street to The Barracks. Chesty's departure from my office was, of course, after he had farted a dozen times. I suppose it could have been worse, he could have left me a souvenir or two.

I developed more than a strong dislike for English Bull Dogs... above all, our mascot. Strange, I always thought of mascots as something majestic. At worse, maybe humorous. Our country has the American Bald Eagle...imposing and powerful. Penn State a lion. Southern Cal a Trojan Warrior. What do we true warriors have? Chesty, a slobbering, farting, ugly, bow-legged mutt. And to make matters shoddier, most folks, the crowds here on Friday night, love him. Except of course the visitor with the stuffed rabbit and ol' Melon Head's guests.

I have no idea why they didn't keep him in his pen. I asked one time but received a command response. "It's better this way." That means, "I don't know" or "I don't have a good reason." Maybe it was just a method to chastise me for my antics. Someone might have gotten in the CO's ear. Because of Chesty's very presence, and his nauseating habit, I spent most of my late Friday afternoons wandering around Building 58, talking to the troops or plopping down in a platoon commander's office and talking.

Had my final haircut here just a few minutes ago...high and tight, from LCpl Crandell, our company barber. He's a sharp, wiry, quiet and almost as tall as me young man. He replaced Corporal Cross this past year as my Company Guidon-Bearer. He snaps the guidon straight out at present arms as if spearing something with its gleaming chrome tip.

You can see it shudder and up close you can hear the polished oak pole vibrate.

Have said my personal goodbyes to my officers, Lieutenants, Spike Splittier, Dan Looke, Ron Stover, Mike McDuffy, and Slick Willie Howard. Same for the Staff NCO's although most are new this year. Gunny Elms is long gone…replaced with SSgt Lee Bradley…good man. Blank is also gone. I spend time with his replacement, our new Color Sergeant, Gunny Shelton Eakin. He's one sharp Marine…true poster type. Gonna' miss the likes of him.

Now I meander through the squad bays…just out of habit and speak with many of the Snuffies that are busy shining shoes, cap visors, brass and rubbing linseed oil into rifle stocks. The fact is most use Linspeed; a synthetic substitute and not authorized but it makes the stocks shinier, but brittle. Break easier especially with the pounding they take here, particularly crashing the rifle butt on the cement when coming to order arms. They're just getting the spit and polish chores done before weekend liberty.

Damn, they're great troops. Been a bunch over the years…Skip Wray, Bob DiLossi, Dave Addison, Terry Poole; Slack, Mione, Powers, Van Weel, Strickland and so many others. Be good anywhere but they are super sharp on the parade deck. Sure can pitch some wild liberties too. Hell, tipping over the cannons on Leutze Park outside our building is a Rite of Passage after a blow uptown. Do it at least once a quarter.

As I pass through the Drill Team squad bay I remember the time I cornered McCloskey, a DT member. I told him and his buddies, Tallick and Griffin, they had to knock-off the cannon-tipping routine. He said, "Skipper, the cannons are beneath us. No creativity. We had more fun driving around the city and tossing Salvo Tablets in the fountains."

"Salvo tablets? Jesus, you didn't?"

"Oh yes, sir. Then go back and watch them bubble up and fill with suds. Great sport."

"You should have spent more time in Dobkins Bar. Maybe Molly would have kept you there, and out of mischief."

"Maybe, Captain. She was good to all of us regulars, and it is 'the' favorite watering hole of the troops."

I smiled and said, "And the Tavern."

"Yes, sir…and the Tavern."

We left it at that. The cannons still are tipped over once a quarter. As I said, a Rite of Passage.

Dobkins Bar and Molly will go on forever I suppose. Certainly as long as there is a Barracks. Dobkins is on The Barracks side of 8th Street, not but a block from the "M" Street Gate of the Navy Yard. Molly and her husband, Mel are the owners. Mel is pleasant, but business like; Molly more like a Mom away from home. She made the best liverwurst sandwiches, and would gladly extend a bar tab to her regulars...and for them, Molly was the first stop on paydays.

I go get myself another cup of coffee and return to my office. I shout, "Chesty, get off my damn couch." He glares at me. I grab his collar and say, "Get down." He moves and drops to the deck but not before leaving me a token reminder. "You did that on purpose." He growls and waddles over to the corner and lays down...with his back to me, probably locked and loaded. I sit, take a sip of coffee, relax and think of all the parades, ceremonies and such I've stood these last forty-three months.

Jesus, there was a ton of them. Remember some better than others, and have told stories about them. Just a helluva lot of shows but I sure have loved dancing in the spotlight, so to speak.

I've stood some one hundred twenty-two consecutive Iwo and Friday night parades and a rehearsal for each on top of the real show. Another twenty plus Special Thursday night parades at The Barracks and a few at Iwo. On top of that, probably about twenty-four or so huge street parades like the LBJ Inaugural, Fourth of July's, Memorial Day's, Columbus Day's, and Veteran Day's...even took the D&B, DT, and Color Guard to Austin, Texas to march in Governor Connelly's Inaugural Parade in early '63...before he was shot when riding with JFK. Then all the ceremonies around , at the White House, Pentagon, Andrews, Leutze Park...big and small; newsworthy or not...well over a hundred.

Then there were the special shows with the D&B, DT, and Color Guard, like at Fort Henry, World's Fair, State Fairs, Naval Academy Plebe Summer, Valley Forge and so forth. Dozens of those it seems.

And, of course, the funerals at Arlington...for just me, maybe fifty or sixty, or more. Big ones, small ones; all take something out of your soul. The funeral I remember the most was for Major Don Koelper, my former Platoon Commander in Force Recon Company. He was killed in Vietnam in early '65; was awarded the Navy Cross for his actions. All of my old buds from Force Recon were there as well as Major Meyers and Captain Taylor, the CO and XO. Those troops gave me my sword, the one I carry here, as a gift when I was commissioned. It felt heavy in my hand this day. I had known Koelper for years, before he was my Platoon Commander, when he was a young lieutenant. His wife, Nancy, along with Meyers and Taylor who knew I was here, asked that I command the troop formation. It was granted even though he rated a Major for the ceremony. I left the formation after the casket was taken inside the chapel at Fort Myer so I could attend the service. Then I returned to the formation to take Don to his gravesite in Arlington, and another white stone, like white caps on a churning sea of green.

My troops put extra effort in it for me. Like I say, these men were special; they had character. It was an emotionally tough day for me. Don Koelper was a "true" mentor of mine, as were Taylor and Meyers.

Of all the ceremonies, parades, and events, the one that had the largest impact on me was the JFK Death Watch. Never could quite wash that experience from my mind and soul. I guess I don't want to.

I take another sip of coffee; let it singe its way down my throat. *Man, this is good. Wonder what happened. Usually tastes like battery acid.*

I have time before I have to change out of utilities and put on my "A", then go to Colonel Marney's office for my last visit. I'm tired from the packing and scurrying around checking out, and getting all those damn shots before going to Vietnam. The Corpsmen love to jam those needles in Marines' arms and butts. They always have a sinister grin on their face that grows with each stab...like shooting darts. Have more to get I suppose when I get to the West Coast. So be it.

I sit back, put my feet up on the imitation whatever, marred coffee table, and let my mind slide down the banister of barracks life... drift away...not that difficult to do. What a tour I've had here...like the Little Rock trip...maybe a lifesaver.

* * *

Little Rock, Arkansas...home of the Arkansas State Fair and here I am with Slick Willie, the DT, D&B and Color Guard for five days. It's early October '65. Weather is clear, warm but not humid and a smell of a rodeo in the air. Nice time of year, everywhere in the US.

328

We'll do two shows a day; one in the afternoon and one in the evening...at the rodeo...in the plowed up arena. Not exactly a parade ground. Difficult to slide and glide, and do facing movements, and real hard on the white trousers. Tough goin' but we do the Battle Color Ceremony and the crowd's reception is off the chart. Hoots, hollers, cheers, whistles, and a bunch of cowboy "Yahoos and Yippees"...maybe an Oouh-Rah or two, but definitely horseshit, bull-riders, ropers and blue white dress. What a combo! People everywhere love the red, white and blue. It's all part of the US of A, and these folks eat it up, and I love bein' part of it all.

After our first evening performance we, meaning Slick, the D&B Drum Major, the Color Sergeant and I are invited downtown to the Gaslight Club, for dinner and drinks...*gratis,* the Club Manager, a retired Army Master Sergeant. The Gaslight is a Little Rock styled Playboy club, with their own version of Bunnies. I'd say, healthier lookin' and prettier than their namesakes. Yep, a lot healthier.

Slick is married, to Anna, so he is on his good behavior. The other two are as well, and they eat and run. Slick stays to guard me while he is in his "can-look, no-touch" mode. I've not been out on a true date since Gabby's death. Her friend, Harriet, has tried to ease the pain on occasion. She introduced me to some honeys at a couple of her parties. They were nice but not in Gabby's league, nor copper haired, so I stayed out of their eddies.

However, this first night here a gorgeous, outgoing, long-legged copper haired wench...in her tiny serving costume stuns me. Whoa!

She's been our only server and she hasn't said much so far but has eyed me each trip to the table. First with a curious look, then with one of interest or so it seemed. After these, the looks took on those of a hunter stalking its prey. Finally, at the end of the evening as she brings our last drink, she says, "I saw the rodeo this afternoon."

"Good. Did you see our part?"

"Yes. Loved it. Saw you."

"Great."

She paused, then leaned over and said, "I mean you were lookin' handsome out there."

"And now I'm not?"

"Yes. No. What I mean was, it was really something...made me tingle and shiver. My brother is in the Marines. He's in Vietnam. I worry about him."

I bet. So do all of us. Things have been heatin' up over there since the 9th Marine Expeditionary Battalion (MEB) landed in DaNang early in '65. Now more units have landed and have enclaves at Chu Lau and Phu Bai, to go along with DaNang. It's the III Marine Amphibious Force now, much larger, and growing. I've got buds there now, like Milsap, Kruger... and others.

I say, "Well, good, and I hope he's doin' okay."

"He writes my mom. He's doin fine, I guess, or as fine as you can over there."

"Yeah, I suppose. He'll be okay. Aren't you goin' to get in trouble spending all this time hanging around just our table?"

"Nope. Frank, the Manager, told me to stick to you like glue, and if you don't mind, I'm goin' to."

"Well, I appreciate that but we're leaving in a few minutes."

"You comin' back tomorrow night?"

"Hadn't thought about it, but--"

"Think about it. I'd like to see you again. Maybe we can go out for a coffee or something afterwards?"

"Okay, I'll think about it...won't be hard to do."

She leans over close to my ear again...warm breath feelin' close, and whispers, "By the way, my name is Nancee. Nancee Moreau."

I turn my head and up, just missing the tip of her nose as she returns upright, "Sounds French."

"It is. But I was born and raised in Arkansas so I'm country fresh."

"Fresh or sassy?"

"Both. I just came here, faster than an eight-legged dog, to get the straw out of my hair and get a good paying job. Goin to be movin' on soon."

She smiles, then strolls away and I take a better look. Wow! This is scary. Red hair, long legs...just two, and has her own natural SCUBA gear. Probably can stay down for a long time.

Slick grins and says, "Scary, huh?"

"Yeah. You've noticed. I think we ought to come back tomorrow night."

"You bet, as long as the food and drinks are free, and she's here. If we have to pay, I'm out of here...but I think you should return no matter what."

"Think I will. Let's go."

* * *

We do shows the next four days and nights. Seems like the crowds get larger and noisier. Frank treats us each night. Slick comes but leaves early, as do the other two. I stay and get to know Nancee better. In the end we become more than casual acquaintances. She says she wants to write, stay in touch. I say, "Okay, but it will only be for a short time."

"Why's that?"

"Because I'll be leaving The Barracks in November sometime. Goin' to Vietnam."

She's quiet, glum looking for a moment. Then says, "So, they won't deliver mail to you there?"

"Of course, but I'll have to send you my new unit address."

"Okay, do that if you wish. If so, then I guess I'll know if you're really interested."

She pauses again. A slow smile spreads across her face. "Will you be coming through here on the way?"

"Don't know. Have to bring my Vette to the coast and store it or something so I'll be driving. Suppose I could."

"Do."

* * *

My mind is back to the present with me on the couch and staring at the standard government pea green bulkheads and Chesty glaring at me from the deck. He moved to keep an eye on me. Good, he's pointed away, and it looks like some scorch marks on the bulkhead.

Pea green walls, chipped and scratched gray metal desks, and hand-me-down furniture. Gotta love it.

I get up, fetch another cup of coffee, and mosey back to my office and the relic. The now stale coffee tastes terrible. Is almost as bad as the Black Death that's in C-Rations. I take a few sips, little ones so I don't overdose, and I go over in my mind what I want to say to the Colonel during our visit. Then think about my remarks to the D&B and later, my Play-Off monologue.

My XO, Lieutenant Splittier pokes his head in the door and says, "You doin' okay, Skipper?"

"Yep, just reminiscing a bit."

"Okay, let me know when you are ready to go. We all want to walk up 8ᵗʰ Street with you to The Barracks...one last time."

"Sounds great. Will do." We always did that on parade nights. *Damn fine Exec; outstanding Marine. Hope I find one near as good where I'm goin'.*

I take a last gulp of coffee, stand up and shudder as it goes down. Time to change into the uniform of the day and head-up to see Colonel Marney. I hate to leave...but it's time. I hope I can choke my way through all this.

I change and inspect myself in the full length mirror on the wall. Got these in every office and every squad bay, and on the quarter-deck. *Lookin' tuff, Stoneface.*

I snap to attention, heels click sharply. Love that sound. I place my Barracks Cap on my head with two hands on the side so as to not touch the spit-shined visor. Face about smartly and look around my lair.

It's been a great tour...God I loved it here, and the troops. Gonna miss it.

I open my door and holler, "Spike, I'm ready."

CHAPTER 45

The Marine Barracks
CO's Office
1600 Hours
19 November 1965

MY LIEUTENANTS ACCOMPANY ME ON the walk up 8th Street to The Barracks. These are fine Marine officers, the best of the Corps. The clicking of our cleated heels beat out our brisk cadence as we traverse the pavement. We pass Dobkins and one of our other watering holes. Regardless of our strides it seems like a stroll that takes forty-three months.

We arrive, the gate sentry pops to attention, salutes. "Good afternoon, Captain Quinn. Lieutenants."

We respond jointly, "Afternoon Marine. Oough Rah!"

"Oough Rah," as he cuts away his salute I recall that Boomer brought that to The Barracks from his last duty station.

At the Center House steps, Spike and the others chorus, "By your leave, sir."

"Granted."

They go up and into the quarters. I continue on to the CO's office.

There I wait briefly, then I'm told it's time. I knock and enter. Center myself on Colonel Marney's desk and say, "Captain Quinn reporting as ordered, sir."

"Hi, Barney. Sit and we'll chat before we get on with the proceedings. Still doing okay?"

"Yes, sir. It's been a year. I'm fine."

"And Gabrielle's parents. How are they?"

"Just talked to them yesterday. Are doin' as well as can be expected, I guess. No one has figured out what exactly happened for sure. Someday, I will. I've got some ideas."

He shakes his head, pauses, and starts talking about all the performances I've participated in and the good they've done. His questions about Gabby cause my mind to wander, thinking of her, and all our favorite places...how every time coming from the parades and we passed Hogates Restaurant, she'd say, "There it is, BQ. The site of just one of your moments of acclaim, in front of your adoring masses." She loved to jerk my chain about that and my now famous Center House statement, "There's not enough bourbon in this bar to get me drunk." When she did I always reminded her of her response to the well-endowed waitress in Ocean City of, "I'll have a BLQ...Oh! I already have one."

I snap out of the moment as the Colonel asks, "Well, Barney... any parting shots or suggestions?"

"No parting shots, sir. Never. I love this place. Do have some ideas for the parade." I give him several suggestions including putting in a true spotlight for the rifle inspections during the drill routine...like they do on Broadway. I mean, it is a show, for the public, the American people...not a personal party for the Commandant.

* * *

The Marine Barracks
Center Walk
1630 hours
Friday

We leave his office, head towards Center Walk. As I approach the line of Staff NCO's I suck in some air. Don't want to choke now. I get through the handshakes okay, and the Colonel and I position ourselves on the Center Walk spot. As we do, the D&B strikes up their concert for me. As they get into the first few bars of the music, I remember it from New York. My mind won't stay focused, won't stay here. It's gone, and this time to earlier this year at the New York Worlds' Fair. Man oh man, what a five days that was...

* * *

I take the Drill Team under Lieutenant Slick Willie Howard, the D&B, and the Color Guard to the Fair in the spring, before our parade season. As I've said before, sort of an out-of-town show revue before our season starts. We'll stay at the Brooklyn Navy Yard and will be taken by bus to the Fair Grounds at Flushing Meadows in Queens. We'll change into our Blue White Dress in the Federal Pavilion Building.

We'll do two shows daily at the central plaza, with its huge Bronze Sphere depicting the world. An afternoon and evening show. The Fair has one hundred forty commercial, twenty-one state, and thirty-six foreign pavilions. Over the two sessions in '64 and '65, it is estimated that fifty-one million people will attend.

The first afternoon we form up at the Federal Pavilion and march up a tree-lined boulevard to the plaza. It's several city blocks. Since the street has pedestrians, I use our supernumeraries along with the Fair security to help clear the path. The D&B is playing, the Drill Team is doing its various street manuals, and a crowd is pulled along like mice following the Pied Piper.

Our opening Battle Color Ceremony at the plaza dazzles those present. The crowds are a little small, but highly appreciative. All the normal hoots, yells, cheers and whistles. New Yorkers and tourists alike. It's a red, white and blue day.

We return to the Pavilion, change out of our unnies, prepare them for the next show, and head out to enjoy the Fair ourselves before our evening performance.

This first evening, I have my first inkling that we have a problem brewing. The crowd outside the Federal Pavilion has increased a thousand fold. The word of our presence and performance is out and spreading like a California brush fire riding a Santa Ana wind. The street leading up to the plaza is jammed to overflowing. It seems like all fifty-one million are here tonight. I have to get the Pinkerton Agency, who is providing security for the Fair, to provide additional assistance in getting us to the plaza. As we march and play, the crowd whistles, cheers and pushes in toward us... trying to touch us, shake hands, trying to grab brass buttons from our coats for souvenirs. All well and good, except the button bit. That would be a problem. I'd say it was close to a well-intentioned patriotic mob scene, if there is such a thing.

I see a little old, blue-haired lady standing on the roadside waving a small American flag. Tears stream down her cheeks. I read her lips as she says, or yells, over and over again, "God bless you boys." Hard to keep the ol' eyes dry when the emotions run this high.

The cheers and noise increase as we continue up the boulevard. The crowd is swelling and I can sense the Pied Piper surge behind us.

My God, they're goin' crazy.

At the plaza, the people are jammed around it and I can see more still coming, some running, most hastily scurrying The crowd explodes into a enthusiastic roar when the D&B starts the first number of its drill and concert routine. Continues with outbursts from the crowd at each break, and the start of another number. The same thing occurs during the drill team routine, and they burst again in a riotous roar with the first rifle inspection throwback, and go completely bananas on the second, the double, both with fixed bayonets. Corporal Ski is more than an ample replacement for Collins.

When we present the colors, the crowd hushes. Amazing, it's like no one is here. Then as the Battle Color Narration ends, and the colors are posted, applause begins. It builds. I can see the waves of clapping hands flow from the front edges of the crowd to the back. The applause gives way to whistles, hoots, hollers, yells and cheers. I wait for a break, and then command Forward March, and we march off the plaza playing the Marines Hymn. As soon as they recognize the Hymn, a roar, like a sonic boom, erupts from the crowd. I swear I can feel a shock wave. Then it lingers as we fade from the plaza…with the mice behind us once again. If one can't feel a love for country at this point, they should move to Lower Slobovia and stay. I'm standin' taller than a California Redwood.

Back at the Federal Pavilion, a representative approaches me from Kodak, and one from the Danish restaurant that are along our return route which is different from our entry. They ask if we will stop, do a short performance on the way back. Kodak offers some refreshments inside if we do. The restaurant manager is more conservative and offers dinner to Slick and me. I convince him to include the D&B Drum Major and the Color Sergeant. I decide we'll do both, what the hell.

Then I get an off-handed compliment. At least I see it as such. I'm told that the managers of the commercial corporate pavilions adjacent to the plaza have complained that we're stealing crowds and business, from them at critical hours. Hell, we didn't steal them...they're ours!

So, starting the second day we make the runs past Kodak and the Danish eatery, after "stealing our crowd" at the plaza. The numbers of people at the Federal Pavilion has increased. It's a madhouse just getting out of here and to the plaza for the ceremony. The crowd is also quick to form at the Kodak Pavilion. When we stop and play, it's a huge magnet snapping people to the area. The D&B plays a couple of numbers here. I would wager that Kodak sold one helluva lot of film.

The best sight, more of a treat, are the young boys, inching close, staring in awe at the troops...wanting to touch the men, the horns, the rifles. Just a reaching out. All with break-your-heart expressions...*Norman Rockwell* cover stuff.

I wait, along with a few security troops, watching the gear while the rest are inside enjoying their Kodak moment. I spend my time talking to the kids, elderly ladies, gents and others. Most are glassy eyed, and some in tears. They all want to tell me where they're from, hoping I'm from their hometown of Davenport, Broken Bow, Elkins Park, Mule Shoe, Brooklyn, or wherever.

The Danish restaurant is jammed. More chow hounds than our Mess Hall when they serve SOS on a cold morning. Shoot, maybe they are. We approach, stop, play, do a quick manual of arms, and leave. The manager is ecstatic. He has SRO for dinner at "Sixish." It's all theater. And oh yes, the food and drinks after were great...and free for the four of us. The troops don't care about us. They're too busy with the young ladies, or seeing the Fair.

When you put the D&B in their Red White Dress, and the Drill Team and Color Guard in Blue White Dress out in the American public, the folks unite as Americans and respond. If any of us had been claustrophobic, we'd have been in deep trouble. The crowds grow larger and louder each performance, and there is scarcely room to march to the plaza, or perform once there.

I guess this performance and the one in Fort Henry, Canada in '63 were about the two most vocal and appreciative audiences I've experienced...well, and the Naval Academy. Although I must say that our half time show at the University of Cincinnati football game against the Quantico Marines in the fall of '63 was crazy. The Barracks CO got a letter from the concessionaires complaining that they lost money because no one left their seats at half time. They wanted to be reimbursed. The answer was of course a polite "No", meaning, "TS".

* * *

I snap back to the present when I hear the D&B break into my choice of a number, *British Grenadier.* They finish and I'm about to walk toward them when they strike up *Men of Harlech.* They added a number for me. Great guys.

They're all smiles as I approach. They're proud of themselves and know I appreciate the extra number. I talk to them, briefly recanting our good times together on the road and other things...private inside stuff just between them and me. We smile and laugh aloud together. The moment is wonderful, rewarding, and to be cherished. I say goodbye, give them my best ceremonial salute, and turn about before I choke up. I return to Colonel Marney, he faces about and we head for Center House.

* * *

The Marine Barracks
Center House
1700 hours
Same day, my last

Everyone orders a drink of some sort. The group settles as Colonel Marney starts to speak. As he does, I look around at the faces of my fellow officers. My imagination allows me to also see those who have left, McKay, Milsap, Kruger, Dennehy, Smokey Beard, Van Dell and others...even Goen, Paquette, and Light Horse Harry Gimletti, although these latter three come with a twinge and a silent chuckle.

The Colonel finishes his remarks. He presents me my souvenir, a silver plated, engraved mug. Gunny Richards fills it with beer. I take off my tie, let the beer settle, look about...I think they expect me to make it. I'm not a beer drinker but this is goin' down in a hurry.

Up the mug comes, head back as far as it will go, mouth wide open as a cavern entrance, and pour...not drink, POUR.

I finish. The Colonel looks at his stopwatch, pauses, and then smiles and says, "Captain Quinn, Barney, you made it, with some to spare. Three point four seconds...your name goes on the plaque. The minimal spillage coming from your mouth I'll attribute to drool...which I might add is normal for you."

"Thank you, sir. And now I have a few thousand words for the group. But first, let me buy the house a drink."

With that, I ring the ship's bell at the end of bar, near my right elbow. This means that since my Center House account has been closed, all of my drinks and any that I buy are pro-rated across the board. Everyone gets a part of the bill...even the soda popers and those not present, like the Band Director with his baton and poison-dipped pen. After a funeral ceremony at Arlington earlier this year he wrote a stinging memo to the CO. I had criticized the uniform appearance and posture of the band unit at graveside...and the music. His opening line in the memo was, "I've dealt with this green-eyed music critic before." It's hard for me to believe, but he doesn't like me. Colonel Marney was amused and took great sport in calling me to his office and giving the memo to me with a humorous endorsement. Anyway, my clanging of the bell is followed by a groan from the majors and married officers.

I deliver my monologue in true Captain McKay fashion, minus the Carolinian slurping and mumbling. He would have been proud. Then I ring the bell again. Louder groans, particularly from the field grade officers, however cheers from the lieutenants.

Soon the usual folks depart, leaving only the hard core...mostly parade deck lieutenants. We party some more, and I continue ringing the bell. I planned this. I wanted to leave one last legendary antic with The Barracks. One that certainly will erase the Mrs. Haney tea party incident. When the club bills arrive in the mail they will think of Ol' Barney one more time.

I don't drink, except for the one beer and a bourbon and Seven I've been nursing all evening. I have a long drive, starting tonight.

Eventually there is only my lieutenants and one Captain...the Elf, Burl Likens. I choke through my last goodbyes, take one final look around and go to my Vette.

Outside, standing in the parking lot, I look up the length of the parade deck. I swear I can see all of the faces...and hear the bugler play Officers Call.

I suck in some air, let my eyes dry, and say aloud,

"Barney ol' boy, lets go to Little Rock."

EPILOGUE

LONG AFTER I LEFT THE Barracks, and Vietnam, and while stationed in San Diego, I received a carbon copy of a memo. It let me know that one is never free of the triumvirate, and always a candidate for the Dubious Achievement Award.

I quote the memorandum:

25 November 1968

From: J. F. Kruger
To: J. B. Dennehy
Subj: 1968 Award; for Dubious Achievement in Ice Hockey
       1.The subject award is recommended for Bernarr Leslie Quinn, based on observation by this undersigned at the San Diego Sports Arena on 23 November 1968. As possible lesser awards it is felt the "Light Horse Gimletti" trophy for poor public appearance would also be appropriate.

       2.The incident leading to this recommendation was observed by the undersigned, along with eight thousand, five hundred, sixteen spectators at a San Diego Gulls, Denver Spurs ice hockey game. Between the second and third periods of the game, B. L. Quinn was seen, along with a fifteen-year-old junior high school student, at the edge of the rink. Both Quinn and the female were practicing with hockey sticks and pucks. B.L. Quinn gave the impression he knew what he was doing. It was subsequently announced that there was to be a contest, sponsored by MJB Coffee, and it became apparent that B.L. Quinn and the fifteen-year-old female were to be the contestants. Signs were placed in front of both the north and south goals. Each sign had a small hole in the bottom, and the object of the contest was to put the puck through the hole in the MJB sign using a hockey stick.

3. The fifteen-year-old female student was the first contestant. She was allowed two shots at the south goal to win a year's supply of free coffee. Her first shot was wide by ten feet; her second attempt hit the sign but was wide of the target hole by about a foot. She was allowed one shot at the north goal for a possible prize of $1,000. Again, she hit the sign but was wide of the hole. It should be noted here that this young fifteen year old junior high school student was wearing a mini-skirt, and it was obvious that she was distracting B.L. Quinn during his warm-up.

4. B.L. Quinn then took up a position at the center of the rink, and it was announced that Barney Quinn was a Major in the Marines. (I immediately denied having knowledge of him or of having ever seen him before. Further, I was able to convince those in the crowd around me that the announcer had actually said, "Merchant Marines.") B.L. Quinn's first shot at the south goal was wide by at least twenty feet; his second attempt was better...he only missed by fifteen feet. He then faced the north goal, and it became obvious that he had not been interested in such an insignificant prize as a year's supply of coffee. He was after the big prize, the $1,000 in cash. As the arena hushed, B.L. Quinn took a couple of very professional looking practice swings, gave the eight thousand, five hundred and sixteen spectators the ol' "You-ain't-got-enough-bourbon-in-this-bar-to-get-me-drunk" grin. Then carefully lined up his aim and fired a tremendous shot, wide of the mark by thirty feet.

5. As B.L. Quinn dejectedly left the ice, to the shouts of a few people yelling, "Bum", it was announced that he would receive a

month's supply of free coffee. He has never touched the stuff as all well know. A very sad ending for The Great Stoneface.

Copy to:
B.L. Quinn
M.G. McKay
J.G. Milsap

There is no escape from the Boys in Blue White Dress.

EXCITING AND HUMOROUS SEQUEL TO THE BOYS IN BLUE WHITE DRESS

*** It received a Five-star review from the Military Writers' Society of American ***

And

*** Judged the North Texas Book Festival 2007 Winner in its category ***

The Light Side of Damnation

By

William F. Lee

Follow Captain Barney Quinn to Vietnam where he first serves as the Company Commander of Lima Company, 3rd Battalion, 3rd Marines... and later in the same position with India Company. Meet the men of Lima and India; enjoy their humor; and live with Barney and the wild and bizarre events that take place. Enjoy his relationship and banter with his Battalion Commander.

Later, continue the adventure with Barney as he is snatched away from his rifle company and becomes the Aide-de-Camp for a three-star general that commands all of the Marine forces in Vietnam. This general knows Barney well from the past and sees himself as a mentor. Barney tries unsuccessfully to get out of this duty and stay with his company and takes his irreverent manner with him in his new unfamiliar role. The two personalities clash and this provides for an interesting, humorous, and wild ride for Barney. Again, in this role, you'll meet many more engaging characters with Barney. The General extends Barney's tour of duty so the two can serve out their time in Vietnam together, and in the end become fast friends.

If you like Captain Barney Quinn, join him for another tour with "The Light Side of Damnation" by William F. Lee.

For review and PURCHASE, go to: www.williamflee.com or call 1-888-728-8467

or

Get it at www.Barnesandnoble.com or www.amazon.com

REVIEWS---

"This book is fast moving, poignant and sensitive...outstanding humor...lively personalities." (Mary Elaine Hughes, Former Editor; TV Program Director.)

"Bill Lee's fast moving account describes a seldom seen dimension of the Vietnam War...fascinating and humorous...through the eyes of a battle-tested Marine rifle company commander." (John Grider Miller, Col.,USMC, Ret'd; Vietnam vet; author; former DepDir,MarCorps History; former Managing Editor, U.S. Naval Institute.)

I hope you enjoyed The Boys in Blue White Dress. These are the folks that helped me along the way.

ACKNOWLEDGMENTS

I thank my wife, Jodi, and my dear friend Mary Hughes, who assisted in the day-to-day editing and proofreading during the long but delightful process of writing and rewriting this fun endeavor. In addition, I express my deep appreciation for their constant encouragement and countless suggestions.

My deep appreciation to John Grider Miller, Colonel, United States Marine Corps, (Retired), a good friend, a fellow former Marine, author in his own right, and one of "The Boys in Blue White Dress" for his input and assistance. His guidance and continual championing of my writing efforts is sincerely appreciated. A true mentor.

In addition, to other "Boys in Blue White Dress", Jack Krebs, John Donovan, Burl Landes, John Speicher, and Bob Reed, for their input.

To my many friends and co-writers at the Lesser North Texas Writers' Group in Plano, Texas, a profound thanks for the hours of listening, suggestions, valuable critique, interest and moral support... thank you, thank you, thank you.

In addition, much appreciation to Fred Hansen, an old friend from EDS for his interest, proofing, suggestions and editing assistance.

To Marilyn Thomas who helped with local research and bringing a fictitious character to life...my gratitude.

To the men of the Drill Team and all of the troops of Ceremonial Guard Company, I thank you for the memories. The hot days standing in a blistering sun at rigid, mannequin-like attention and the unseen shivering hours in the cold, wet, snowy sparsely attended ceremonies were proud moments made easier with your support. The memories of our times together on the parade deck, at the ceremonial sites, and at the Tavern and at Center House are cherished beyond imagination. You are the finest group of men that ever served in Blue White Dress, Forest Green, or in camouflaged utilities.

Again, thanks to former Sergeant Thomas P. Lee, not related except for our time together in Ceremonial Guard Company, for his poem and dedication at the front of this book.

42881883R00224

Made in the USA
San Bernardino, CA
12 December 2016